Hiking
Yosemite National Park

Suzanne Swedo

FALCON®

HELENA, MONTANA

*A*FALCONGUIDE®

Falcon® Publishing is continually expanding its list of recreation guidebooks. All books include detailed descriptions, accurate maps, and all the information necessary for enjoyable trips. You can order extra copies of this book and get information and prices for other Falcon® books by writing Falcon, P.O. Box 1718, Helena, MT 59624 or calling toll free 1-800-582-2665. Also, please ask for a free copy of our current catalog. Visit our website at www.Falcon.com or contact us by e-mail at falcon@falcon.com.

All photos by author unless otherwise noted.
Cover photo by Bill Hatcher.

Elevation profiles provided by TOPO!/Wildflower Productions
375 Alabama Street, Suite 230/San Francisco, CA 94110
415-558-8700/www.topo.com

Cataloging-in-Publication Data is on file at the Library of Congress.

Project Editor: Jay Nichols
Copyeditor: Richard Chapman
Maps by Sue Cary
Page Compositor: Darlene Jatkowski
Book design by Falcon Publishing, Inc.

CAUTION

Outdoor recreational activities are by their very nature potentially hazardous. All participants in such activities must assume the responsibility for their own actions and safety. The information contained in this guidebook cannot replace sound judgment and good decision-making skills, which help reduce risk exposure, nor does the scope of this book allow for disclosure of all the potential hazards and risks involved in such activities.

Learn as much as possible about the outdoor recreational activities in which you participate, prepare for the unexpected, and be cautious. The reward will be a safer and more enjoyable experience.

♻ Text pages printed on recycled paper.

Contents

Dedication vi

Acknowledgments vii

Overview Map viii

Legend ix

Introduction 1

How to Use This Guide 1

Life in Yosemite 2

Geology 4

History 5

Zero Impact 6

Wilderness Permits.. 8

Bears 9

A Few Words of Caution 10

Trail Finder Table 13

Author's Favorites 16

THE HIKES

The Valley Floor 17

   1 East Valley Floor 19

   2 West Valley Floor 22

   3 Glacier Point via the Four Mile Trail 26

   4 Happy Isles to the Top of Nevada Fall 28

   5 Mirror Lake–Tenaya Canyon Loop 32

   6 Yosemite Falls 35

   7 Half Dome 38

The South Rim of Yosemite Valley 42

   8 Taft Point and The Fissures 44

   9 Sentinel Dome 46

  10 McGurk Meadow 47

  11 The Pohono Trail 49

  12 The Panorama Trail—Glacier Point to Nevada Fall 53

The North Rim of Yosemite Valley 57

  13 Tioga Road to the Top of Yosemite Falls 59

  14 El Capitan from Tamarack Flat 62

  15 Porcupine Creek to North Dome 65

  16 The North Rim 67

  17 Tuolumne Grove 70

The High Sierra Camps 73
  18 Merced Lake High Sierra Camp 74
  19 Vogelsang High Sierra Camp 79
  20 May Lake High Sierra Camp 84
  21 Glen Aulin High Sierra Camp 85
  22 Sunrise High Sierra Camp 89
  23 The High Sierra Camp Loop 92

The Southern Park 97
  24 Mariposa Grove of Big Trees 98
  25 Alder Creek 102
  26 Chilnualna Fall 104
  27 Buena Vista Crest 107
  28 Wawona Meadow 111
  29 Ostrander Lake 114
  30 Ottoway Lakes 116
  31 The Clark Range 120
  32 Merced River High Trail 121

South of Tuolumne Meadows 125
  33 Tenaya Lake 126
  34 Clouds Rest 128
  35 Tenaya Lake to Half Dome 130
  36 Cathedral Lakes 132
  37 Elizabeth Lake 135
  38 Lyell Fork 136
  39 Lyell Fork to Donohue Pass 139
  40 Mono Pass 141

North of Tuolumne Meadows 144
  41 Waterwheel Falls and the Grand Canyon of the Tuolumne 145
  42 Harden Lake 149
  43 Lukens Lake 151
  44 Ten Lakes 153
  45 Soda Springs and Parsons Lodge 156
  46 Dog Lake 159
  47 Lembert Dome 161
  48 Young Lakes 163
  49 Polly Dome Lakes 166
  50 Gaylor Lakes 169

Hetch Hetchy 171
  51 Wapama Falls 173
  52 Rancheria Falls 175
  53 Lake Vernon 177
  54 Jack Main Canyon and Tilden Lake 179

The North Boundary Country **182**

    55 Saddlebag Lake and 20 Lakes Basin 184

    56 Lundy Canyon 188

    57 Green Creek 190

    58 Virginia Lakes Basin 192

    59 Hoover Lakes 194

    60 Matterhorn Canyon 195

    61 Benson Pass 199

    62 McCabe Lakes 202

    63 Peeler Lake 205

Two Famous Trails **209**

    64 The John Muir Trail 211

    65 The Pacific Crest Trail 214

Appendices

Appendix A: Further Reading 217

Appendix B: Hiker's Checklist 218

About the Author 219

For my sister Jo.

Acknowledgments

Thanks to the many park rangers and other personnel and volunteers of the National Park Service in Yosemite who have been so generous with their time and assistance, especially Laurel Boyers and Dave Gansci, Linda and Alan Estes and Deanna Petree. All have provided much valuable information and have helped to smooth the way. The biggest debt of gratitude is owed to wilderness ranger Mark Fincher, who knows everything there is to know about the trails of Yosemite, and who, during his busy summer season, reviewed the manuscript and made comments and suggestions that were always right on target. What a joy to work with people whose lives have been dedicated to caring for and sharing their love of the most beautiful place in the world! Also deeply appreciated are the support and assistance of Penny Otwell and all the hardworking staff at the Yosemite Association, whose purpose it is to initiate and support interpretation, education, research, and scientific and environmental programs in Yosemite. For their aid and encouragement and plain good company in the field, thanks also to Joellyn Acree, Erica Crawford, Melinda Goodwater, Jane Magid, and Sally McKinney, and for infinite patience and tolerance and caring, Rex.

Overview Map

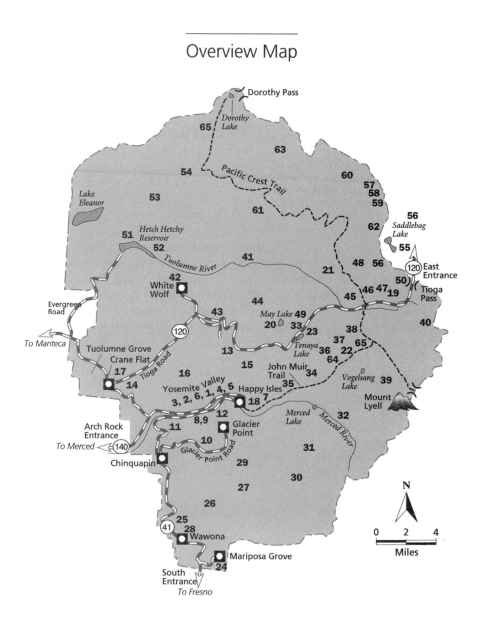

Legend

Interstate		Campground		
U.S. Highway		Picnic Area		
State or Other Principal Road		Cabins/Buildings		
Forest Road	22512	Peak/Elevation	9,782 ft.	
Interstate Highway		Dome		
Paved Road		Gate		
Gravel/Dirt Road		Mine Site		
Trailhead		Town		
Main Trail(s)/Route(s)		Pass		
Alternate/Secondary Trail(s)		Meadow		
Parking Area	P	Point of Interest/Overlook		
River/Creek/Falls		Powerline		
Intermittent Stream		National Forest/Park Boundary		
Spring		Map Orientation	N	
Glacier		Scale	0 0.5 1 Miles	
Lake				

ix

Introduction

Yosemite National Park occupies the heart of John Muir's "Range of Light" in the Sierra Nevada. The name means "snowy range" in Spanish, and in winter more than 60 feet of snow may accumulate. Yet the Sierra has also been called the gentle wilderness, because extremes of temperature are not great and the hiking days of summer are comparatively dry and sunny. It is a land of amazing diversity. Elevations in Yosemite range from 2,000 to over 13,000 feet, from the rolling oak woodlands of the western slope to the jagged mountain crest, where offspring of the great glaciers that carved the spectacular topography still lie in shady hollows above thousands of lakes. Then, to the east, the land abruptly drops away to the apparently endless sagebrush desert of the Great Basin. There are three groves of giant sequoia trees, the largest living things on earth, miles of forests and meadows, and a rich and varied collection of wildflowers, wildlife, and history galore. Then there is the incomparable valley itself, Yosemite, surrounded by massive granite domes and spires and booming waterfalls, and in the summer season, teeming with tourists.

More than 4 million people visit the park each year. Most concentrate their activities in Yosemite Valley, a mere 1-by-7 mile corner of the park. Those who are willing to explore on foot, however, can expect a genuine, uncrowded wilderness experience. Yosemite's borders encompass almost 1,200 square miles, and almost 800 miles of excellent trails travel through some of the most dramatic and beautiful scenery on earth.

This book describes the best of them, how to find them, how to plan and equip yourself to tackle them, and what special, natural wonders to enjoy along the way.

HOW TO USE THIS GUIDE

The purpose of this guide is to help you choose and plan a day hike or backpack in Yosemite best suited to your time, energy, experience, and personal preferences. It offers a preview of what you are likely to see and experience along your chosen route: geological features, historical sites, trees, birds, flowers, and mammals. It helps you anticipate places where the trail is faint, where it is clear, where and when rivers and streams are special sources of delight or where they may be obstacles to travel.

Trail descriptions are intended to be used along with U.S. Geological Survey topographic maps, available at wilderness outfitting and sporting goods stores, at visitor centers and shops in Yosemite, and through the USGS at P.O. Box 25286, Federal Center, Denver, CO 80225. Phone (800) USA-MAPS; on-line at www.mapping.usgs.gov.

Each trail description begins with a statistical section for quick reference to the characteristics of the hike. The **General description** lets you know whether the route is a loop, in which you return to the place where you started without retracing your steps; an out-and-back hike, in which you return to the trailhead the same way you came; or a shuttle hike, in which you begin at one trailhead and end at another, requiring two vehicles, a shuttle bus, or another driver to pick you up or deposit you at either end.

Total distance is described in miles.

The **Difficulty** rating is bound to be interpreted differently by hikers in varying degrees of physical condition, including their adaptability to high elevation. In general, Easy trails can be negotiated by anybody who can walk. Moderate trails are of greater length or involve some elevation gain and loss, and may challenge those who are not accustomed to much physical activity. Moderately strenuous hikes are for experienced hikers or those who are very physically fit. Strenuous hikes will challenge the most experienced and energetic of hikers.

Trail traffic: A rating of Light means that you may or may not see another hiking party along the way. Heavy means that you will regularly meet others on the trail and cannot expect to contemplate a well-known landmark or picnic spot without plenty of company. Moderate covers the wide range between these two extremes.

Elevation gain will give you some idea of how much climbing and descending you can expect, but don't forget that there may be many ups and downs between the lowest and highest elevations.

Permits are discussed in the special section on wilderness permits.

Key points are landmarks on the trail, usually trail junctions. The distances are based on the official National Park Service measurements, but the park service cautions hikers to be aware that trails have been rerouted over the years to avoid obstacles like rockslides or washouts, or to protect fragile vegetation in boggy meadows. The signs marking these trails have not always been corrected. Sometimes new signs have been added to one end of a trail but not to junctions along the way, so you will find that the miles don't always add up. Still, I have walked every trail in this book and have found none of the stated mileage between points to be inaccurate by more than a quarter mile.

At the end of each hike description, the **Best months** section refers in most cases to the only time that trails are open and safe to use at all. The hiking season in Yosemite is all too short. Most trails are passable only on skis, showshoes, or with special winter climbing equipment for most of the year. More specific times to visit areas especially noteworthy for their seasonal displays of wildflowers or fall colors or flowing waterfalls will be mentioned here.

Facilities refers to sources of supplies or contact with emergency services nearest the trailhead.

LIFE IN YOSEMITE

Yosemite is a hiker's paradise because of its wonderful diversity. The range is only about 400 by 70 miles in extent and is mostly gray granitic rock, yet every nook and cranny, every stream drainage or mountain peak, is different from the rest. The main reason for this variety is Yosemite's wide elevation range. Extremes of topography lead to extremes of weather, temperature, and soil. These in turn provide habitats for a wide variety of plants and animals. More than 1,300 species of flowering plants, 223 kinds of birds, and 77 kinds of mammals are found here. Summer days in the western foothills can reach 100 degrees F; winter nights at the crest of the range may be 30 degrees below zero. The foothills may receive as little as 15 inches of precipitation in a year while the forests at 8,000 feet may get 65 feet. Still, the Sierra Nevada is a gentle wilderness to hike because 95 percent of its precipitation falls as winter snow. Summers are usually sunny and dry, and though thundershowers can be expected in July and August at higher elevations, they are usually of short duration.

The hiking season can begin as early as April in the western foothills between elevations of 2,000 and 4,000 feet. The rolling hills are covered with a mixture of shrubby chaparral and oak woodland, green and carpeted with flowers usually through May, becoming hotter and drier later in the season. As elevations increase, wispy gray bull pines appear on the hillsides, along with the showy white wands of California buckeye.

At 4,000 to 6,000 feet a mixed coniferous forest of ponderosa pine, Douglas-fir, and incense-cedar flourishes, along with live oaks, deciduous black oaks, and maples. Warm, moist pockets support three separate groves of giant sequoias. Yosemite Valley, at about 4,000 feet, is at its finest in May and June. Waterfalls pour over the cliffs and dogwoods and azaleas bloom along the streams. Mule deer, black bears, and several kinds of ground squirrels are active in spring, summer, and fall, along with a great variety of birds.

Lodgepole pine and red fir dominate at 6,500 to 8,000 feet. This is the zone of heaviest snowfall in winter. Moisture from the Pacific Ocean is wrung from the air and piled up here in deep snowdrifts that remain well into July. Forests are dark and deep with fairly open, bare floors, because little sunlight reaches the ground. Yet strange little parasitic and saprophytic plants, including several kinds of orchids, thrive here, nourished by dead and decaying material in the soil.

The subalpine zone from 8,000 to 10,000 feet is considered by some to be the beginning of the true High Sierra. The landscape is more open and rocky and the views are the finest. The sky is intensely blue because the air is thinner. Graceful mountain hemlocks stand tall at the lower end of this zone, but the lodgepole and whitebark pines near timberline are often gnarled and stunted, forced to hunker down to avoid howling winter winds. Belding ground squirrels and marmots whistle in the meadows, and showy black, white, and gray Clark's nutcrackers squawk among the trees.

The region of high peaks and passes above timberline is true arctic-alpine country. The temperature is low, winds high, and the growing season short, so plants keep their heads low. Most of the alpine wildflowers are perennials that wait underground for the few short weeks of sunshine and freedom from snow. Beginning roughly in mid-July and continuing through August, they burst forth to carpet the high meadows and decorate the rock crannies with masses of color. Across the late-lying snowfields, rosy finches chase insects that have been blown upward from below. Pikas scurry among the rock piles, gathering food to see them through the winter.

Then at the crest, all at once, the mountains fall away to the Great Basin. On the steep eastern slope, mountain and desert species mix together. Sagebrush and pinyon pines appear. The very rock is different on the eastern side of the crest. Ancient red and white metamorphics remain above the much younger granite that underlies most of Yosemite. Many points along the crest reveal stupendous views of Mono Lake, the Owens Valley, and the White Mountains.

GEOLOGY

Yosemite occupies the central part of the Sierra Nevada, a 400-mile-long active dynamic classroom of geologic forces and features. The range was formed by the collision of vast plates of the earth's crust, lifting what had once been seafloor and offshore volcanic islands to become mountain peaks. Roughly 150 million years ago, huge globs of molten material called magma from beneath the earth's crust forced their way toward the surface, cooking the surrounding and overlying seafloor sediments to a new kind of rock known as metamorphic. Most of the molten material cooled and solidified beneath the surface to become granitic rock. Then, about 80 million years ago, mountain building ended for a time. For millennia rain and wind and weather washed away almost all of the overlying ancient seafloor to reveal the gray granite that gives Yosemite its distinctive appearance today. A few remnants of the old metamorphic rock can still be seen in a narrow belt low in the western foothills, and in another high on the Sierra crest, but more than 95 percent of the Sierra Nevada is granite.

About 25 million years ago, the range began to rise again, this time as a result of movement on the famous San Andreas Fault. North of Yosemite volcanoes erupted, blanketing the land in lava and ash. The entire range broke apart along its eastern border, the Sierra crest thrusting upward, the Owens Valley dropping down, so that the current range slopes gradually upward from west to east, till it reaches the crest, then drops away in a vertical cliff. Eventually the mountains gained enough height to block the flow of the moist winds that blow from the Pacific, which dropped their loads of rain and snow on the western flank of the range, cutting rivers and streams. The sediment washed away to the west, filling the great central valley of California with rich and productive soil. The land to the east, now deprived of water, became desert.

The movement of ice applied the finishing touches to Yosemite's scenery. About 2 to 3 million years ago, the climate of the earth cooled just a bit. Enormous ice caps formed over the poles and spread outward. While they did not reach Yosemite, the snows that did fall accumulated to great depths, then compressed to ice. The ice, under its own weight, began to flow down the previously cut stream courses, gouging them wider and deeper, scraping and polishing their bottoms and sides, sharpening the mountaintops into spires and horns, forming knife-edged ridges called aretes and amphitheaters called cirques. The ice dug out basins in the rock, and when it melted, it left thousands of sparkling alpine and subalpine lakes, many of which over time filled in with silt to become flower-filled mountain meadows. The glaciers in Yosemite today are not remnants of the original ice flows. The global climate has warmed and cooled in cycles since then, and the glaciers have melted and re-formed in response. The current glaciers are only a few hundred years old, but they lie in the hollows created by their larger predecessors, and the weather processes that created them are still at work. The mountain-building processes are work, too. The mountains are still being steadily, though not smoothly, uplifted. The Sierra is alive and growing. All along the western slope, hot springs steam and bubble along numerous faults, and earthquakes rattle local residents. As recently as 1872, an earthquake struck the Sierra to the south of Yosemite, lifting the mountains 15 to 20 feet in that area and devastating the small town of Lone Pine.

In Yosemite we can see the evidence of more than 600 million years of geologic history, and as the mountains build and erode away, witness the process as it happens.

HISTORY

The southern Sierra Miwok people, who hunted, fished, and gathered a rich variety of plant materials, especially acorns, inhabited Yosemite for more than 800 years. They conducted trade with the Piute from the east side of the mountains for obsidian for arrowheads, salt, and various foods. Both made beautiful baskets.

Yosemite was first seen by outsiders in 1851 when the Mariposa battalion chased a band of Indians led by Chief Tenaya into the valley. Shortly thereafter the native people were forced to leave their villages in the area. By 1855 the first tourists had arrived, followed by the first homesteaders. Stagecoach routes, then railroads, were built to reach the valley. Sheep and cattle were turned into the meadows to graze and trample the grasses, and loggers began to cut the trees. Fortunately, a few farsighted individuals recognized the need for protection and set in motion the appropriate political machinery leading to President Abraham Lincoln's signing of the bill that placed Yosemite Valley and the Mariposa Grove under the protection of the state of California. In 1868 the legendary John Muir arrived in Yosemite and led the movement for federal protection.

Yosemite National Park was created in 1890. All parks were patrolled by the U.S. Cavalry until 1916, when their function was taken over by the National Park Service. Many trails and other facilities were constructed or expanded by federal agencies like the WPA and the CCC during the Great Depression of the 1930s. After World War II, people and cars poured into the park in ever-increasing numbers. Now, Yosemite gets four million visitors each year, forcing the National Park Service to walk a tightrope between two somewhat contradictory mandates. It must "conserve the scenery and the natural and historic objects and the wildlife therein . . . " and it must "provide for the enjoyment of the same in such manner and by such means as will leave them unimpaired for the enjoyment of future generations."

5

Providing access to the parks and accommodations within so that everyone can enjoy them without disrupting and changing them forever is an ongoing challenge. Roads, trails, campgrounds, other lodging, emergency services, administration, and sources of supply, no matter how carefully planned and constructed, inevitably make an impact on the natural environment. Hikers can do their part by respecting park rules and practicing Zero Impact principles.

ZERO IMPACT

While the primary aim of this book is to encourage people to experience and appreciate the beauty of Yosemite up close and on foot, the backcountry is heavily used, and the environment is fragile. To prevent further wear and tear on the land, each hiker must accept personal responsibility for his or her impact on the environment by practicing Zero Impact principles. You can do your part by reading and following the suggestions and regulations you receive when you pick up your wilderness permit.

Guidelines for day hikers can be found in the Yosemite Guide, which is given to every park visitor at all entrance stations and at visitor centers and wilderness centers.

On the trail

When traveling on trails, group size is limited to 15 people. Groups traveling cross-country are limited to 8 people. All routes described in this book are on trails. Hiking on trails leaves the least impact on the land, so all the hikes in this book follow established trails. To prevent damage to the trails themselves, do not shortcut switchbacks. They have been built to retard erosion as well as to create a more comfortable grade for gaining and losing elevation. When the trail is wet or muddy, try to avoid walking alongside it, trampling vegetation and wearing a parallel trail. Many of Yosemite's meadows are scarred by a series of wide parallel ruts across the landscape that look like the work of vehicles. On the other hand, if you must cross a meadow with no conspicuous pathway, and are part of a group, spread out so that you do not create a new rut by numerous feet passing over the same route.

Good manners and consideration for others, not to mention safety, dictate that foot travelers yield to pack animals on the trail. Step off the trail and stand quietly until the last horse or mule has gone completely past. Bicycles or mechanized travel of any kind is prohibited in the backcountry (as are pets and firearms). Downhill hikers should yield to those heading uphill so that the climbers can maintain their rhythm and momentum.

Selecting a campsite

Camping is prohibited within 4 trail miles of Yosemite Valley, Hetch Hetchy Reservoir, Wawona, Glacier Point, and Tuolumne Meadows, and within 1 mile of any road. Otherwise you may camp anywhere you choose in the Yosemite wilderness so long as you observe a few restrictions designed to reduce your impact on the land and on other campers.

Choose a site at least 100 feet from water, and whenever possible, 100 feet from the trail, or at least out of sight of passers-by. Pitch your tent or spread your tarp on sandy ground or pine duff, never on growing vegetation. In the afternoon sunshine, green meadows are deceptively inviting, but are cold, damp, and buggy at night. Use an established and designated campsite, one that has been used before, and do not modify the area in any way by digging trenches around tents, building new fire rings, or breaking limbs off trees.

Campfires

Campfires are prohibited above 9,600 feet in Yosemite and are discouraged even at lower elevations. If you must have a fire, keep it small and cozy, and take only firewood that is dead and lying on the ground. Do not remove branches from standing dead trees. They provide homes for dozens of different creatures and are important parts of the ecosystem. High-elevation fires are proscribed not because of wildfire danger, but because the 9,600-foot mark is the average timberline elevation in Yosemite, where vegetation grows slowly, and the few trees that manage to hang on to life near timberline are evergreens that do not drop much organic material on the ground. The soil needs protection from compaction that the litter on the forest floor supplies, especially where people are moving around and pitching tents. Compaction prevents the soil from absorbing vital water and oxygen, and removes the source of organic material that is returned to the soil as it decomposes.

Backpacking stoves are so light and efficient, and modern fabrics so warm, that fires are no longer needed for cooking or warmth, but for social atmosphere alone. As attractive as going "back to nature" seems, there are too many of us now, and too little truly wild nature left to afford an extravagant campfire. Keep it small if you must have it, and of course, make sure it is completely out when you leave.

Housekeeping

There is one simple rule for good housekeeping in the wilderness: Do not put anything in the water. That includes soap, food scraps, and fish guts. Biodegradable soap is not the answer. To biodegrade means to decompose; that is, to rot. Biodegradable soap does not poison organisms in the water like detergent can, but it does encourage the growth of bacteria that can upset the chemical balance of the water to the detriment of the organisms that live in it. Hot water and a little sand do fine for washing dishes, but if you must use soap, wash and rinse everything at least 100 feet from any water source. The same goes for your own body. A refreshing swim in a mountain pond won't do any damage, and you can surely survive a few days in the wilderness without contacting some dread disease if you do not use soap; but if you feel you must, wash and rinse at least 100 feet away from water.

Keep your camp clean of crumbs and other edibles. Learn to take just what you need to eat, and pack out your leftovers. At very popular campsites jays, squirrels, mice, and marmots have come to expect human food scraps, and have acquired bad habits like snatching food from your hand, or chewing holes in your pack or tent to investigate appetizing smells. In popular camping areas, leave pack zippers and flaps open when you are asleep or away from camp so that varmints can crawl in to investigate and crawl back out again, without gnawing their way through the fabric.

Human waste disposal is one of the most difficult problems in the backcountry. There are simply too many of us concentrated in too few areas to avoid having a serious impact. The park service has constructed solar composting toilets at the most popular campsites in the park and encourages campers to use them. Otherwise, find a spot 200 feet from water where there is some organic material on the ground and dig a hole about 6 inches deep, then cover everything. Take extra plastic bags along and pack out your toilet paper. A teaspoon of powdered bleach in the plastic bag will prevent odors. Do not bury it. It is sometimes dug up again by animals, and takes many years to decompose underground. Burning toilet paper is no longer recommended since the practice has started more than one serious fire.

WILDERNESS PERMITS

Wilderness permits are required year-round for all overnight trips into the Yosemite backcountry. They are not required for day hikes. The permits are free of charge.

Permits are issued under a quota system designed to prevent overcrowding and damage from overuse in popular wilderness areas. They are based on trailhead entry, not on final destination. Half of the number of permits available for each trailhead can be picked up within 24 hours of your trip at wilderness centers throughout Yosemite on a first-come, first-served basis. The Yosemite Valley Wilderness Center, the Tuolumne Meadows Wilderness Center, the Big Oak Flat and Wawona visitor centers, and the Hetch Hetchy Entrance Station all issue permits. Reservations for the other half of the permits are available in advance by mail, but you must pick up the permit in person before your hike. There is a $3 per person charge for advance reservations. Currently, Yosemite's advance reservation system is under revision. For information about where and when to apply for advance reservations, call (209) 372-0200. You can also keep up with permit changes on-line at www.nps.gov/yose/wilderness.

If your hike begins outside Yosemite, obtain your permit from the Forest Service permit station nearest your entry point. All hikes described in this book that originate outside the park begin in the Hoover Wilderness. Trails north of Lundy Canyon are administered by the Bridgeport Ranger District of the Toiyabe National Forest. Permits are available from the USDA Forest Service Office in Bridgeport. Call (619) 932-7070. Trails south of Lundy Canyon are administered by the Mono Ranger District of the Inyo National Forest. Permits are available from the Mono Basin Visitor Center at Mono Lake near Lee Vining. Call (619) 647-6525.

The purpose of wilderness permits is not merely to maintain trailhead quotas. They help the National Park Service determine how much use each trail gets, so that priorities for trail maintenance and patrols can be established and funds allocated. They also allow a point of contact at which hikers can be informed of current trail conditions or any special regulations that might be in effect due to bear activity, fires, or any other emergency.

Wilderness permits are not a form of trail registration. Your itinerary is on file so that search and rescue teams have some idea of where to begin if you are reported lost, but it is up to you to leave word with someone at home who will contact the park service if you do not return when expected.

BEARS

Black bear management has become such a serious issue in Yosemite that it deserves special discussion. All of Yosemite's bears are black bears, regardless of their color. The grizzly, the California state mammal, is now extinct in California. Black bears are neither as unpredictable nor as aggressive as grizzlies. No human has ever been killed by a black bear in Yosemite, but there have been numerous injuries, lots of property damage, and many vacations spoiled. The fault is not with the bears. For many years Yosemite bears were fed scraps from local hotels, to the delight of tourists who came to watch the evening show. When the practice was discontinued, the bears resorted to raiding garbage containers all over the park. When bear-resistant garbage containers were installed, the bears mastered the art of opening ice chests in campgrounds, and when bear-proof boxes were installed in campgrounds, the bears moved into the backcountry to feast on freeze-dried backpacker cuisine. At the same time, they discovered what culinary delights are to be found in vehicles left in parking lots. The National Park Service has tried tagging, relocating, and even killing hundreds of Yosemite's bears, to no avail. Current park policy is to attempt to change the behavior of the humans, not the bears. After all, we created the problem in the first place.

The best way to help save Yosemite's bears, your expedition, and your vehicle is to carry a bear-proof food canister in the backcountry and to store any food you must leave behind in the bear-proof boxes located in parking lots and at trailheads. Bear-proof canisters are not perfect; they are bulky, weigh about three pounds, hold only a few days' food, and cost about $75. Still, the bears have not figured out how to get into them. You can rent one in locations all over Yosemite for only $3 for your entire trip. Once you learn to select and pack your food carefully, you can carry enough food for two people for several days. The alternatives are few. The counterbalance method of hanging food is illustrated in the handout you will receive along with your wilderness permit. The technique appears simple on paper, but it is very difficult to find a tree of the proper height with a branch of the proper diameter, and to balance your food sacks perfectly. The counterbalance method should be considered a delaying tactic only. Bears are much stronger, more patient, more determined, and much more intelligent than you think. If you can get it up there, they can get it back down again. Attach pots and pans or other noisemakers to your food sacks so that when the bear goes to work you will have some warning and can chase it away.

In 1998 over 1,100 vehicles were broken into in parking lots. Bears break windows, tear off doors, and tunnel through upholstery to reach the trunk from the inside. Do not store any food, garbage, anything that smells like food, or any containers that look like they might contain food like ice chests or paper bags, even if they are empty, in your car. Not even in the trunk. Do not assume that if food is sealed in plastic or foil and has not been opened that a bear cannot smell it. Their sense of smell is extremely acute, and they have learned that food comes in certain kinds of containers even if they can't read the labels or smell what's inside. They have been known to open cans of motor oil just to check. All parking lots, campgrounds, and trailheads in Yosemite have bear-proof food storage boxes nearby. Use them.

The National Park Service considers proper food storage to be your responsibility. Don't expect sympathy if you lose your food. You are liable for a fine for not storing it properly.

A FEW WORDS OF CAUTION

Weather patterns
While most Sierra summer days are clear and sunny, high mountains create their own weather. Hikers must be prepared for anything. Snow can fall at any time of year, including July and August, though it is not common. Afternoon thundershowers, sometimes accompanied by violent hailstorms, can build with amazing rapidity on summer days that begin without a cloud in the sky. They are usually of short duration, but long enough to drench and chill an unprepared traveler. Never set out without rain gear. Lightning can be a serious hazard on open ridges above timberline. If a storm threatens, head downhill to the cover of timber as quickly as possible. If you're caught in an exposed area with no time to descend, get away from your pack or any metal equipment and *squat* until the danger passes—do not sit.

Drinking water
In spite of the clear and sparkling appearance of Yosemite's lakes and streams, water from even the most remote of sources has been found to contain *Giardia lamblia*, a microorganism that causes diarrhea and other intestinal upsets. It is not life-threatening illness for normal healthy adults, but it is debilitating and persistent, and must be treated with antibiotics whose side effects may be equally unpleasant. The symptoms do not appear for more than a week after exposure, so victims sometimes do not associate their malady with their wilderness experience. Treat all water with a water filter guaranteed to remove *Giardia,* with iodine, or by boiling. Since the bug is killed at temperatures far below boiling, even at high elevations, just bringing water to a rolling boil is treatment enough. Iodine is lightweight, convenient, and effective if fresh, but some people are allergic and some object to the taste.

Wild animals
Injuries caused by bears in Yosemite are almost invariably due to human ignorance or carelessness. Take care to avoid moving between a mother and

her cubs, and do not try to touch or feed a bear, or to reclaim food the bear has already taken from you. More injuries are caused by deer than by bears in the park since people are more likely to approach a deer and risk being sliced by sharp hooves when the animal is startled.

Mountain lions have been spotted in Yosemite, but they are very shy, and attacks are extremely rare. If you should encounter one, do not run or you might be mistaken for prey. Hold your ground, wave your arms to make yourself appear larger, and shout. Then congratulate yourself on being given the gift of a glimpse of a beautiful animal in its native habitat.

You'll find rattlesnake habitat at lower elevations where there is plenty of brush to provide cover for small animals like rabbits, squirrels, and mice. Rattlers are most active at dawn and dusk and blend beautifully with their surroundings. They prefer to save their venom for catching their prey and do not strike at people unless they feel threatened. Stay alert and watch your step. The chances of being bitten are extremely slim and snakebites are rarely fatal.

Stream crossings

This is one hazard that is not exaggerated, unlike perceived threats from wildlife. Most of the larger streams in Yosemite have sturdy bridges across them, but in exceptionally wet years, even some of these get washed away. Be sure to research trail conditions in advance if your proposed route involves a major river crossing. More frequently, it is the smaller creeks swollen with snowmelt early in the year that are most dangerous. Some have rock or log crossings that must be managed with great care. A stout stick is a great stabilizer. Be sure to plant it upstream so that rushing water does not

If you decide to wade, always overestimate the depth and strength of the current.

grab it and pull it out from under you. Always unbuckle your pack straps so that if you should fall in, you can free yourself from being dragged and held underwater.

If you decide to wade, always overestimate the depth and the strength of the current. Sierra streams are so clear they are usually deeper and swifter than they seem. Do not wade through water higher than your knees. The recommended method is to remove your socks and cross in your boots, which will give you temporary protection against the numbing cold and more stability on underwater obstacles. Do not try to cross barefooted. Seek out the widest part of the stream, even though the temptation is to pick a narrower spot to make the crossing quicker. The widest spot is usually the shallowest, slowest, and the safest. If you are not sure whether you can cross safely, you can try again early in the morning when the snow upstream has begun to melt in the morning sun. Do not take chances. You can always return.

Losing the trail
Yosemite trails are much more defined, well marked, and better maintained than those you will find in most other wilderness areas. Still, some are used more regularly than others and are easier to follow. High water, avalanches, rockslides, and fast-growing meadow vegetation and brush can obscure a clear trail in a single season. Watch for trail blazes on the trees, made by cutting away the outer bark, usually in simple geometric shapes at approximately eye level. In open rocky places, watch for cairns, also known as ducks—piles of rocks that indicate the presence of a trail. Stay alert for sawed logs, metal tags, sometimes even plastic strips. If you become confused on the trail, go back to a point where you were absolutely certain of your location, and start over. If you feel you are hopelessly lost, stay put and wait for help.

Trail ducks, also called cairns, mark many of Yosemite's trails.

Trail Finder Table

	EASY	MODERATE	DIFFICULT
Backcountry Lakes	20 May Lake HSC 33 Tenaya Lake 43 Lukens Lake	18 Merced Lake HSC 19 Vogelsang HSC 22 Sunrise HSC 27 Buena Vista Crest 29 Ostrander Lake 36 Cathedral Lakes 37 Elizabeth Lake 42 Harden Lake 44 Ten Lakes 46 Dog Lake 48 Young Lakes 49 Polly Dome Lakes 53 Lake Vernon 55 Saddlebag Lake 58 Virginia Lakes Basin	30 Ottoway Lakes 31 The Clark Range 50 Gaylor Lakes 57 Green Creek 59 Hoover Lakes 60 Matterhorn Canyon 61 Benson Pass 62 McCabe Lakes 63 Peeler Lake
Waterfalls	1 East Valley Floor 9 Sentinel Dome 51 Wapama Falls	4 Happy Isles to Nevada Fall 12 Panorama Trail 21 Glen Aulin HSC 25 Alder Creek 26 Chilnualna Fall 52 Rancheria Falls 57 Green Creek	6 Yosemite Falls 32 Merced River High Trail 41 Waterwheel Falls 54 Jack Main Canyon and Tildan Lake 56 Lundy Canyon
Alpine Country, Ridges, Passes, and Plateaus		19 Vogelsang HSC 39 Donohue Pass 40 Mono Pass 44 Ten Lakes 55 Saddlebag Lake 60 Matterhorn Canyon 62 McCabe Lakes 63 Peeler Lake	31 The Clark Range 50 Gaylor Lakes 56 Lundy Canyon 59 Hoover Lakes 61 Benson Pass
Really Flat Trails with No Hills	1 East Valley Floor 2 West Valley Floor 5 Mirror Lake 28 Wawona Meadow 33 Tenaya Lake		

	EASY	MODERATE	DIFFICULT
Overnight Backpacking Trips	21 Glen Aulin HSC 29 Ostrander Lake 37 Elizabeth Lake	11 The Pohono Trail 13 Tioga Road to the Top of Yosemite Fall 19 Vogelsang HSC 22 Sunrise HSC 35 Tenaya Lake to Half Dome 36 Cathedral Lakes 48 Young Lakes 52 Rancheria Falls 55 Saddlebag Lake 57 Green Creek	30 Ottoway Lakes 44 Ten Lakes 59 Hoover Lakes
Trails to Avoid if You Want Solitude	1 East Valley Loop 5 Mirror Lake–Tenaya Canyon Loop 24 Mariposa Grove 33 Tenaya Lake 38 Lyell Fork 45 Soda Springs and and Parsons Lodge	4 Happy Isles to the Top of Nevada Fall 12 The Panorama Trail 18 Merced Lake HSC 19 Vogelsang HSC 20 May Lake HSC 21 Glen Aulin HSC 22 Sunrise HSC 23 High Sierra Camp Loop 36 Cathedral Lakes 37 Elizabeth Lake 42 Harden Lake 46 Dog Lake 47 Lembert Dome 55 Saddlebag Lake	3 Glacier Point via the 4 Mile Trail 6 Valley Floor to top of Yosemite Falls 7 Half Dome 34 Clouds Rest
Early Season (before July) Trails	1 East Valley Floor 2 West Valley Floor 5 Mirror Lake–Tenaya Canyon Loop 24 Mariposa Grove 28 Wawona Meadow 51 Wapama Falls	25 Alder Creek 26 Chilnualna Fall 52 Rancheria Falls 53 Lake Vernon	
Wildflowers	1 East Valley Floor 2 West Valley Floor 10 McGurk Meadow 28 Wawona Meadow 43 Lukens Lake 45 Soda Springs and and Parsons Lodge	18 Merced Lake HSC 25 Alder Creek 29 Ostrander Lake 36 Cathedral Lakes 37 Elizabeth Lake 38 Lyell Fork 42 Harden Lake 51 Wapama Falls 52 Rancheria Falls 53 Lake Vernon	39 Lyell Fork to Donohue Pass 54 Jack Main Canyon 56 Lundy Canyon

	EASY	MODERATE	DIFFICULT
Wildlife (especially bears)	10 McGurk Meadow 28 Wawona Meadow	4 Happy Isles to the Top of Nevada Fall 18-23 All High Sierra Camps 36 Cathedral Lakes 38 Lyell Fork 44 Ten Lakes 52 Rancheria Falls	

Author's Favorites

For Photography	1 East Valley Floor	39 Lyell Fork to Donohue Pass
	2 West Valley Floor	44 Ten Lakes
	4 Happy Isles to the Top of Nevada Fall	48 Young Lakes
	7 Half Dome	54 Jack Main Canyon and Tilden Lake
	11 The Pohono Trail	55 Saddlebag Lake
	12 The Panorama Trail	56 Lundy Canyon
	16 The North Rim	57 Green Creek
	23 The High Sierra Camp Loop	58 Virginia Lakes Basin
	31 The Clark Range	59 Hoover Lakes
	32 Merced River High Trail	60 Matterhorn Canyon
	34 Clouds Rest	63 Peeler Lake
	35 Tenaya Lake to Half Dome	
	36 Cathedral Lakes	
For High-Altitude Scenery	19 Vogelsang HSC	55 Saddlebag Lake
	31 The Clark Range	56 Lundy Canyon
	39 Lyell Fork to Donohue Pass	57 Green Creek
	40 Mono Pass	58 Virginia Lakes Basin
	50 Gaylor Lakes	59 Hoover Lakes
		61 Benson Pass
For an Easy Day Hike	2 West Valley Floor	28 Wawona Meadow
For a Moderate Day Hike	21 Glen Aulin HSC	52 Rancheria Falls
	40 Mono Pass	55 Saddlebag Lake
	50 Gaylor Lakes	
For a Long, Hard Day Hike	7 Half Dome	56 Lundy Canyon
	11 The Pohono Trail	57 Green Creek
	34 Clouds Rest	59 Hoover Lakes
	48 Young Lakes	
For a True Wilderness Adventure	31 The Clark Range	61 Benson Pass
	32 Merced River High Trail	63 Peeler Lake
	54 Jack Main Canyon and Tilden Lake	

The Valley Floor

The Valley Floor

Yosemite Valley is one of the natural wonders of the world. Almost vertical walls rise up to 4,733 feet above the valley floor, where the Merced River winds its way through flower-filled meadows and shady forests. The famous profile of Half Dome dominates the east end and El Capitan the west. Some of the world's highest waterfalls pour from the cliffs. It is a Mecca for hikers, climbers, photographers, fishermen, rafters, cyclists, and just plain tourists from everywhere on earth. While it covers only about 7 square miles of a national park that sprawls over 1,200 square miles, the majority of visitors stay in the valley, and indeed, many believe that Yosemite Valley and Yosemite National Park are one and the same. Do not expect a wilderness experience in Yosemite Valley, but don't assume that hiking there is not worthwhile just because it's popular. The valley's attractions draw so many sightseers because they are well worth seeing, but there are also many beautiful, quiet, out-of-the way corners to enjoy on foot and in solitude.

Spring and fall are the best times to hike the valley. The crowds and traffic are heaviest in summer and temperatures can be uncomfortably hot for strenuous hiking. Springtime is more comfortable; the waterfalls are full, and the wildflowers are blooming. In fall the air is clear and brisk and the changing colors of the oaks, dogwoods, maples, and willows are spectacular.

All hikes on the valley floor are day hikes because no camping is allowed outside established campgrounds. Permits are not necessary, but it's a good idea to drop by the visitor center and the wilderness center for information about trail conditions and weather reports. You can help reduce traffic and pollution in the valley by parking your car and using the shuttle buses that run every 10 minutes and go to most valley trailheads.

If you are planning a backpack that originates in the valley, you can pick up your wilderness permit at the wilderness center, between the Ansel Adams Gallery and the post office in Yosemite Village. You can also get a parking permit there to display in your window in the backpacker's parking lot just east of Curry Village. The other lots are for day use or for lodge or tent cabin guests only. If you arrive the day before your trip, remember that all accommodations—campgrounds, lodges, and hotels—are usually full and require reservations many months in advance. Sunnyside walk-in campground on the north side west of Yosemite Lodge is your best bet. Be sure to stow all food, food containers, garbage, and ice chests in the bear-proof containers at the parking lot any time you leave your car.

The valley is open year-round and can be reached from the west via California 41 from Fresno, California 140 from Merced, and California 120 from Manteca. In summer California 120, Tioga Road, is open all the way through the park to the east side of the Sierra near Lee Vining on U.S. Highway 395. There is a $20 fee per car to enter the park from any direction.

Contact Yosemite at (209) 372-0200 or e-mail at www.nps.gov/yose/ for more information.

1 East Valley Floor

General description:	A leisurely, flat loop hike with views of North Dome; Happy Isles Nature Center.
Total distance:	2.6 miles.
Difficulty:	Easy.
Elevation gain:	100 feet.
Trail traffic:	Light to heavy.
Best months:	Year-round.
Maps:	USGS Half Dome quad.
Permits:	None.

Finding the trailhead: Board the Yosemite Valley shuttle bus from any-place in the valley and get off at Stop 1 or Stop 14, Curry Village, or leave your car in the big parking lot at Curry Village at the southeast end of the valley.

Trailhead facilities: Food, supplies, phones, water, and restrooms at Curry Village.

Key points:
- 0.0   Curry Village parking lot/trailhead.
- 0.1   Backpackers' parking lot.
- 0.9   The Fen.
- 1.0   Happy Isles Nature Center.
- 1.1   Happy Isles Bridge on Shuttle Bus Road.
- 2.0   Stables.

The hike: From the raised patio area in front of the bustling Curry Village snack bar/grocery/bike rental complex, look be-yond and above the enormous parking lot on your left to towering North Dome and

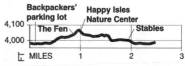

Elevation data provided by TOPO! www.topo.com

the Royal Arches, serene and indifferent to the hubbub below. Then follow the paved footpath eastward past a line of tent cabins fronted by a row of large, brown, steel bear-proof boxes for nighttime storage of food, toothpaste, and other aromatic bear-tempting articles.

If you set out before 9 A.M., a good idea in midsummer when valley temperatures climb into the 80s, you are likely to pass a row of bleary-eyed tent cabin guests brushing teeth, applying deodorant, and generally prepar-ing for the day. A few hundred yards beyond the tent cabins and the tooth-brush brigade, a driveway turns right into a parking lot for backpackers. Go into the lot, turn left, and walk to the southeast end. Take the unmarked, but wide and obvious trail into the shady ponderosa pine and incense-cedar forest.

Pass a little A-frame structure used for ranger/naturalist talks, and at 0.9 mile reach a swampy area known as the Fen. Here a boardwalk runs through a lush growth of water-loving horsetails, sedges, and fragrant mints. An

East Valley Floor

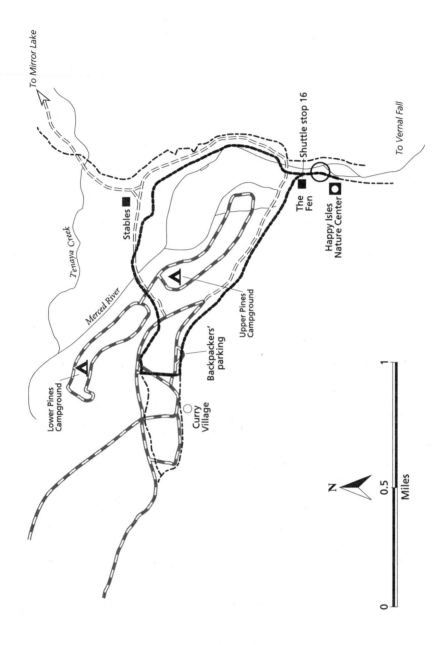

To Mirror Lake

Shuttle stop 16

Stables

The Fen

Happy Isles Nature Center

To Vernal Fall

Tenaya Creek

Merced River

Upper Pines Campground

Backpackers' parking

Lower Pines Campground

Curry Village

N

0   0.5   1
Miles

interpretive panel tells about the living things inhabiting soggy places like this one. The trail crosses a paved path at 1 mile just before meeting the Merced River. To the right is the Happy Isles Nature Center, with wonderful exhibits and books inside. Behind the building you can see the rubble and smashed trees left by the 1996 rockslide where a hiker was killed. The footbridge across the Merced was so battered by recent flooding that it is no longer safe for foot traffic, so you must detour to the left and follow the riverside path to the shuttle bus road (Stop 16 at 1.1 miles). There are restrooms and a snack bar here.

This hike crosses the road and continues downstream along the north bank of the Merced. Take a tiny detour and walk out onto the bridge over the road for views of the river, which rushes toward the bridge in noisy whitewater rapids, then emerges more quietly from the other side. The view of North Dome over the river on the downstream side is a photographer's favorite.

Once you have crossed the road, you leave the crowds behind and follow a path through incense-cedar and pine, streamside alder and dogwood. Big, showy white azaleas perfume the air in May and June. The river changes character at every turn, sometimes gurgling busily, sometimes green and placid, occasionally splitting to flow around wooded islands. This section of the trail is shared by horses and mules because it connects their stables to the John Muir Trail. Remember to step off the trail to let them pass, since pack animals always have the right-of-way.

At 2 miles the stable area appears across the road on the right, and simultaneously Upper Yosemite Fall comes into view ahead. Turn left here and cross back over the Merced on the road on the Clark Bridge. Pass between

View of Yosemite Falls from East Valley floor.

the entrances to Upper and Lower Pines Campgrounds. A sign on the right directs you to Curry Village. Shortly thereafter you will spot straight ahead the cabins for Curry Village employees. Just beyond the cabins and to the right (or west) you'll find the Curry Village parking lot and the end of the hike.

2 West Valley Floor

General description:	An almost flat loop around the west end of Yosemite Valley.
Total distance:	6.5 miles.
Difficulty:	Easy.
Elevation gain:	330 feet.
Trail traffic:	Light, except at popular roadside attractions.
Best months:	Spring, summer, and fall.
Maps:	USGS El Capitan and Half Dome quads.
Permits:	None.

Finding the trailhead: From Yosemite Village, take Northside Drive (one-way, westbound) to El Capitan Drive and turn left (south). From any of the west side park entrances take Southside Drive (one-way, eastbound) to El Capitan Drive and turn left (north). Park along the road on either side just west of the El Capitan Bridge.

Trailhead facilities: None; restrooms at Bridalveil Fall.

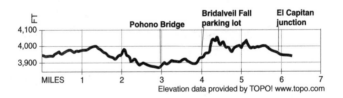

Elevation data provided by TOPO! www.topo.com

Key points:
- 0.0   El Capitan Bridge.
- 0.3   Northside Drive.
- 0.6   El Capitan spur 2.
- 2.7   Pohono Bridge.
- 4.0   Bridalveil Fall parking lot.
- 4.3   Southside Drive.
- 5.8   El Capitan junction.

The hike: Valley floor trails are surprisingly quiet and unvisited if you stay away from the big attractions. If you start early, you can have the whole western valley to yourself.

The trail begins beside an apple tree at the west end of the bridge over the Merced River. Upstream, to the north is the 7,569-foot monolith of El

West Valley Floor

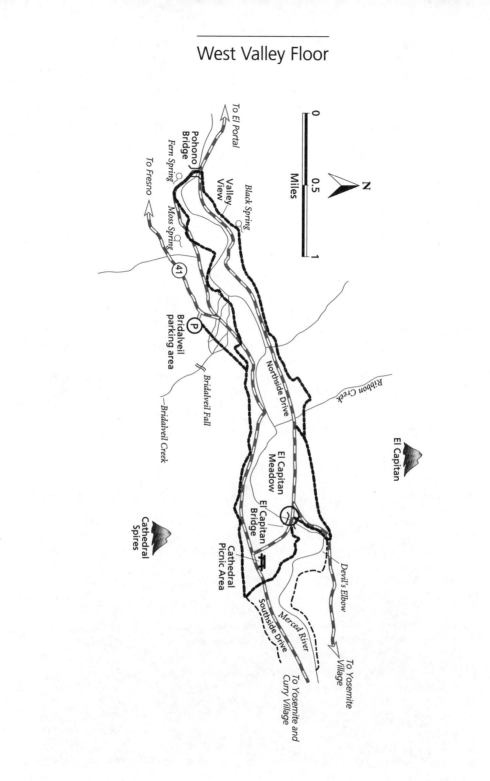

Capitan; downstream are the Cathedral Rocks and Cathedral Spires. These and many more of Yosemite's granite walls draw climbers from all over the world. Set off upstream (northward) alongside the quiet, green river on a path of partly eroded asphalt, following the curve of the river as it swings eastward and parallels the road for a short distance. This curve is called the Devil's Elbow. In midsummer the water-level drops to reveal a sandbar in midstream, popular with swimmers and sunbathers. The bank was badly trampled until the park service revegetated the area and constructed an unobtrusive fence between the path and the river, with signs directing traffic upstream to openings in the fence, allowing access to the river by a less fragile route.

Where this fence ends at 0.3 mile, cross Northside Drive, and make a sharp hairpin turn back westward. The trail sign across the road says "El Capitan 0.4 mile." As you walk westward, the famous North American wall of El Capitan looms directly overhead. It was named for a patch of darker-colored mineral in the granite that is shaped like the North American continent. You are close enough here to see—without binoculars—the figures clinging to the rock above and hear them shouting back and forth. As you approach the nose of El Capitan, cross several spur routes used by climbers to reach the base of the wall from the road. Two of these have signs (in four languages) setting out rules and warnings for climbers. At the second climber warning sign at 0.6 mile, the trail sign says "Bridalveil Fall 3.7 miles." Some distance beyond, another sign says exactly the same thing: "Bridalveil Fall 3.7 miles." Continue straight ahead past both signs along the trail that parallels the road. If the season is early spring and Ribbon Creek is flowing fast

Bridalveil Fall spills over the southern wall of Yosemite Valley.

and deep and is too dangerous to cross, cut downhill (left) to the road and walk along the shoulder of the road to get across the creek. Ribbon Creek falls over the cliff just west of El Capitan as Ribbon Fall and, like Bridalveil across the valley, dissolves into a mist toward the bottom in early summer, and dries out entirely by mid-July.

Rejoin the trail beyond the creek. It's still partly eroded asphalt, remnants of an old road. The blackened lower trunks of the trees are signs of a 1970s controlled burn. The trail comes almost all the way out to the road at an open place close beside the Merced, where there is a good view of Bridalveil Fall. Also, on the north side of the road, an interpretive panel explains glacial features and the origin of the waterfall. The trail ducks back into the forest of white fir, incense-cedar, black oak, and a few ponderosas, and presently passes to the right around Black Spring, where water-loving cattails, horsetails, and willows thrive in the muck. It's a wonderful place to pause and listen to the songs of blackbirds and warblers. The trail comes to the road again at a spot called Valley View, one of the most popular photo stops in the valley. There are toilets here at a turnout on the road.

At 2.7 miles, cross the road and the river on the Pohono Bridge. Turn upstream (east) and walk between Southside Drive and the river past a gauging station. This must be one of the loveliest little corners of Yosemite, especially in May and October when the dogwoods are in bloom or turning red. The Merced quickens its pace, and its racing over the rocks masks the sound of nearby traffic. There are two springs here, Fern Spring on one side of the road, Moss Spring on the other; in May the trail is muddy, but the moisture allows the growth of some beautiful pink bleeding hearts or frilly white false Solomon's seal lilies.

The trail hugs the riverside for a time, then emerges into sunshine next to Southside Drive, skirting Bridalveil Meadow. Across the road, a sign marks the site of the famous confab between John Muir and Teddy Roosevelt about the need for the protection of land in the national park system. In mid- to late season when Bridalveil Creek is low, you can follow the trail along the Merced, but earlier in the year you must leave the trail where it once again nears the road and walk along the shoulder to get over Bridalveil Creek. It is at this point that Southside Drive and California 41 come together. Backtrack just a few feet on California 41 to visit Bridalveil Fall on the right (south) side of the road at 4.1 miles. Bridalveil flows over the southern wall of Yosemite Valley through a defile between Cathedral Rocks and the Leaning Tower, but before it reaches the bottom, 620 feet below, the wind catches, tatters, and flings the droplets into graceful lacy patterns.

Leave the Bridalveil Fall area on a wide, beaten path and continue east, parallel to Southside Drive. Turn right at the junction that directs you to Curry Village. Climb over the Bridalveil moraine a bit above the road and walk along a tumble of mossy rocks to get a great view of El Capitan across the valley. To your right the cliffs loom impossibly high and straight over your head. The path is lovely, with the sun slanting through the oaks and maples. The trail leads you back down beside the road, where you can see the back of El Capitan Meadow beyond, then swings away again through a stand of Douglas-fir and incense-cedar. At the signed junction at 5.8 miles, turn left (north). Cross Southside Drive at the Cathedral Picnic Area turnoff and follow the trail through a dense growth of baby ponderosa pines. The trail finally meets the El Capitan road on the east side of the bridge. Cross the bridge to your car.

3 Glacier Point via the Four Mile Trail

General description:	A steep out-and-back day hike to views of almost the whole of Yosemite Valley.
Total distance:	9.2 miles.
Difficulty:	Strenuous.
Elevation gain:	3,200 feet.
Trail traffic:	Moderate.
Best months:	Spring, summer, or fall. Trail closed in winter.
Maps:	USGS Half Dome quad.
Permits:	None.

Finding the trailhead: Drive east (the only way you can go) on one-way Southside Drive to the parking area on both sides of the road just beyond the Sentinel Beach/Yellow Pine picnic areas. Watch carefully for the trailhead sign on the right—if you miss it, you'll have to drive all the way around the valley to get back. You can also use the Yosemite Valley shuttle bus, if you don't mind walking an additional mile each way. The nearest bus stop is 8, Yosemite Lodge. Follow the bike path across Swinging Bridge, turn right, and walk 50 yards to the trailhead. For an easier hike, take the shuttle bus to Glacier Point and hike downhill to the trailhead.

Trailhead facilities: None; Glacier Point has food, water, toilets, and telephones.

Key points:
- 0.0 Interpretive panel; Sentinel Rock.
- 4.6 Glacier Point/snack bar.

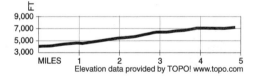

The hike: The Four Mile Trail is really 4.6 miles long because it had to be rerouted since its original construction. An interpretive panel with historical information about the early days of tourism in Yosemite marks the beginning of the trail. Towering overhead is the vertical flat slab of Sentinel Rock. The asphalt trail begins its switchbacking ascent among huge mossy boulders beneath shady live oaks, laurels, and maples. Mariposa lilies, catchfly, and alum root line the path, which soon crosses a little creek lined with thimbleberry, lupine, and monkey

Glacier Point via the Four Mile Trail

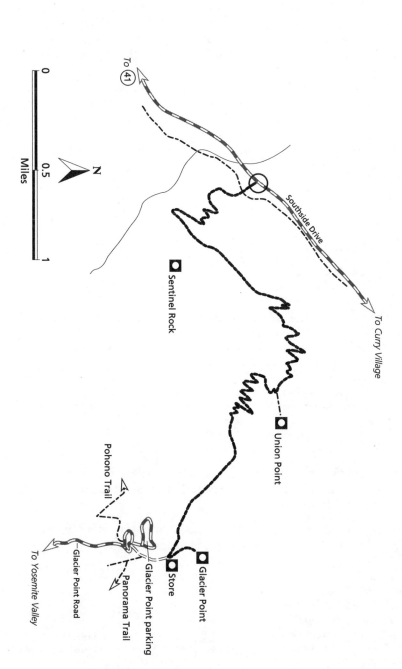

flowers. The route works gradually eastward as it climbs. If you begin your hike by 8 A.M., watch for hang gliders suspended in air right beside the trail, on their way to the landing area in Leidig Meadow. Still climbing, the trail comes even with Yosemite Falls, roaring across the valley. At about three-quarters of the way, you arrive at a short spur trail to Union Point, where Tenaya Canyon, North Dome, Clouds Rest, and Half Dome appear briefly, then disappear as the trail heads in a more southerly direction. The switchbacks become a bit less short and steep and the way becomes sunnier and more open. At last, the trail loses a bit of elevation, rounds a shoulder, crosses a tiny rivulet, then makes a short climb to top out at the Glacier Point Snack Bar. Enjoy the several stupendous views of the park in the Glacier Point area, then return the way you came. Descend carefully; the loose gravel can be slippery.

4 Happy Isles to the Top of Nevada Fall

General description: A loop to the top of Nevada Fall, returning via the John Muir Trail.
Total distance: 5.8 miles.
Difficulty: Moderate.
Elevation gain: 1,950 feet.
Trail traffic: Heavy.
Best months: May–June for spectacular waterfalls; October–early November for foliage.
Maps: USGS Half Dome quad.
Permits: None.

Finding the trailhead: Board the Yosemite Valley shuttle bus from any-place in the valley (Curry Village has parking nearest the trailhead) and get off at Stop 16, Happy Isles.

Trailhead facilities: Restrooms, snacks, and nature exhibits; pit toilet at the top of Nevada Fall on the north side of the river.

Key points:
- 0.0 Happy Isles.
- 0.8 Vernal Fall Bridge.
- 0.9 Mist Trail junction.
- 1.5 Silver Apron Bridge above Vernal Fall.
- 2.5 Top of Nevada Fall.
- 2.7 Panorama Trail junction.
- 5.0 Vernal Fall Bridge via John Muir Trail.

Elevation data provided by TOPO! www.topo.com

Happy Isles to the Top of Nevada Fall

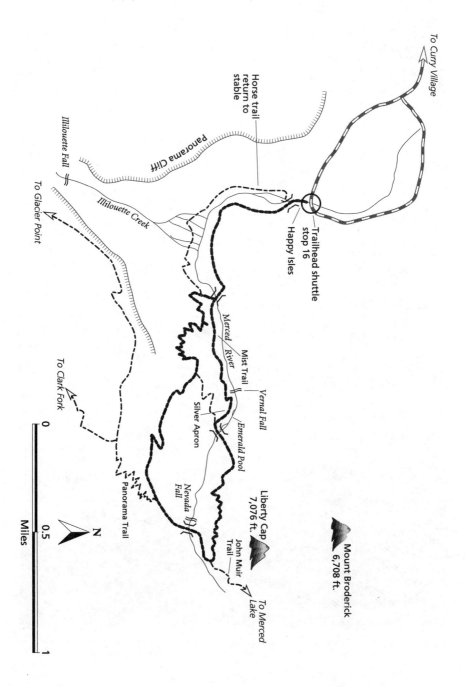

The Merced River's plunge over Nevada Fall before the flat floor of Yosemite Valley.

The hike: If you have time for only one hike in Yosemite, whether you want to spend the day on the trail or take only a short stroll, this is the one. This is what Yosemite is about; massive granite cliffs, classic glacial features, and views of at least four of the valley's biggest and best waterfalls. The Merced River plunges over the steps of the Giant Staircase as Nevada (Spanish: Snowy) Fall, then as Vernal (Latin: Springtime) Fall before it meanders over the flat floor of Yosemite Valley. Take your rain gear if you're hiking beyond the Vernal Fall Bridge in springtime, or choose a warm day. The trail skirts the falls so closely that you'll be drenched from the spray. Later, if time permits, hike or drive up to Glacier Point for a spectacular view of your entire route up the Giant Staircase as well as the rest of Yosemite Valley.

Happy Isles is the site of the notorious rockfall of July 1996 that killed a hiker. A huge sign there marks the beginning of the John Muir Trail, showing mileage to various points all the way to trail's end at Mount Whitney, 211 miles to the south.

The first part of the trail was paved at one time, but the asphalt has washed away in places over the years, so it's sometimes rough and rocky. Don't expect a true wilderness experience here. This is a popular spot for good reasons, but the farther you go, the more solitude you'll find. It's popular not only because it is spectacular, but because it's one of the few routes out of the valley to the high country.

The trail climbs gently through black oak and pine forest among enormous lichen-draped boulders up along the north bank of the Merced. A little spring trickles out of the rocks a few hundred yards up on your left. Don't drink the water without purifying it. The trail steepens gradually as you climb, but you'll want to stop frequently anyway to enjoy the roaring river through openings in the trees. In about a half mile across the Merced to your right, tucked back up in Illilouette Gorge, Illilouette Fall pours 370 feet down the Panorama Cliff to meet the Merced River. If you stop now and then to glance behind you, Upper Yosemite Fall is visible. The trail suddenly descends to the bridge at 0.8 mile, where dozens of visitors will be taking photos or staring in open-mouthed wonder at 317-foot Vernal Fall upstream. There are restrooms, a water fountain, and dozens of freeloading Steller's jays and ground squirrels. For their health and your safety, do not feed them.

Cross the bridge to the south side of the Merced, and turn left (upstream). The crowd will soon thin noticeably. At 0.9 mile the Mist Trail leaves the John Muir Trail to the left. To follow the loop clockwise, take the left fork, and return on the John Muir Trail. Where the sign says "Foot Trail Only, Top of Vernal Fall via Mist Trail .3 mile," get out your rain gear. The Mist Trail climbs steeply by big wet stone blocks. Watch your step! The thunder of the falls is almost deafening in early season; morning sunlight through the spray has a diffuse, mystical quality, and there's always a rainbow or two if the sun is shining. At the top of the falls is an oak-shaded bench where you can shake off excess water. Beside this bench, the Merced pauses to collect itself in the deceptively quiet Emerald Pool, before crashing over the cliff. A long, slanting ramp called the Silver Apron tempts the sweaty hiker to ride this water slide into the pool. Don't do it! In an instant you'll be washed over the rim to the rocks 320 feet below. There are several warning signs along the riverbank reminding hikers to keep away from the edge and out of the water. Some who have ignored the warnings have been killed.

At 1.5 miles, cross the bridge at the Silver Apron back over the Merced and begin climbing steeply again along its north shore, sometimes through a light mist from Nevada Fall in early season. Another set of switchbacks brings you out onto the sunny bench above the falls, where you'll meet the junction with the John Muir Trail; follow the trail, turning right (south) toward Yosemite Valley. There are plenty of viewpoints with protective railings where you can watch Nevada Fall rush over the lip and drop 594 feet. It's a perfect place for sunbathing and picnicking. Keep an eye on your lunch! The local squirrels and jays will make off with it if your attention wanders for even a moment.

After gaping awestruck at the roaring water, cross the bridge and follow the slope upward a short distance where you pass the junction with the Panorama Trail at 2.7 miles. It takes off to the left toward Illilouette Fall, Glacier Point, and beyond. Your trail, to the right, is cut into the side of the cliff beneath a weeping rock overhang that gently drips onto the trail. Delicate ferns and columbines are tucked into the cracks. Continue to descend on well-graded switchbacks, enjoying views of Upper Yosemite Fall across the valley, until you reach Clark Point. This is where the hiker who is heading upward on the Muir Trail catches the first jaw-dropping view of Nevada Fall with Mount Broderick and Liberty Cap looming above. There is a lateral trail here that cuts back to the Mist Trail, but if you want to stay dry this time, keep left and stay on the John Muir Trail. Just before you reach the Vernal Fall Bridge again, you'll pass the junction to the Mist Trail where you went up, then another junction for horses only that leads back to the stables. You cross the Vernal Fall Bridge at 5 miles and return to Happy Isles the way you came.

5   Mirror Lake–Tenaya Canyon Loop

General description:	A short, easy day hike leading to one of the most isolated corners of the valley.
Total distance:	4.2 miles.
Difficulty:	Easy.
Elevation gain:	100 feet.
Trail traffic:	Moderate.
Best months:	Accessible year-round, but finest in May and June.
Maps:	USGS Half Dome and Yosemite Falls quads.
Permits:	None.

Mirror Lake–Tenaya Canyon Loop

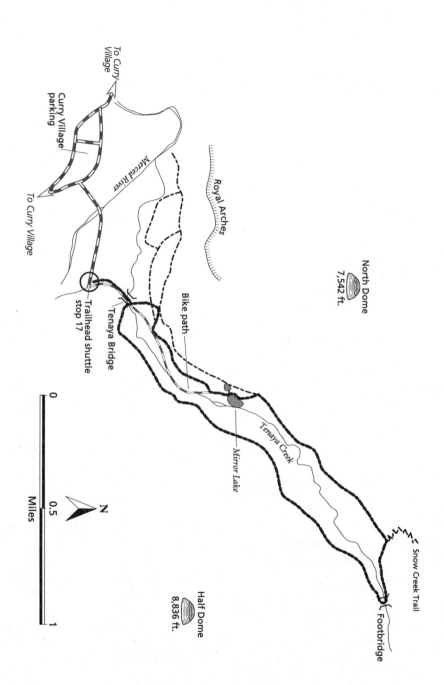

Finding the trailhead: Board the Yosemite Valley shuttle bus from anyplace in the valley (Curry Village has parking nearest the trailhead) and get off at Stop 17, Mirror Lake.

Trailhead facilities: Restrooms, but no potable water.

Key Points

0.0   Mirror Lake Trailhead.
1.0   West end of Mirror Lake.
2.1   East end of Mirror Lake
         footbridge.

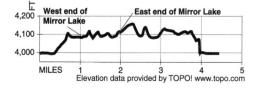

The hike: Mirror Lake was created when a rockslide dammed up a section of Tenaya Creek, which promptly went to work to reclaim its original course. Every spring it washes tons of silt down the canyon to refill the lake basin, extending fingers of earth out into the water. These fingers invite colonization by water-loving plants like sedges and willows, which soon come alive with the songs of redwing blackbirds. Mirror Lake is well on its way to becoming Mirror Meadow. Eventually, as the basin fills in and dries out, trees will move in, and soon the land will again be a conifer forest with Tenaya Creek running through it, perhaps leaving the canyon as though Mirror Lake had never been—at least until the next rockslide. For years the park service periodically dredged the lake, slowing the natural succession from lake to forest in order to preserve the popular reflection, but the practice was finally discontinued. Interpretive exhibits along the way help visitors appreciate the way the natural world is continually transformed.

To hike the loop in a clockwise direction, skirting the west shore of Tenaya Creek and Mirror Lake and returning along the eastern shore, follow the sign to Mirror Lake along the paved road (no longer in use except for bicycles) across the Tenaya Creek Bridge past the interpretive panel on the right, which tells about the Yosemite flood of January 1997. That year, an unseasonable thaw sent runoff from a wetter-than-normal snowpack raging through the valley, gouging out the streambed and raising the water level to as much as 20 feet above normal. It washed out roads, bridges, campgrounds, and housing, and closed down the park. Just beyond this panel you can leave the road and follow a signed footpath to the left or continue on the road. The road is the more scenic route since it follows the creekside. Both road and trail rise slightly, passing through a quiet forest of ponderosa pine, white fir, Douglas-fir, incense-cedar, and dogwood. At 1 mile, the forest opens to reveal tranquil Mirror Lake, reflecting Half Dome above it. Mount Watkins provides the backdrop to the north. There are sandy beaches along the lakeshore for picnics and wading.

The majority of visitors stop here, but those who continue on upstream will discover one of the more isolated, less hectic corners of Yosemite Valley. The forest floor is deeply carpeted with pine needles and bracken fern. Wild ginger, incongruously tropical looking in this setting, sprawls along the ground. Look for its weird, three-petalled purplish green flowers hidden beneath the big, shiny heart-shaped leaves. There are dozens of species of butterflies in patches of sunlight, and you can often hear canyon wren songs echoing off the cliffs upstream. A trail junction appears at 2.1 miles marking the Snow Creek Trail, which climbs steeply up out of Tenaya Canyon to the rim of the valley. Just past the big trail sign, cross the bridge over Tenaya Creek and return downstream along the eastern shore. Your trail meets the road again just where it crosses the Tenaya Creek Bridge, within a few hundred yards of the shuttle bus stop.

6 Yosemite Falls

General description: A steep out-and-back day hike or backpack to views of Sentinel Rock, Half Dome, and Upper Yosemite Fall.
Total distance: 6.8 miles.
Difficulty: Strenuous.
Elevation gain: 2,630 feet.
Trail traffic: Heavy.
Best months: Late spring and early summer.
Maps: USGS Half Dome and Yosemite Falls quads.
Permits: None, if done as a day hike; for backpackers, available in advance or from the wilderness center in Yosemite Village.

Finding the trailhead: Take the shuttle bus from anywhere in Yosemite Valley to Stop 8, Yosemite Lodge, or drive to the parking lot behind (north of) the lodge, then cross the road to Sunnyside Campground. A sign in front points the way through the campground to the Upper Yosemite Fall trailhead, marked by another, larger, sign.

Trailhead facilities: Food, lodging, phones at Yosemite Lodge.

Key points:
0.0   Upper Yosemite Fall Trailhead.
1.0   Columbia Rock lookout.
3.2   Yosemite Creek junction.
3.4   Yosemite Falls overlook.

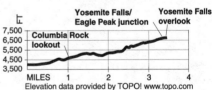

The hike: Begin climbing immediately up rocky switchbacks, winding your way among house-sized boulders shaded by canyon live oak, ponderosa pine, and incense-cedar. Slowly more and more of the flat valley floor comes into view through the trees. At 1 mile, you reach an overlook protected by iron railings; it's known as Columbia Rock. Directly across the valley is Sentinel Rock. You can trace the path of the glaciers that flowed down Tenaya Canyon in front of Half Dome and down Merced Canyon behind it, to where they met and scooped out the wide valley floor.

Leaving Columbia Rock, the trail ascends a few soft gravelly switchbacks, then descends for a short distance, crosses several springtime rivulets, rounds

Upper Yosemite Fall in winter. Note the mound of snow formed by the fall's frozen spray.

Yosemite Falls

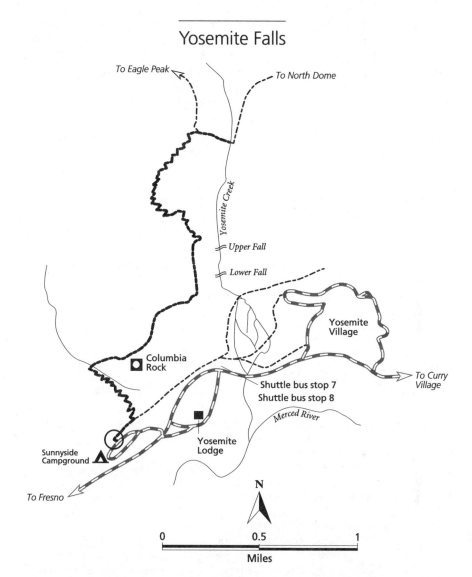

a corner, and suddenly reveals 1,430-foot Upper Yosemite Fall, booming like thunder early in the summer. The refreshing mist supports little moss–and-fern gardens growing among the rocks. Over the roar of the falls, listen for the sweet descending notes of the canyon wren's song. The trail now ascends very steep, rough stairsteps past the top of the lower falls and all of the middle falls (675 feet). Notice the trickles of water seeping out of the cracks between the layers of exfoliating (peeling) granite. Partway up the upper falls the trail ducks behind a ridge, concealing the falls from view until you reach the top. Climb the sunny gully densely clothed in scrub oak, except where a huge pile of talus has spilled into the gully. Above the rock pile you can see a white scar on the cliff above where the darker, lichen-stained rock broke away in 1980 and killed three hikers. This part of the trail can be hot. As you near the top of the gulch, firs, Jeffrey pines, and a refreshing springtime trickle make a rest at the Yosemite Creek junction at 3.2 miles welcome. Follow the right fork for a few yards, then follow the signs to the overlook, an area filled with weirdly sculptured rocks and twisted Jeffrey pines, to an iron railing at 3.4 miles. Directly across the valley, the upside-down bowl of Sentinel Dome rises alone and to the west of Glacier Point. Farther in the distance is Mount Starr King, also somewhat rounded and isolated from the surrounding ridges. Farther beyond, beautiful Mount Clark and the Clark Range define the horizon.

Upper Yosemite Fall pours through a notch just to the left (east) of the overlook. You might be tempted to get closer for a better view, but be very careful scrambling over the smooth rocks. There is nothing to stop your fall into the creek and over the precipice if you lose your footing.

You can return the way you came, or if you are planning to spend the night, return to the main trail and follow it a little farther upstream. Do not camp in the trampled and overused forested spot just ahead. Camping within one-quarter mile of the rim is prohibited. If you continue north along the ridge a short distance, you will find several good campsites.

7 Half Dome

General description: Out-and-back day hike or backpack to some of the valley's most spectacular views.
Total distance: 16 miles.
Difficulty: Moderately strenuous as a backpack, very strenuous as a day hike.
Elevation gain: 4,842 feet.
Trail traffic: Heavy.
Best months: All summer.
Maps: USGS Half Dome and Yosemite Falls quads.
Permits: None for a day hike; for backpackers, available in advance or from the wilderness center in Yosemite Valley.

Finding the trailhead: Board the Yosemite Valley shuttle bus from any-place in the valley and get off at Stop 16, Happy Isles. If you are backpack-ing, leave your car in the backpackers' lot near Curry Village.

Trailhead facilities: Food, phone, and toilets in Yosemite Valley.

Key points:
   0.0   Happy Isles.
   4.8   Little Yosemite Valley.
   6.0   Half Dome Trail.
   8.0   Summit.

Half Dome

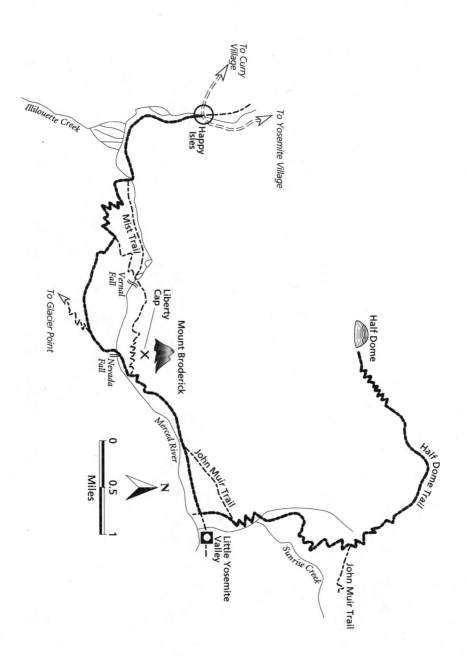

Majestic Half Dome with cables to help negotiate the last 400 feet to the summit.

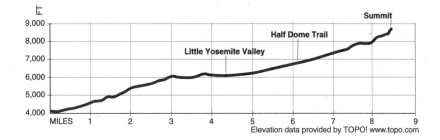

Elevation data provided by TOPO! www.topo.com

The hike: This is a very popular hike, and a grueling one. It is more enjoyable as a backpack, spending a night in Little Yosemite Valley, but Little Yosemite Valley is a popular spot and permits are very hard to come by, especially on weekends. In earlier days, it was possible to camp on the summit, but camping is now prohibited to protect the rare Mount Lyell salamanders that shelter under the rocks on top. This is probably just as well because there are no sanitary facilities on the summit and you can't dig holes in solid granite. The top is reached by pulling yourself up a set of steel cables fastened to the slickrock. If you don't like heights, don't try it. Make sure you get a weather report before you start. Thunderstorms have killed hikers on top. Start very early in the morning, both to beat afternoon thundershowers and to beat the crowds. Gloves make hanging on to the cables easier.

Follow Hike 16 to Little Yosemite Valley at 4.8 miles. There is an earlier turnoff to the Half Dome Trail at 4.3 miles, but ignore it and keep right. If you are backpacking, you'll be going to Little Yosemite Valley anyway, and the shorter trail is steeper and does not save much time. Head north out of Little Yosemite Valley Campground, passing the junction with the shortcut trail and climbing steeply, first along Sunrise Creek, continuing generally northward (and upward!) until reaching the Half Dome Trail junction at 6 miles. Leave the main trail here.

About a half mile farther along the wide and dusty path, keep an eye out for a small spur trail to the right (east) where there is a spring. *This is your last source of water.* The trail swings west to reveal a view of Half Dome to the left and Clouds Rest to the right. Across the way are Basket Dome and North Dome. The trail swings a little farther south now and faces the huge, sparsely timbered shoulder of Half Dome. A sign warns hikers not to proceed if bad weather threatens. Believe it! Now you switchback steeply on sometimes slippery gravel up and over the crest of this shoulder to at last come face to face with the famous—or infamous—cables that help you negotiate the last 400 feet to the summit.

The top of Half Dome flattens out considerably and is furnished with flat, oddly weathered granite slabs. When you have recovered from your climb, wander around to take in the 360-degree panorama. Below, Yosemite Valley is spread out like a map, with El Capitan at its west end. North Dome and Clouds Rest flank the bare and smooth Tenaya Canyon. Farther east, Merced Canyon points toward the Cathedral Range, and the colorful Clark Range is visible to the southeast.

If you are day hiking, you'll have to tear yourself away after only a short visit to make it back to the valley before dark. You can vary your trip back by taking the Mist Trail down to Happy Isles.

The South Rim of Yosemite Valley

The South Rim of Yosemite Valley

All of the south rim trails begin along the Glacier Point Road, which cuts off Wawona Road (California 41) at a junction called Chinquapin, about 14 miles from Yosemite Valley. It starts at about 6,000 feet amid ponderosa and sugar pines, climbs through a beautiful red fir forest at almost 8,000 feet, then drops to 7,200 feet at Glacier Point, 16 miles away. Glacier Point is an extremely popular overlook 3,000 feet above the valley floor; it offers the best views of Half Dome, the valley, and indeed, most of the whole park, accessible by road. Almost all of the hikes beginning from this road have spectacular views of the valley, too. There is a snack bar, gift shop, phones, and toilets, along with an amphitheater for nighttime astronomy programs and an area from which hang gliders are launched before 8 A.M.

It was also the site of the infamous firefall. The bark of hundreds of the magnificent old red firs from the nearby forest was set ablaze just after dark on summer evenings. Then the glowing coals were raked over the cliff to form a fiery "waterfall" in the dark. The spectacle was magical to see, but the lichens and other organisms inhabiting the rock face below were seared away and the beautiful old forest was threatened. The National Park Service ended the practice in 1968.

The only accommodations anywhere on Glacier Point Road are at first-come first-served Bridalveil Creek Campground. There is no place to stay overnight near the trailhead, if you arrive late on the day before your hike, and you must get your wilderness permit for a backpacking outing down in Yosemite Valley or at Wawona.

The road is open all the way to Glacier Point spring through fall, but in winter it's plowed only as far as the ski area at Badger Pass. There are plenty of bears around. Do not leave ice chests or food in your car. Most trailheads have bear-proof boxes for food storage.

A hiker's shuttle bus runs daily from the valley during the summer. You can get a schedule and fares at the visitor center or call (209) 372-1240.

8 Taft Point and The Fissures

General description:	A short day hike with views of Yosemite Valley and spectacular geologic features.
Total distance:	2.2 miles.
Difficulty:	Easy.
Elevation gain:	250 feet.
Trail traffic:	Moderate.
Best months:	Spring, summer, or fall; whenever Glacier Point Road is open.
Maps:	USGS Half Dome quad.
Permits:	None.

Finding the trailhead: Drive 13 miles up Glacier Point Road from Chinquapin. Parking and the marked trailhead are on the left.

Trailhead facilities: Pit toilet, no water.

Key points:

- 0.0 Taft Point/Sentinel Dome Trailhead.
- 0.4 Pohono Trail junction.
- 0.9 The Fissures.
- 1.1 Taft Point.

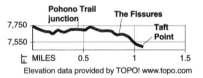

Elevation data provided by TOPO! www.topo.com

The hike: Before setting out, remember that this is an upside-down hike. After the easy cruise downhill, the uphill return will take more time, so plan accordingly and take water. The trail begins at a sign in a sandy opening in the mixed pine and fir forest. Take the left (west) fork. The right fork goes to Sentinel Dome (Hike 9). The trail passes through a flat, fairly open stretch past a big outcrop of almost pure white quartz on the right, then swings south and starts downhill where the forest closes in. At 0.4 mile you reach the Pohono Trail continue walking left (south). The trail sign here says you have come only 0.2 mile from the trailhead, but it is out of date and inaccurate. The forest deepens and a little creek you will soon hop across nourishes a colorful garden of water-loving cow parsnip, senecio, corn lily, knotweed, and shooting stars. All at once the trail emerges from the shady forest onto open rock, and then steepens. The flower-filled gully on your right abruptly narrows, deepens, and drops through a notch that sends the little creek plummeting toward the valley floor.

Descend carefully down the rocks past low patches of manzanita and the occasional Jeffrey pine. Stay alert here. At 0.9 mile, a sign says simply "The Fissures," but by the time you reach it, you will already have skirted several of them. They are not visible until you are standing on their rims. The fissures are narrow, deep cracks in the granite, perhaps 30 to 40 feet long, extending inward from the edge of the overhanging cliff. Peering over the side, you can see that they slice completely through the rock, revealing a stomach-lurching glimpse of the floor of Yosemite Valley several thousand

Taft Point and The Fissures and Sentinel Dome

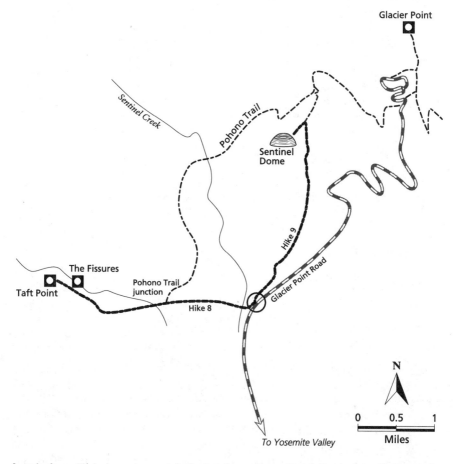

feet below. This is not a good choice for an evening hike in low light, or for a walk with small, unrestrained children.

Once your internal butterflies have settled, proceed toward a slightly rising point of the cliff that leans out over the valley like the prow of a ship with a protective iron railing around it. This is Taft Point (1.1 miles). A look over the edge is guaranteed to reawaken the butterflies. Directly across from the point are the Three Brothers. To the left (west) is the massive face of El Capitan, to the right (east) is Yosemite Falls. Wander westward along the rim for a look at the dramatic knife edges and needle-like spikes of the Cathedral Spires.

When you are ready to return, descend the slight rise to a trail junction. The left fork returns to the trailhead and parking, the right one heads westward along the Pohono Trail toward Inspiration Point (Hike 10.)

9 Sentinel Dome

See map on page 45

General description: An out-and-back day hike with the best views of Yosemite Valley for the least effort.

Total distance: 2.2 miles.

Difficulty: Moderate.

Elevation gain: 373 feet.

Trail traffic: Moderate.

Best months: Spring, summer, or fall; whenever Glacier Point Road is open.

Maps: USGS Half Dome quad.

Permits: None

Finding the trailhead: From Wawona Road (California 41) drive 13 miles up Glacier Point Road from Chinquapin. Parking and the marked trailhead are on the left.

Trailhead facilities: Pit toilet, but no water.

Key points:

0.0 Trailhead.
0.4 Service road.
0.6 Glacier Point Trail.
1.1 Top of Sentinel Dome.

Elevation data provided by TOPO! www.topo.com

The hike: The location of Sentinel Dome above Yosemite Valley provides a complete 360-degree sweep of just about the whole park. Carry water and wear good sturdy shoes for this one. Smooth-soled sandals invite accidents. This dome, like the others in Yosemite is the result of the nature of the rock itself; it is not formed by the movement of glaciers (though the scouring action of ice may polish and smooth the rough edges). Granitic rock forms when molten material under the earth's crust rises toward the surface, but cools and solidifies before it gets there. When the surface material is eroded away by time and weather, pressure on the underlying granite is decreased and the rock expands. The kind of granitic rock that forms Sentinel Dome and others in Yosemite is so solid and massive that it does not break into pieces when it expands; instead, great sheets of rock pop loose like layers of an onion and are eroded away.

The trail begins at a sign in a sandy opening in the forest that directs you to the right (northeast). The other fork goes to Taft Point and The Fissures (Hike 8). The rough and rocky path crosses a brook, then undulates gradually upward, slowly revealing the top of the dome. Soon it curves to the left (north) and proceeds more steeply over smooth and featureless rock. Stenciled metal signs keep you on course. At 0.4 mile, an old partly paved service road joins the trail from the right. Continue around the base of the dome on your left. When you have reached the "back," or more gradually sloping side of the dome at 0.6 mile, a trail splits off to the right and heads down to Glacier Point. Turn left just past this point and head up the steep open slope on an indistinct trail of sorts. Don't worry if you lose the path; the only way to go is up. At the summit is a gnarled Jeffrey pine, now dead but still picturesque. It was once the subject of innumerable photographs and postcards.

When you have caught your breath, make a slow circle around the summit. To the west, Yosemite Valley flanked by the Cathedral Rocks on the left and El Capitan on the right stretches toward the coast. If the Great Central Valley is free of smog (a rare occurrence) you can see all the way to the Coast Ranges. Moving clockwise, the entire length of Yosemite Falls comes into view, and in early summer you can hear its roar from here. Farther east is smoothly rounded Basket Dome and North Dome and, beyond them, Tenaya Canyon, with the sheer face of Half Dome glowering over it. Clouds Rest is just beyond Half Dome, and far behind it lies the Cathedral Range. Further east the Merced River Canyon and Nevada Fall appear, then comes Mount Clark and the colorful Clark Range, providing a backdrop for the rounded tops of Mount Starr King. The lower, forested country to the south closes the circle.

When you are ready, descend very slowly and carefully, avoiding loose sand and gravel whenever possible, and return the way you came. Take care to follow the metal signs directing you to the parking lot.

10 McGurk Meadow

General description:	Short, out-and-back day hike leading to a vast array of wildflowers.
Total distance:	1.6 miles.
Difficulty:	Easy
Elevation gain:	150 feet.
Trail traffic:	Moderate.
Best months:	All summer, but wildflowers are best in July.
Maps:	USGS El Capitan and Half Dome quads.
Permits:	None.

Finding the trailhead: Drive about 8.5 miles up Glacier Point Road from Chinquapin. The trailhead is on the left just before you reach the entrance to Bridalveil Creek Campground. It's easy to miss. The campground is on the right (south) side of the road. The easiest way to find the trailhead is to drive to the campground entrance, turn around, and head back the way you came. Park in the first turnout on the right. The trailhead sign is about 100 yards ahead.

Wildflowers adorn McGurk Meadow and many others in Yosemite.

McGurk Meadow

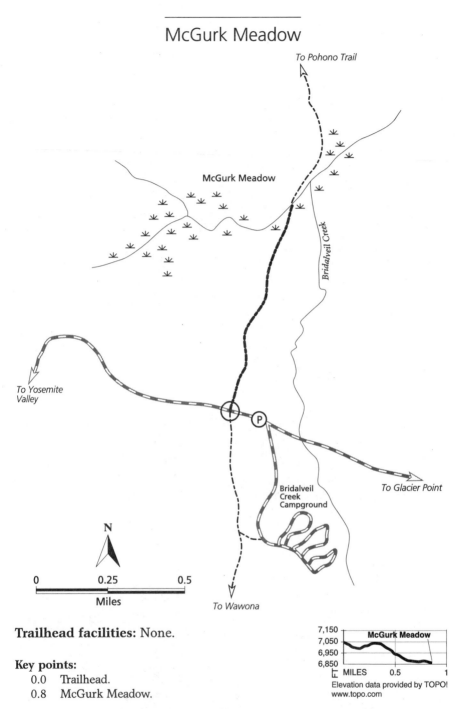

To Pohono Trail

McGurk Meadow

Bridalveil Creek

To Yosemite Valley

N

P

To Glacier Point

Bridalveil Creek Campground

N

| 0 | 0.25 | 0.5 |

Miles

To Wawona

Trailhead facilities: None.

Key points:
  0.0   Trailhead.
  0.8   McGurk Meadow.

McGurk Meadow

7,150
7,050
6,950
6,850

MILES   0.5   1

Elevation data provided by TOPO!
www.topo.com

The hike: This is one of Yosemite's prettiest and "bloomingest" meadows. The path descends through quiet lodgepole forest. Alongside, currants, strawberries, lupines, and larkspur flourish. Just before reaching the meadow, watch for an old log cabin on the left. Beyond lies the meadow, threaded by a little brook and spangled with wildflowers of every color: shooting stars, lungwort, corn lily, monkey flower, paintbrush, and more. The meadow is a fairly long one that invites a longer stroll around its periphery. If you prefer, you can find a pleasant spot to linger alongside. Such a meeting of forest and meadow is one of the best places for wildlife watching during the morning and evening hours. Retrace your steps to the trailhead.

11 The Pohono Trail

General description: Shuttle backpack or a long day hike, affording a series of stunning panoramic views.
Total distance: 13.8 miles.
Difficulty: Moderate as a backpack, strenuous as a day hike.
Elevation gain: 2,800 feet.
Trail traffic: Light to moderate.
Best months: All summer, though creeks are dry by mid-August.
Maps: USGS El Capitan and Half Dome quads.
Permits: Available in advance or from the wilderness center in Yosemite Valley.

Finding the trailhead: Follow Glacier Point Road to its end 16 miles from Wawona Road at Chinquapin, or take the shuttle to Glacier Point. If you are driving, park all the way at the upper level of the parking lot. Walk straight toward Half Dome, which looms ahead of you, then, near the rim of the cliff, turn right (east) on the worn path and look uphill to find the big trailhead sign. You will need to leave a car or arrange to be picked up at the Tunnel View parking lot, just east of the Wawona Tunnel on California 41.

Trailhead facilities: Food, supplies, water, toilets, and phones at Glacier Point. Phones and toilets at Tunnel View.

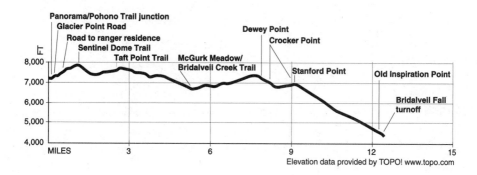

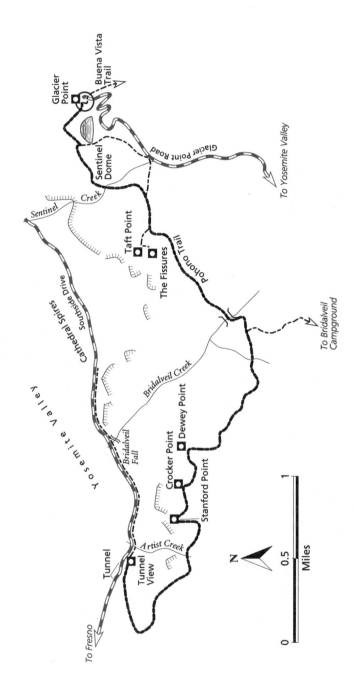

Buena Vista Trail

Glacier Point

Sentinel Dome

Glacier Point Road

To Yosemite Valley

Sentinel Creek

Taft Point

The Fissures

Pohono Trail

Cathedral Spires

Southside Drive

To Bridalveil Campground

Yosemite Valley

Bridalveil Creek

Dewey Point

Crocker Point

Bridalveil Fall

Stanford Point

Tunnel

Artist Creek

Tunnel View

To Fresno

N

0   0.5   1

Miles

Key points:
0.0   Trailhead.
0.1   Pohono/Panorama Trail junction.
0.1   Glacier Point Road.
0.4   Road to ranger residence.
1.0   Sentinel Dome Trail.
2.0   Taft Point Trail.
5.0   McGurk Meadow/Bridalveil Creek Trail.
8.7   Dewey Point.
9.3   Crocker Point.
10.0   Stanford Point.
12.7   Old Inspiration Point.
13.2   Bridalveil Fall turnoff.

The hike: Take a minute to recover from the overwhelming immensity of the panorama at Glacier Point before setting off. To the left is North Dome, capping the graceful Royal Arches; in the center is Half Dome, the monumental symbol of Yosemite. Tenaya Canyon stretches away to the northeast, and to the west runs the Merced River canyon, down whose Giant Staircase flow Nevada and Vernal falls. Walk slightly uphill to the right. At the junction at 0.1 mile, take the Pohono Trail to the right (west). At 0.2 mile, cross Glacier Point Road, then ascend a few switchbacks beneath white and red firs to 0.4 mile, where a dirt road leads to a ranger residence on the left. Continue right on the trail that for a short time parallels the road. At 1.0 mile, meet the junction with the Sentinel Dome trail. To see Sentinel Dome, turn left at the junction and follow it a half mile to the top (see Hike 9).

To continue on the Pohono Trail, go straight (southwest) along the valley rim. Watch for Yosemite Falls across the valley as the route climbs, levels, then descends on switchbacks. You can catch occasional glimpses of Sentinel Dome pushing up out of the forest uphill on your left. Cross Sentinel Creek, often dry later in the year, and wind through the forest over gently rolling terrain until you reach a junction, at 2 miles, with the trail between Glacier Point Road and Taft Point. The forest deepens and a little creek you will soon hop across nourishes a colorful garden of water-loving cow parsnip, senecio, corn lily, knotweed, and shooting stars. All at once the trail emerges from the shady forest onto open rock, and steepens. The flower-filled gully on your right abruptly narrows, deepens, and drops through a notch that sends the little creek plummeting toward the valley floor. Descend carefully down the rocks past low patches of manzanita and the occasional Jeffrey pine. Stay alert here. A sign says simply "The Fissures," but by the time you reach it, you will already have skirted several of them. They are not visible until you are standing on their rims (see Hike 8). Beyond, a few yards above the trail to your right (north), is Taft Point, protected by an iron railing. It's well worth a short detour for great views of the Three Brothers across the valley.

Return to the trail and continue west, first over open rock, then into forest, dipping down to meet Bridalveil Creek and crossing it on a footbridge. This is the first legal place to camp on the Pohono Trail. A short distance beyond, at 5 miles, keep right at the junction with the trail that heads south to meet Glacier Point Road via McGurk Meadow. The trail rises and falls through the forest, crossing a few more creeklets that dry out by midsummer, until it at last ascends to Dewey Point at 8.7 miles. You can scramble carefully out to the very top to a granite aerie from which, laid out before you, is a panorama of almost the whole of Yosemite Park. To the west you can see the Wawona Tunnel parking lot, your end point, and beyond it, Cascade Creek Falls. Directly across the valley, Ribbon Fall drifts down in early springtime, and just beyond that, El Capitan. You can hear climbers' shouts from here if the wind is blowing in the right direction.

Mount Hoffman is on the horizon to the east, marking the geographic center of Yosemite. If the day is clear you can see Mount Conness on the northern park boundary. Tenaya Canyon, heading straight for the Cathedral Range, cuts the sheer granite at the base of Clouds Rest and Half Dome, partly hidden behind Sentinel Dome.

Return to the trail, which now alternates between forest and open spots with chinquapin, pinemat manzanita, ceanothus, and huckleberry oak— spiny shrubs unfriendly to hikers in shorts. The trail dips to pass Crocker Point at 9.3 miles. Be sure to detour the short distance out to the point, for from here you can see Bridalveil Fall shooting down between the Leaning Tower and Cathedral Rocks.

The trail dips again and hops an ephemeral little creek lined with willow, currant, monkey flower, and wild geranium. It reaches Stanford Point at 10 miles, then veers away from the valley rim and climbs a rise through a garden of lupines to reach willow-choked Meadow Brook. This little creek drops over the cliff as delicate Silver Strand Falls, seldom seen past late June. The trail rises, then drops, more steeply now, to Artist Creek, dry in summer, then continues on a knee-pounding descent through shady forest to Old Inspiration Point, at 12.7 miles. You can see remains of the asphalt road that led to this original Inspiration Point years ago. Descend rocky switchbacks now to 13.2 miles, where a trail cuts off to the right (east) toward Bridalveil Fall. Continue straight ahead down the rough trail to the Wawona Road and the parking lot at Tunnel View.

12 The Panorama Trail—Glacier Point to Nevada Fall

General description: A day hike along the rim of Yosemite Valley for views of five famous waterfalls.
Total distance: 10.4 miles.
Difficulty: Moderate.
Elevation gain: 1,400 feet.
Trail traffic: Heavy.
Best months: Spring and early summer when the falls are full, but worth the effort all through the summer. Trail is closed in winter.
Maps: USGS Half Dome quad.
Permits: None.

Finding the trailhead: Follow Glacier Point Road to its end 16 miles from Wawona Road at Chinquapin, or take the shuttle to Glacier Point. If you are driving, park all the way at the far (upper) end of the parking lot. Walk straight toward Half Dome looming ahead of you, then, near the rim of the cliff, turn right (east) on the worn path and look uphill to find the big trailhead sign.

Trailhead facilities: Glacier Point has a snack bar and gift shop, water, and restrooms; pit toilet at the top of Nevada Fall on the north side of the river.

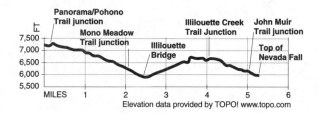

Key points:
0.0   Glacier Point Trailhead.
0.1   Panorama/Pohono Trail junction.
1.2   Mono Meadow Trail junction.
2.1   Illilouette Fall Bridge.
4.0   Illilouette Creek Trail junction.
5.0   John Muir Trail junction.
5.2   Top of Nevada Fall.

The hike: Take a minute to recover from the overwhelming immensity of the panorama before setting off. To the left is North Dome capping the graceful Royal Arches; in the center is Half Dome, the monumental symbol of Yosemite. Tenaya Canyon stretches away to the northeast, and to the east runs the Merced River canyon, down whose Giant Staircase flow Nevada and Vernal falls. Beautifully sculptured Mount Clark and the Clark Range stretch off to the east.

Staircase of the Merced River.

The Panorama Trail—Glacier Point to Nevada Fall

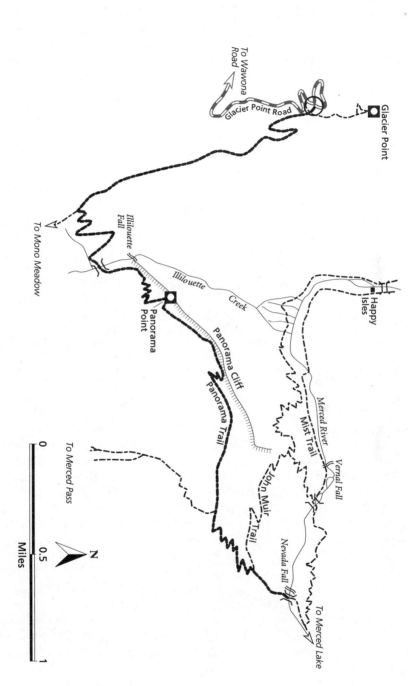

Begin at the big trailhead sign slightly uphill to the right. Farther on, at 0.1 mile there are two more signs and two trails. To the right is the Pohono Trail, which skirts Yosemite Valley to the west. The Panorama Trail, described here, goes left (south) toward Illilouette Fall. The first mile of the trail switchbacks downward through an area burned in 1987. Fragrant ceanothus and chinquapin with its spiny green fruits line the path. This is a good place to listen for the booming call of the blue grouse in spring and early summer. Males find a territory to their liking then sit and hoot, hour after hour, day after day, sometimes for weeks at a stretch, hoping to encourage a mate and discourage competitors. Their call is like the sound blowing over the mouth of a bottle produces.

At 1.2 miles, a trail coming from Mono Meadow to the south joins this one. Keep left (northeast) and continue to descend into the Illilouette Gorge. Shrubs give way to forest and the rush of Illilouette Creek becomes audible. Other hikers have worn a little turnout to the left of the trail to get a look at the fall, which is just out of sight from the trail itself. This is the only way to see most of Illilouette Fall from any direction because it is tucked so tightly back into the gorge. Just before the trail reaches the bridge over Illilouette Creek, you might spot what appears to be an idyllic campsite on the right, but camping is not permitted here. It's too near the water, too near the trail, and too near the road. It's a nice spot for lunch, though. Cross the footbridge over the creek at 2.1 miles. The fall is not visible from the footbridge over the creek, but the creek cascades down in picturesque wedding cake fashion, and in springtime, the blooms of western azaleas lining the banks perfume the air.

From the bridge the trail climbs fairly steeply up out of the gorge, then follows the brow of the Panorama Cliff. There is no sign to mark Panorama Point, but it is the obvious place to step off the trail a few yards to the left to take in the view. You can get a good look at the notorious rockslide of 1996 that damaged much of Happy Isles. Yosemite Valley winds off to the left and Yosemite Falls is just visible on the far side. Soon the trail winds far enough around the hill to reveal spectacular 594-foot Nevada Fall, and shortly after that, reaches a junction at 4 miles. Here, a trail heads right (south) through a badly burned area, eventually to rejoin Illilouette Creek several miles upstream from Illilouette Fall. The Panorama Trail stays left and switchbacks down fairly steeply past several little rills and mossy rock gardens to meet the John Muir Trail coming up from Yosemite Valley, at 5 miles. Follow the signs to the right to meet the top of Nevada Fall, at 5.2 miles.

Join the crowd there picnicking, sunbathing, and watching the Merced River shoot over the lip of the sheer cliff. Be sure to stay behind the protective rails and away from the slippery edges. The river has claimed several lives here. You can continue on down the John Muir Trail to Yosemite Valley from here (if you have a ride back up to Glacier Point), or you can just return the way you came.

The North Rim of Yosemite Valley

The North Rim of Yosemite Valley

Hikes on this side of the valley start later in the year than those on the south because the snow lasts longer in the shady hollows and valleys, and many of the streams are too fast, too wide, and too deep to cross safely until well into July. Because of the deep gorges cut by these streams, along with differences in the nature of the rock that makes up the cliffs, north rim trails cannot skirt the valley rim as closely as the south rim trails do. There are many breathtaking views from the tops of landmarks like El Capitan and North Dome, but the trails sometimes retreat through forest back toward Tioga Road for several miles between one scenic point and the next. Furthermore, many of the south rim overlooks can be reached in a relatively short day hike, while most of the north rim trails are very strenuous as day hikes and may be more enjoyable as overnighters. For these reasons, the north rim is not so heavily used as the south, providing more opportunities for solitude (and for obtaining wilderness permits.) The nearest source for permits for these hikes is the Big Oak Flat Entrance Station; they are also available at Tuolumne Meadows and Yosemite Valley.

All of the hikes in this section are reached from California 120, known as the Big Oak Flat Road, west of Crane Flat, and Tioga Road, to the east. There are several first-come, first-served campgrounds off the road: Porcupine Flat, Tamarack Flat, Yosemite Creek, and White Wolf. The Hodgdon Meadow Campground at the Big Oak Flat entrance and the Crane Flat Campground require reservations. White Wolf has a High Sierra camp as well, for which reservations many months in advance are needed.

The nearest (minimal) source of supplies is the gas station at Crane Flat. Both Tuolumne Meadows and Yosemite Valley have more, but are about an hour's drive in either direction. There is no gas in Yosemite Valley.

13 Tioga Road to the Top of Yosemite Falls

General description:	Out-and-back day hike or overnight backpack to the Yosemite Falls overlook.
Total distance:	16 miles.
Difficulty:	Moderate.
Elevation gain:	860 feet.
Trail traffic:	Moderately heavy.
Best months:	Summer and fall.
Maps:	USGS Yosemite Falls quad.
Permits:	Available in advance or from the wilderness center at Yosemite Valley or Tuolumne Meadows. No permits required for a day hike.

Finding the trailhead: On Tioga Road (California 120), drive about 20 miles east of Crane Flat, 26 miles west of Tuolumne Meadows. There is parking on both sides of the highway. The Ten Lakes Trail departs from the north side, the Yosemite Creek trail from the south. The trailhead is not obvious from the parking area. To find it, walk a few feet to the west along the narrow shoulder of the road and look for a small sign partly obscured by brush.

Trailhead facilities: None at trailhead. Phones and restrooms at Yosemite Creek Campground, but no piped water.

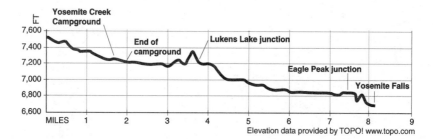

Elevation data provided by TOPO! www.topo.com

Key points:
- 0.0 Trailhead.
- 1.5 Yosemite Creek Campground.
- 2.2 End of campground.
- 3.7 Lukens Lake junction.
- 7.5 Eagle Peak junction.
- 8.0 Yosemite Falls.

The hike: It is possible to save 3 miles and some elevation gain and loss as well as a potentially difficult stream crossing by parking in the Yosemite Creek Campground and beginning your hike from there. The road to the campground cuts off to the south from Tioga Road several miles to the east

Tioga Road to the Top of Yosemite Falls

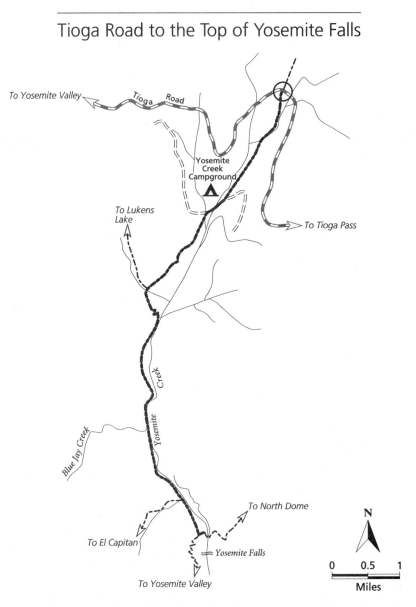

of the parking area. The "official" trailhead, however, begins at Tioga Road. From the inconspicuous wooden sign, descend through lodgepole pines to the crossing of Yosemite Creek, which can be difficult in early season when the water is high. Then descend very gradually until you reach the Yosemite Creek Campground at 1.5 miles. Follow the paved road all the way through the campground, over the bridge across Yosemite Creek, and past the campground entrance. Just after crossing another smaller branch of the creek, turn left at a sign marked "Trail Junction," and leave the road and the campground at 2.2 miles.

The trail wanders through fairly flat forest, then climbs over a rocky shoulder marked with ducks where the route is obscure. Some handsome junipers grow from cracks in the rock. Shortly after descending from this shoulder, a trail cuts back to the right (northwest) at 3.7 miles, heading toward Lukens Lake and White Wolf. Continue straight ahead (south) and cross a tributary of Yosemite Creek. There are a few campsites here. Gradually the smooth, rounded granite walls force the trail and the creek into a narrow defile, and the lovely aquamarine water races over the smooth rock, hypnotizing one with its swirling patterns. Then the valley widens and the creek and the trail meander more slowly through the forest, where more good campsites can be found. Cross Blue Jay Creek carefully on rocks that are sometimes slippery, then cross two wide, sandy flats, reenter the forest, and meet the Eagle Peak Trail in a ferny glen at 7.5 miles. Descend a slot that crosses a couple of bumps to reach the Yosemite Falls junction at 8 miles. This is where you meet the steady stream of sweating, gasping hikers laboring up from the valley floor. Follow the signs to the overlook a short distance to the east. Be careful scrambling over the slick rocks near the creek. There is nothing to stop your fall into the water and over the precipice if you lose your footing.

If you plan to spend the night, retrace your steps to the main trail and follow it back upstream before pitching your tent. The area just at the top of the falls is trampled and overused, and camping within 0.25 mile of the rim is prohibited anyway.

14 El Capitan from Tamarack Flat

General description: Shuttle; out-and-back day hike or overnighter with views of Half Dome, Glacier Point, and El Capitan.
Total distance: 16.4 miles.
Difficulty: Strenuous as a day hike, moderate as a backpack.
Elevation gain: 1,240 feet.
Trail traffic: Light to moderate.
Best months: Spring–fall as a day hike; spring–early summer as a backpack.
Maps: USGS Tamarack Flat and El Capitan quads.
Permits: None needed for a day hike; available in advance or from the wilderness center in Yosemite Valley for an overnight stay,.

Finding the trailhead: From Tioga Road (California 120) about 3 miles east of Crane Flat, turn southeast on the road to Tamarack Flat Campground and drive about 3 miles to the end.

Trailhead facilities: None.

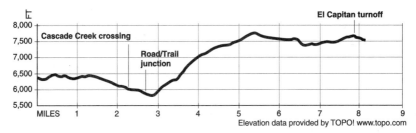

Key points:
0.0 Tamarack Campground.
2.2 Cascade Creek crossing.
2.7 Road/trail junction.
7.9 El Capitan turnoff.
8.2 El Capitan.

The hike: This can be done as a strenuous day hike, but is more enjoyable as a backpack. If you do plan to make it an overnighter, inquire about trail conditions before you start, because the only place to camp, by August Ribbon Creek, might be dry.

Pass the gate at the end of the campground and continue on the now-abandoned road that descends to a junction near Cascade Creek, at 2.2 miles. The creekside is fragrant with azalea and dogwood, and it supports a lush stand of Indian rhubarb, a plant with enormous round leaves and showy flowers that appear to poke right through their centers. Stay on the road that crosses the main branch of Cascade Creek on a bridge. This creek joins with Tamarack Creek lower down, drops in a beautiful waterfall called the

62

El Capitan from Tamarack Flat, Porcupine Creek to North Dome, and The North Rim

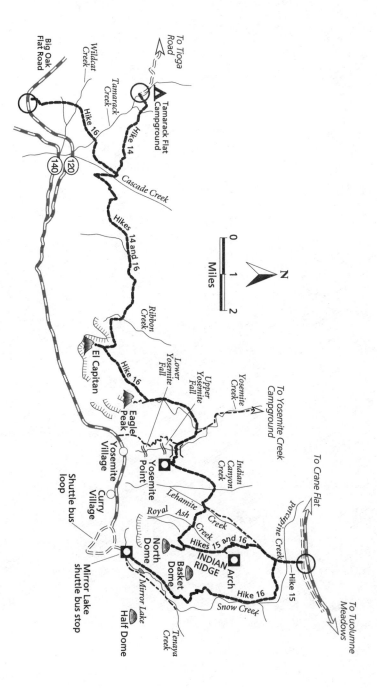

El Capitan rises high above the Merced River.

Cascades south of the Big Oak Flat Road, crashes down beside El Portal Road, and is visible from California 41 all the way across the valley. At 2.7 miles, the road is blocked with a pile of logs that diverts you to the left, where a signed trail begins. The route turns back on itself for a short time and begins a stiff climb up a forested slope to a ridgetop, which it follows, still climbing steadily, to Ribbon Meadow. This area is almost too thickly forested to rightfully be called a meadow, but it is boggy (and buggy) enough early in the year to deserve that designation. A little way beyond is Ribbon Creek, the only camping along the route. Cross the creek, then follow the trail as it cuts back north around the edge of El Capitan Gully, down which there is a stomach-lurching view of the valley. El Capitan is now visible ahead. Contour along the slope over brushy, open rocks to the spur trail to the top of El Capitan at 7.9 miles, and head out to the summit. You will already have noticed that the summit is not as flat as it appears from below, but is somewhat rounded and domelike, slanting downward toward the valley. Don't wander too near the edge. The rock is smooth and it's a long way down.

The view is all you would expect from such a perch. Half Dome rises out of Tenaya Canyon to the left (east) with Merced Canyon behind it. Off in the distance is Mount Lyell, highest peak in the park. Directly across from you are Glacier Point and Sentinel Dome, and behind them, the dramatic narrow ridge of Mount Clark. When you have had enough, return the way you came. If you have a ride, you can continue east along the North Rim of Yosemite Valley, returning to Tioga Road by several roughly parallel routes. (See Hikes 15 and 16.)

15 Porcupine Creek to North Dome

See map on page 63

General description:	Out-and-back day hike to one of the finest views in Yosemite from North Dome.
Total distance:	8.8 miles.
Difficulty:	Moderate to strenuous.
Elevation gain:	650 feet.
Trail traffic:	Moderate.
Best months:	All summer.
Maps:	USGS Yosemite Falls quad.
Permits:	None.

Finding the trailhead: On Tioga Road (California 120) drive 14 miles west of Tuolumne Meadows, or 23 miles east of Crane Flat. The trailhead and parking area are on the south side of the road.

Trailhead facilities: None.

Key points:

   0.0   Trailhead.
   0.7   Porcupine Creek crossing.
   1.5   Four-way junction.
   3.9   North Dome spur trail.
   4.4   Summit.

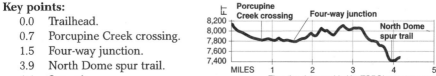

Elevation data provided by TOPO! www.topo.com

The hike: Although this hike is only moderate in length and the net elevation gain and loss is minimal, there are lots of steep ups and downs and some tricky footing. Allow plenty of time; it will probably take longer than you think.

From the east end of the parking area, head downhill on the eroded remains of a road. At 0.7 mile, cross Porcupine Creek. If the water is high, there is a log crossing just upstream. Continue through red fir forest, climbing slightly, to a junction at 1.5 miles. Your trail goes straight ahead. A few feet beyond this, another sign directs you straight ahead to North Dome and Yosemite Falls. Then, just a few feet beyond that sign, the trail splits again. Take the left (south) fork again, toward North Dome. Wind steadily uphill, partly through forest, partly over open rock lined with manzanita until you reach the top of Indian Ridge. A short detour cuts off to the left (northeast) to a very unusual rock arch, a geologic feature seldom seen in granite. There's nothing else like it in Yosemite, so don't miss it.

The main trail follows the top of Indian Ridge, drops sharply off to the left, then picks up the ridgeline again. Here in an open rocky space, another short spur trail goes right (south) for a stupendous view, and your first look at the bald rounded top of North Dome just below. Yosemite Valley stretches away to the right, flanked by Sentinel Rock and El Capitan. To the left, Half Dome looms impossibly huge just across the gorge and Clouds Rest rises even higher in smooth curves farther back along the same ridge.

Return to the main trail and make your way carefully down the slickrock to a junction at 3.9 miles. Follow the spur left (southeast) down toward North Dome. At first you drop down the east side of the ridge crest, passing to the right of Basket Dome to a timbered saddle, then back up the smooth exfoliating crown of North Dome, reaching the summit at 4.4 miles. North Dome's position above the confluence of several major drainages makes it one of the finest viewpoints in Yosemite. From left to right Tenaya Canyon, Merced Canyon, Illilouette Gorge, and Yosemite Valley itself fan out in all directions. When you have run out of film and/or time, return the way you came.

16 The North Rim

See map on page 63

General description:	Shuttle, overnight route following the North Rim of Yosemite Valley from west to east, skirting the tops of El Capitan, Yosemite Falls, and North Dome.
Total distance:	30 miles.
Difficulty:	Moderate to strenuous.
Elevation gain:	3,360 feet.
Trail traffic:	Light, except near the top of Yosemite Falls and at North Dome.
Best months:	All summer, but ask about trail conditions in early season. Snow lies late in the shady gullies well into summer, and some of the creek crossings are dangerous at high water.
Maps:	USGS El Capitan, Half Dome, and Yosemite Falls quads.
Permits:	Available in advance or from the wilderness center in Yosemite Valley and the Big Oak Flat Entrance.

Finding the trailhead: From the junction at the west end of Yosemite Valley, drive 4 miles north on Big Oak Flat Road (California 120). The trailhead is on the right, immediately past the Foresta Road turnoff on the left (south). There is no space to park at the trailhead itself, but there is a big turnout a few hundred yards back downhill on the road. The shoulder is very narrow between the parking area and the road; walk carefully.

Trailhead facilities: Groceries, accommodations, supplies, and phones in Yosemite Valley.

Key points:
```
 0.0   Trailhead.
 4.0   Old Big Oak Flat Road.
 4.5   Cascade Creek.
 9.7   El Capitan spur.
10.3   Return to main trail.
11.8   Eagle Peak spur.
12.6   Return to main trail.
14.8   Upper Yosemite Creek junction.
15.3   Lower Yosemite Creek junction.
17.7   Lehamite Creek.
19.0   North Dome spur.
20.0   Return to main trail.
22.1   Upper Lehamite Creek junction.
26.1   Snow Creek Bridge.
28.4   Tenaya Canyon.
29.0   Mirror Lake.
30.0   Mirror Lake shuttle bus stop.
```

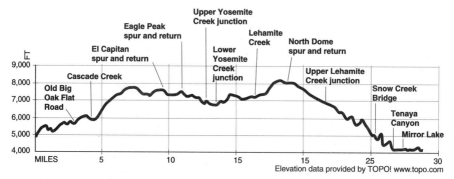

The hike: This route follows the North Rim of Yosemite Valley from west to east, beginning near Old Big Oak Flat Road and skirting the tops of El Capitan, Yosemite Falls, and North Dome, dropping into the valley at Tenaya Canyon above Mirror Lake.

While climbing the chaparral-covered slope recovering from the 1990 Foresta fire, stay alert for rattlesnakes. As soon as you cross to the north side of the ridge, notice the millions of young ponderosa pines jostling one another for growing space. The forest floor, newly opened by fire, hosts a colorful display of wildflowers, especially showy wild irises. Birding is exceptional here because of the number of desirable nesting sites in the hollow, burned-out trees. Leave the burned area behind, cross several tributaries of Wildcat Creek blooming with dogwoods and azaleas, and continue on to Tamarack Creek, which might be tricky to cross at least until midseason. Huge leaves of Indian rhubarb, twice the size of dinner plates, line the creek, and when they are in bloom, their flowers seem to poke up right through the center of the leaves.

A little farther on, cross a small branch of Cascade Creek and reach the now abandoned Old Big Oak Flat Road at 4 miles. Turn right. The left fork leads back up to Tamarack Flat Campground and the Tioga Road. Cross the main branch of Cascade Creek on a bridge and continue down the road to 4.7 miles, where the road is blocked with a pile of logs diverting you to the left (north) at a signed junction. The trail turns back on itself for a short time and begins a stiff climb up a forested slope to follow a ridgetop, still climbing steadily to Ribbon Meadow. This area is almost too thickly forested to rightfully be called a meadow, but it is boggy (and buggy) enough early in the year to deserve that designation. A little way beyond is Ribbon Creek where there is some camping, if the creek is still flowing. Cross the creek, then follow the trail as it cuts back north around the edge of El Capitan Gully, down which there is a stomach-lurching view of the valley. You can see El Capitan ahead of you now. A junction with the spur trail to the top of El Capitan appears at 9.7 miles. The view from the top is all you would expect from such a height, but don't go too near the downward-sloping edge. Return to the main trail at 10.3 miles, descend to the turnoff to Eagle Peak, at 11.8 miles, and climb to the top. At 7,779 feet, this is the highest of the Three Brothers. Directly across from you is Taft Point, and below you can see almost the whole floor of Yosemite Valley. Descend to the main trail again, at 12.6 miles.

Continue north through some mushy ground alongside Eagle Peak Meadows, then meet the Yosemite Creek trail at 10.3 miles. The trail rises and falls until it reaches a second junction at 15.3 miles. This is where you'll meet the sweating, panting hikers toiling up from the valley floor. Turn left (southeast) at the junction for a few yards, then follow the signs to the overlook, an area of sculpted rocks and twisted Jeffrey pines to an iron railing. Directly across the valley the upside-down bowl of Sentinel Dome rises alone to the west of Glacier Point. Farther in the distance is bullet-shaped Mount Starr King, standing isolated from the surrounding ridges. Return to the trail and descend to cross Yosemite Creek on a footbridge, just above where the creek falls over the rim. Continue upstream on switchbacks over mostly open rock to Yosemite Point. Now you are immediately above Yosemite Village, and you can just glimpse Yosemite Falls back to the right.

From Yosemite Point follow the valley rim, climbing steeply at first, then beginning an up-and-down progress through fir forest, crossing Indian Canyon Creek. Just before Lehamite Creek at 17.7 miles, a side trail cuts off to the left, returning to Tioga Road. Your trail continues straight ahead, gaining elevation gradually at first, then more steeply, finally laboring up rough switchbacks to the crest of Indian Ridge. Half Dome rears up in front of you, impossibly enormous at such close range. Downhill to the right is the bald pate of North Dome. Cross over the ridge, following ducks, to a spur trail at 19 miles. Don't miss the experience of descending to the top of North Dome, where Yosemite Valley stretches off to the west, Illilouette Gorge heads south, Merced Canyon comes in from the east, and Tenaya Canyon, from the northeast. Watch your step here. The trail down to the North Dome is very steep and very slippery, with fine gravel sprinkled over smooth rock.

Arch on Indian Ridge.

Return to the main trail at 20 miles, then climb steeply up the slick rock along the east side of the crest of Indian Ridge. Partway up is another spur trail to the left (south), where you can look down on North Dome from a higher point. Continue up the ridge to a saddle where another detour cuts off to the right (northeast) to a very unusual rock arch, a geologic feature seldom seen in granite. There's nothing else like it in Yosemite. Back on the main trail, descend partly through manzanita, partly through forest, to a junction at 22.1 miles. Turn right (east) toward Mirror Lake. Descend slowly until you near the main branch of Snow Creek, and follow the trail as it turns south and drops sharply downhill to meet the Snow Creek Trail, at 25.6 miles. Continue south down very steep switchbacks, beside wonderful examples of exfoliating granite with hanging gardens fed by seeps of water coming from between the layers, to Tenaya Canyon, at 27.9 miles. Turn right (west) and follow Tenaya Creek to Mirror Lake, at 29 miles. From here you can follow the road for a mile back to the backpackers' parking lot or ride the shuttle bus back to Curry Village.

17 Tuolumne Grove

General description:	Easy out-and-back day hike that takes you to the mammoth Tunnel Tree.
Total distance:	2 miles.
Difficulty:	Easy.
Elevation gain:	500 feet.
Trail traffic:	Moderate.
Best months:	Spring, summer, and fall; whenever the road is open.
Maps:	Ackerson Mountain.
Permits:	None.

Finding the trailhead: From Yosemite Valley, drive 16 miles north on Big Oak Flat Road to Crane Flat. Turn right on Tioga Road (California 120) and drive less than a mile to the Tuolumne Grove parking area on the left.

Trailhead facilities: Toilets.

Key points:

0.0   Trailhead.
1.0   Tuolumne Grove.

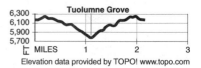

The hike: The Tuolumne Grove of giant sequoias is not as heavily visited as the Mariposa Grove and does not have a tram tour through it, so you can enjoy the beauty and serenity of the forest away from the sounds of

A hiker can find solitude in the less traveled Tuolumne Grove of giant sequoias.

Tuolumne Grove

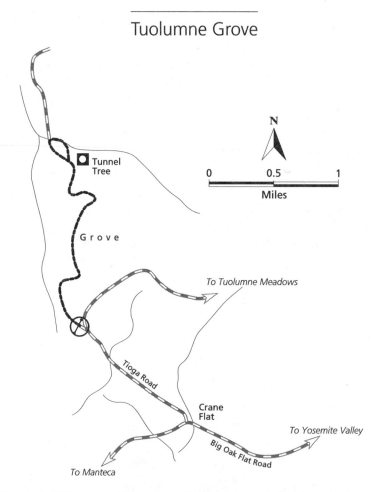

Tunnel Tree

N

0   0.5   1

Miles

G r o v e

To Tuolumne Meadows

Tioga Road

Crane Flat

To Yosemite Valley

Big Oak Flat Road

To Manteca

"civilization." The route follows an old road now closed to vehicle traffic. It passes through a closed gate and descends in a beautiful old forest of white fir, Douglas-fir, sugar pine, and incense-cedar. This last, with its smooth red bark, is often confused with the giant sequoia, but the first of these will not appear for about a half mile. In spring, exquisite white dogwoods bloom in openings in the forest. The first huge sequoia with an interpretive panel beside it appears on the left. A sign to the right directs you to the Tunnel Tree. This tree was already only a stump when the tunnel was cut through it in 1878, but dead or alive, it gives you an eerie feeling to look straight up to the sky while you're inside. Beyond the Tunnel Tree is a picnic area that used to be a parking lot, when cars were allowed into the grove. A nature trail begins here on the right across a little bridge. It has a series of excellent interpretive signs explaining the natural history of the trees: how they reach their great ages of 3,000 years; how they are adapted to survive repeated fires; how they depend on fire, insects, and squirrels to reproduce; and more. The nature trail loop returns to the road at the picnic area, from which you now climb back up to the trailhead.

The High Sierra Camps

The High Sierra Camps

These are a series of five backcountry camps with tent cabins that offer dorm-style sleeping, linens, meals, and showers. They are about a day's hike apart, and a popular trip is to make a loop of all of them, though each is within a day's walk of a trailhead and may be visited individually. They range in elevation from 7,200 feet at Merced Lake to 10,100 feet at Vogelsang and occupy some of the most beautiful settings in Yosemite. The largest, Merced Lake, accommodates 60 people; the smallest, Glen Aulin, holds 32. You can hike the camps on your own, or as part of an organized, naturalist-led group. The High Sierra camps offer a wonderful way to see some of Yosemite's finest backcountry without carrying a pack, but of course, they are extremely popular. They are operated by Yosemite Concession Services and reservations are granted by lottery. Lottery applications are accepted from October 15 to November 30. Call (559) 253-5674.

Each of the High Sierra camps provides good camping for backpackers with solar toilets and bear-proof boxes nearby. Snacks and emergency supplies are available at the camps during limited hours each day, which vary from camp to camp. Even if you are backpacking, these camps are very popular and permit quotas are filled early. The surest way to see them is to go early or late in the season.

This section will describe hikes to each of the camps from their nearest trailhead, then will describe the loop in a counterclockwise direction, beginning at Tuolumne Meadows—since the first camp on the loop, Glen Aulin, is downhill from here, you have extra time to adjust to the higher elevations.

---

18 Merced Lake High Sierra Camp

General description: Overnight backpack to the High Sierra camp nearest Yosemite Valley.

Total distance: 26.8 miles.

Difficulty: Strenuous as a two-day backpack, moderate if you take more time.

Elevation gain: 3,260 feet.

Trail traffic: Heavy.

Best months: Mid-June–September.

Maps: USGS Half Dome and Merced Peak quads.

Permits: Required; acquire in advance or at the wilderness center in Yosemite Valley.

Merced Lake High Sierra Camp

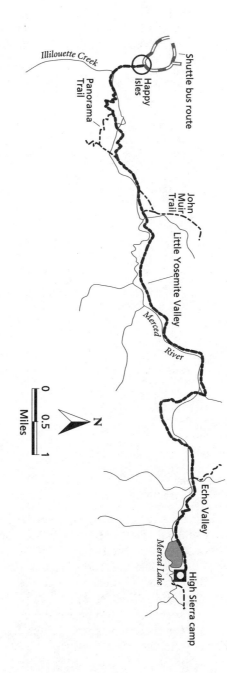

Finding the trailhead: Park in the backpackers' lot east of Curry Village. Either take the Yosemite Valley shuttle bus from Curry Village to Stop 16, Happy Isles, or walk from the parking lot, turn right (east) at the entrance and follow the well-marked path to Happy Isles. This will add 1 mile each way to your hike. From the shuttle bus stop, continue on the paved road over the Happy Isles Bridge, then turn right to the big sign that marks the beginning of the John Muir Trail.

Trailhead facilities: Snacks, water, and toilets.

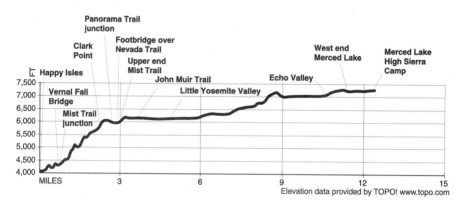

Elevation data provided by TOPO! www.topo.com

Key points:

0.0	Happy Isles.
0.8	Vernal Fall Bridge.
0.9	Mist Trail junction.
2.3	Clark Point.
3.3	Panorama Trail junction.
3.5	Footbridge over Nevada Fall.
3.8	Upper end of Mist Trail.
4.3	John Muir Trail junction.
4.8	Little Yosemite Valley.
11.4	Echo Valley.
12.7	West end Merced Lake.
13.4	Merced Lake High Sierra Camp.

The hike: Merced Lake is the site of the largest of the High Sierra camps and the farthest from any trailhead. The hike up the Giant Staircase along the Merced River allows you to experience the river in its many moods and to appreciate the power of the glaciers that carved and polished the canyon.

The sign at the trailhead shows mileage to various points on the John Muir Trail all the way to Mount Whitney, 211 miles to the south. You will have plenty of company, especially at the beginning of this hike, since it is one of the starting points for the High Sierra Camps Loop, as well as the jumping-off point for the John Muir Trail and the climb to Half Dome.

The trail climbs gently on an eroded asphalt path through black oak and ponderosa pine forest among enormous lichen-draped boulders. In about a half mile, across the thundering Merced to your right, watch for 370-foot

Illilouette Fall tucked back in its deeply cut gorge in the Panorama Cliff. The trail now steepens briefly, then suddenly descends to the Vernal Fall Bridge at 0.8 mile. Upstream, Vernal Fall is perfectly framed by maple, alder, and various conifers as it drops 317 feet over the lowest step of the Giant Staircase. There are restrooms, drinking water, and lots of people here.

Cross the bridge to the south side of the river and turn left, upstream. Pass a lateral trail on the right for horses only that leads back to the stables, then meet the Mist Trail junction at 0.9 mile. This is an alternate route to the top of Nevada Fall (see Hike 4), which is not recommended for backpackers since it is steep, slippery, and wet. Continue climbing on the John Muir Trail, which switchbacks relentlessly uphill. There are plenty of excuses to stop and rest on the way. Across the valley to the northwest is Upper Yosemite Fall. To the northeast across the river gorge, the rounded backside of Half Dome comes into view along with Mount Broderick, Liberty Cap, and finally, 594-foot Nevada Fall. This heart-stopping view is finest at Clark Point (2.3 miles), where a lateral trail cuts over to the Mist Trail, nearer to the river. Continue to ascend the John Muir Trail on well-graded switchbacks, eventually passing beneath a dripping rock overhang decorated with delicate hanging gardens of ferns, columbines, monkey flowers, and other water-loving species. At 3.3 miles the Panorama Trail leading back to Glacier Point joins this one from the right (south). The trail drops a bit, hops a couple of little creeks, then emerges into a wide, sunny expanse of smooth granite at the top of Nevada Fall. Here, at 3.5 miles, a footbridge crosses the river. There are plenty of viewpoints with protective railings where you can watch the falls rush over the lip. Do stay behind the railings

Bunnell Cascade on the Merced River.

and heed the warning signs. Hikers have slipped on the slick rock and been washed over the falls. This is a perfect place for lunch or a snack, but please do not share your food with the panhandling squirrels and jays.

When you have absorbed the scene or run out of time, cross the foot-bridge and follow the north shore of the river to 3.8 miles. There is an outhouse here, and just beyond, the junction with the upper end of the Mist Trail. Continue upstream, climbing the well-defined, heavily used trail over inlaid rocks. The trail soon levels out and passes from sunlight into shade, and the Merced changes from a rushing, raging torrent to become quiet, dark, and deep.

At 4.3 miles, your trail parts company with the John Muir Trail, which heads off to the left (northeast) toward Half Dome. After slogging through heavy sand for a half mile, another lateral trail at 4.8 miles takes off to the left to join the John Muir and Half Dome trails. Ahead is Little Yosemite Valley, your first camping opportunity. It's a busy and popular place, especially for bears. There are plenty of bear-proof boxes for food storage; be sure to use them if you are not carrying a bear canister. There is also an architecturally elegant two-story solar composting toilet here. The National Park Service has constructed two communal fire rings for campers to share. Please do not scar this already overused area by building another one.

Beyond Little Yosemite Valley the trail continues through level forest. Watch for brilliant red snowplants and the drabber brownish pinedrops on the forest floor. These live on decaying material in the soil, so they have no need of green leaves and can survive in deep shade. In little more than a mile, steep granite walls close in, pinching shut Little Yosemite Valley, forcing the river to pick up speed and vigor. It cascades noisily for a short time before slowing and widening out once again through Lost Valley. The trail climbs out of the valley, passing under the enormous dome of Bunnell Point, where the river pours down the long slippery slide of Bunnell Cascade and is finally crossed on a footbridge to the south side. Climb the switchbacks blasted out of the smooth granite, then pause to wipe away the sweat and enjoy the view where the river roars through a spectacular rocky gorge.

Descend once again, cross back over the river, and soon enter Echo Valley, a badly burned-over flat where several creeks flow in to join the Merced. At 11.4 miles, where Echo Creek flows into the valley, a trail to Sunrise High Sierra Camp cuts off to the north. Soon the Merced begins to race beside the trail again as you climb the final mile to Merced Lake. There is a stock gate at the west end of the lake at 12.7 miles. Be sure to close it behind you. Skirt the lakeshore closely until you reach the campground at the far end of the lake. There are toilets and bear-proof boxes here, too. The High Sierra camp lies just beyond at 13.4 miles. Campers may use the water tap at the camp to avoid purifying river water, but are asked to use the toilets at the backpackers' campground. You can buy emergency items and snacks during posted hours at the High Sierra camp. Just beyond is a ranger station, which is manned all summer.

From here you can return to Yosemite Valley or continue north to Vogelsang High Sierra Camp to continue the loop.

19 Vogelsang High Sierra Camp

General description: An overnight backpack loop to the highest of the High Sierra camps.

Total distance: 19.1 miles.

Difficulty: Moderate.

Elevation gain: 2,000 feet.

Trail traffic: Moderate.

Best months: Late June–September.

Maps: USGS Vogelsang Peak and Tioga Pass quads.

Permits: Required; available at the Tuolumne Meadows Wilderness Center.

Finding the trailhead: From the west, drive Tioga Road (California 120) eastward past the Tuolumne Meadows Visitor Center, store, and campground, all on the right (south). Cross the bridge over the Tuolumne River. In about a mile, turn right at the entrance to the wilderness center. Follow the road as it curves around to the left for about a half mile to the Dog Lake parking lot on the left. Chances are you'll see broken glass on the asphalt where bears have broken into cars containing improperly stored food. Leave ice chests and all food in the bear-proof boxes provided. You can also ride the Tuolumne Meadows shuttle bus to Stop 2, Dog Lake Trailhead.

Trailhead facilities: Food, supplies, and phones at Tuolumne Meadows.

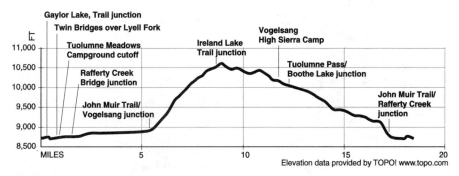

Key points:

0.0	John Muir Trailhead.
0.2	Bridge over Dana Fork and junction with Tuolumne Meadows Lodge.
0.3	Junction with Gaylor Lakes Trail.
0.6	Twin bridges over Lyell Fork.
0.7	Cutoff to Tuolumne Meadows Campground.
1.3	Rafferty Creek Bridge junction.
5.6	John Muir Trail/Vogelsang junction.
8.0	Ireland Lake Trail.
11.5	Vogelsang High Sierra Camp.
12.3	Tuolumne Pass/Boothe Lake junction.
17.8	John Muir Trail/Rafferty Creek junction.

Vogelsang High Sierra Camp

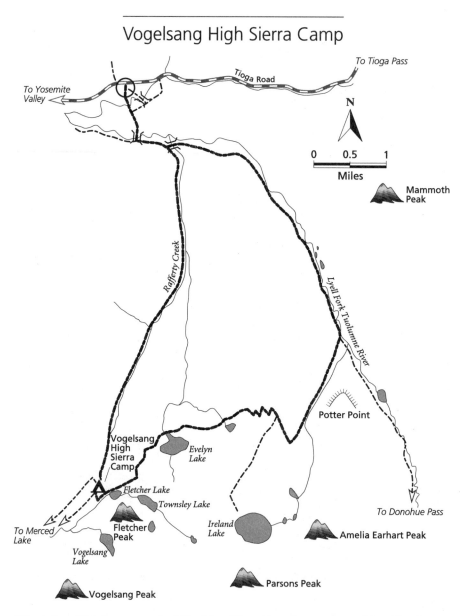

The hike: This loop may be hiked in either direction, approaching Vogelsang from the west via Rafferty Creek, or from the east via the Lyell Fork and Evelyn Lake. If you have only one night to spend, you can make an out-and-back hike of 13.4 miles via Rafferty Creek, but this area really deserves more time, at least three days. This hike will be described in a clockwise direction, that is, via Lyell Fork, returning via Rafferty Creek, because the ascent is more gradual.

To begin, cross the road south of the parking lot to the John Muir Trailhead sign. Follow the trail southeast to the footbridge over the Dana Fork, at 0.2 mile. Ignore the cutoff back to the lodge and cross the bridge, then turn left and follow the river upstream. At 0.3 mile is another cutoff to the left to Gaylor Lake. Keep right here, too. (You have probably noticed that although the trailhead sign was marked "Vogelsang 6.7" and the sign in front of you says "Vogelsang 6.8" you have actually come farther than 0.1 mile. The trail signs have been erected at different times and are not always perfectly consistent.) The route bends slightly to the right, crosses a low rise, and reaches the twin bridges over the Lyell Fork at 0.6 mile. This is surely one of the most sublime vistas in Yosemite, with the clear turquoise river winding toward you through the green meadow. The color of the water comes from glacial "flour," rock ground so fine by the Lyell Glacier upstream that it remains suspended in the water and reflects this lovely green light. In places, deep bowls have been carved into the granite by the scouring force of the silt carried by spring runoff. The massive gray hulk on the left is Mammoth Peak (not to be confused with Mammoth Mountain, the ski resort, which lies farther south). Soon after you leave the twin bridges, another path leads back to the Tuolumne Meadows Campground at 0.7 mile. Continue left on the John Muir Trail through lodgepole forest and over open rock to 1.3 miles, where the Rafferty Creek Trail, the more direct route to Vogelsang, leads uphill to the right (south). You will be returning on this trail. Cross the bridge over the creek on your left and continue through forest and meadows, which, in early season, are a solid mass of pale lavender shooting stars (and mosquitoes.) Soon the sound of the river becomes apparent—it's been hidden for a while behind a low ridge—and another glorious view of Lyell Canyon opens up before you.

Follow the path along the river to 5.6 miles, where the Vogelsang trail leaves the John Muir Trail and angles off to the southwest, leaving the river behind. Near this junction are some good campsites to the right of the trail. This is a notorious bear hangout and *the bears here are intelligent and resourceful.* Consider the hanging of food to be a delaying tactic only. You will sleep more soundly if you carry a bear-proof canister.

Beyond the junction and the camping area, the trail begins to climb, switchbacking through lodgepole pine, sometimes through patches of wild strawberries and alpine prickly currant bushes. As the trail nears the creek on the left, a lovely little meadow appears. Be sure to pause for a moment and look up and ahead for the waterfall flowing from Ireland Lake, just out of sight in the bowl above.

Beyond the meadow the trail leaves the stream, first heads southwest, then makes a dogleg to the north and reaches a junction with the Ireland Lake Trail at 8 miles. The trail sign here incorrectly gives the distance to Ireland Lake as 3 miles. It is actually only 1.5 miles (each way), and is well worth a detour if you have the time. The lake lies in a huge open glacial cirque above timberline beneath Parsons and Amelia Earhart peaks.

Back on the Vogelsang trail, cross a little creek, then climb a rocky slope that becomes steep toward the top, with tight switchbacks. Stay alert. It's easy to zig when you should have zagged and miss the route. Your goal is obvious, however—it is the low point on the ridge ahead. This is the highest point of your hike at 10,600 feet, and it offers sensational views. The

Vogelsang Peak rises high above the High Sierra camp.

vegetation has changed from upright lodgepole pine to whitebark pine forest that is less than knee-high on this windy ridgetop. Behind you to the northeast is the light-colored Kuna Crest, and beyond that, the Koip Crest, which marks the park boundary. To the south are black Amelia Earhart and Parsons peaks, and beyond them the group of tall peaks on the horizon includes Mount Lyell, highest point in Yosemite. To the west, an unnamed lake occupies a broad green bowl with your trail skirting its northwest shore before vanishing over the next ridge.

Descend from the saddle to the outlet of this little lake, noting that the whitebark pines, though still twisted and gnarled, are now growing upright. Hop the outlet stream, cross a low ridge, and enter a larger bowl containing Evelyn Lake. Off to the north beyond Tuolumne Meadows lie the high peaks of Yosemite's north boundary country, crowned by Mount Conness, third highest peak in the park. The trail now crosses the outlet of Evelyn Lake, tops another rise, then descends through a notch that often holds patches of snow well into summer, and as a result, is usually filled with flowers. Downhill to the right are glimpses of Boothe Lake and of the Rafferty Creek Trail leading back down to Tuolumne Meadows. A little farther along, Fletcher Lake, lying at the base of Fletcher Peak comes into view on the left. A long meadow dotted with whitebark pine stretches out ahead.

Vogelsang High Sierra Camp lies at the far end of Fletcher Lake at 11.5 miles. There are plenty of campsites beneath the trees all along the lake. Be sure to camp only on pine duff and not on the fragile green meadow vegetation, and stay well away from the even more delicate lakeshore. There are a few especially fine sites toward the north side of the big meadow near the cliff edge with views of Boothe Lake and Mount Conness. Use the bear-proof boxes provided if you are not traveling with a bear-proof canister. These are located near the distinctive oddly shaped solar composting toilet for backpackers. Please do not use the toilets at the nearby High Sierra camp. There is a tap with potable water near the camp that you may use if you don't want to purify lake water. Emergency supplies and snacks are available during posted hours at the camp.

If you have time, climb up to Vogelsang Lake or beyond to Vogelsang Pass for more breathtaking views. The round-trip distance for this detour is 2.4 miles. On your way, you can see all the way to Half Dome at the head of Yosemite Valley.

When you're ready to return to Tuolumne Meadows, find the signed junction in front of the High Sierra camp and descend north, then northeast, gently down the ridge above Boothe Lake to Tuolumne Pass, where you will find another junction at 12.3 miles. You can make yet another detour of 0.4 mile for a look at Boothe Lake, or continue gently downhill along Rafferty Creek for a long stretch, sometimes through forest, sometimes at the edge of the meadow. Toward the end, the descent steepens and at last switchbacks down to the junction of the John Muir Trail at 17.8 miles, closing the loop. From here, return the way you came to Tuolumne Meadows.

20 May Lake High Sierra Camp

General description:	Out-and-back day hike or overnight backpack to May Lake and Mount Hoffman.
Total distance:	2.4 miles.
Difficulty:	Easy.
Elevation gain:	490 feet.
Trail traffic:	Heavy.
Best months:	All summer; whenever the road is open and free of snow.
Maps:	USGS Tenaya Lake quad.
Permits:	Available in advance or from the wilderness centers in Yosemite Valley or Tuolumne Meadows.

Finding the trailhead: From Tioga Road (California 120), drive 27 miles east of Crane Flat, or 20 miles west of Tioga Pass, to the May Lake Road junction. Follow the narrow road north about 2 miles to the trailhead. Drive with care here—in many places the road is only wide enough for one vehicle at a time. Leave any food or ice chests in the bear-proof boxes at the trailhead.

Trailhead facilities: None. Toilets and potable water at May Lake. (Please use the toilets at the campground, not at the High Sierra camp.) There is also a small store usually open for a few hours each day at the camp, offering T-shirts and a few emergency items.

Key points:

0.0 Trailhead.

1.2 May Lake.

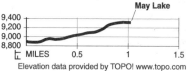

Elevation data provided by TOPO! www.topo.com

The hike: This is the High Sierra camp most easily reached from the road (not counting Tuolumne Meadows Lodge), so you are bound to have plenty of company on the trail. The hike begins in a shady glen with a variety of conifers, lodgepole pine, silver pine, hemlock, and fir, then passes a discolored little pond teeming with fairy shrimp and other interesting creatures. The well-used trail climbs slowly at first, passing through granite corridors where cracks bloom with ferns, mountain pride penstemon, shaggy hawkweed, and other wildflowers. Eventually the trail begins a steeper, winding climb, revealing good views now and then down Tenaya Canyon past Clouds Rest and Half Dome. The dramatic pointy peak in the distance is Mount Clark. Back up the canyon in the other direction, Tenaya Lake is just visible.

The trail flattens out in forest and in just a few yards reaches a fork. To the left is the camping area, to the right is the High Sierra camp. Enjoy the lakeshore, but do not jump in. This is the local water supply, so swimming is prohibited. Mount Hoffman at 10,850 feet, rises dramatically behind the lake. It is well worth a scramble to the top if you have the time, since it lies in the geographical center of the park and offers superb views.

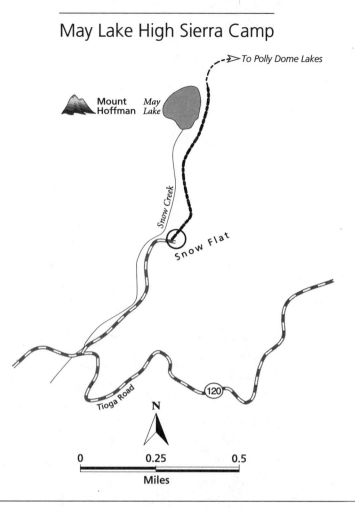

To Polly Dome Lakes

Mount Hoffman May Lake

Snow Creek

Snow Flat

Tioga Road 120

N

0   0.25   0.5

Miles

21 Glen Aulin High Sierra Camp

General description: An out-and-back day hike or overnighter through flowery meadows and lodgepole forests.

Total distance: 10.4 miles.

Difficulty: Easy as a backpack, moderate as a day hike.

Elevation gain: 600 feet.

Trail traffic: Heavy.

Best months: All summer; whenever the Tioga Road is open.

Maps: USGS Falls Ridge and Tioga Pass quads.

Permits: None required for a day hike; available in advance or at the Tuolumne Meadows Wilderness Center for overnight trips.

Finding the trailhead: From the west, follow Tioga Road (California 120) past the Tuolumne Meadows Visitor Center, store, café, and campground,

Glen Aulin High Sierra Camp

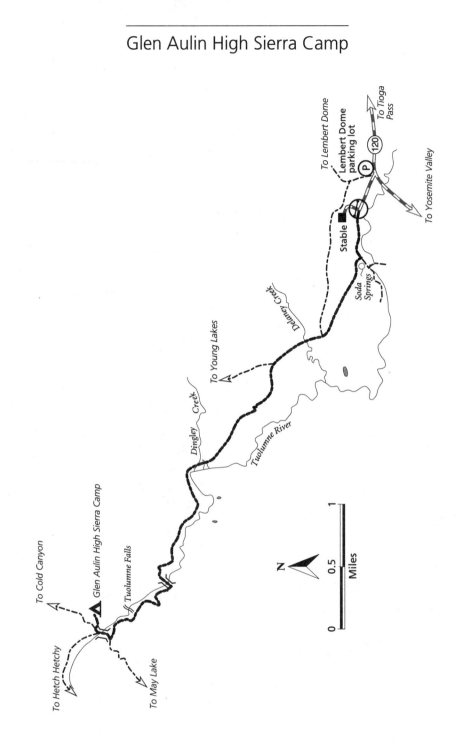

all on your right. Just after crossing the bridge over the Tuolumne River, turn left (north) into the Lembert Dome parking area. From the east (Tioga Pass) follow the Tioga Road past the turnoff to the wilderness center on your left and continue about a hundred yards to the Lembert Dome parking area on your right. You can also ride the Tuolumne Meadows shuttle bus to Stop 4, Lembert Dome. Overnight parking is prohibited in the parking lot, so if you are planning to backpack, park along the paved road parallel to Tioga Road. If there are no spaces left, follow the road around to the right and park at the stables. At a closed gate, this road turns sharply to the right and heads toward the stables. The trail begins at the gate.

Trailhead facilities: None; potable water, toilets, snacks, and emergency supplies are available at the High Sierra camp during posted hours.

Key points:

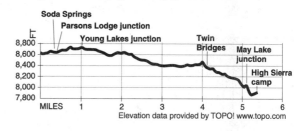

Elevation data provided by TOPO! www.topo.com

    0.0   Trailhead.
    0.5   Soda Springs.
    0.6   Parsons Lodge junction.
    1.2   Young Lakes junction.
    3.5   Twin Bridges.
    5.0   May Lake junction.
    5.2   High Sierra camp.

The hike: Pass through the gate and follow the road (closed to vehicles) westward through the meadow with scattered lodgepoles to the ramshackle log structure at Soda Springs, a naturally carbonated spring bubbling up rusty water. Just beyond is Parsons Lodge, a stone building with historical exhibits, and beyond that, a log cabin used by park volunteers. There is a public restroom behind the cabin. The path splits near the cabin. Head right, around the rear of the building (the road around the front goes to the sewage treatment plant). Nearby, the road intersects a trail with several signs. One says the High Sierra camp is 4.7 miles, another says Glen Aulin is 5.3 miles. That's because the Glen itself is a short distance beyond the High Sierra camp. Walk through flowery meadows and lodgepole forest, then wade shallow Delaney Creek. If it's early season, you can keep your boots dry by crossing on a big log immediately upstream. The trail is heavy and dusty here since it is used by pack trains going to and from the High Sierra Camp.

At 1.2 miles, meet a junction with one of the trails that heads north to Young Lakes. Continue northwest, descending very gradually. In less than a mile you emerge from behind a low ridge to behold the spectacular Cathedral Range, with the Tuolumne River in the foreground. The next couple of miles along the river offer one incredible photo-op after another. Sometimes the trail passes over highly polished granite, buffed by glacial ice to a blinding sheen. Follow the ducks across these open spaces to stay on the trail. Climb around a low shoulder of rock and watch for the Little Devils Postpile on your left, an unusual volcanic feature much younger than the surrounding rock.

The White Cascade drops into a pool in front of Glen Aulin High Sierra Camp.

The trail then turns sharply right and drops down a short steep notch, and very soon it reaches a pair of footbridges across the Tuolumne River, at 3.5 miles. From this point on, the river picks up speed and cascades over a series of falls all the way to Glen Aulin. Tuolumne Falls is the most spectacular of these, and the trail takes you near enough to feel the spray.

Continue descending, enjoying views up Cold Canyon all the way to Matterhorn Peak and Mount Conness on the northern boundary of the park. At times the trail dives into deep forest lined with Labrador tea and corn lily, then emerges again into sunshine on cobblestone paths, or on smooth rock marked by ducks. Finally, in a patch of deep forest, it meets the junction with the trail to May Lake High Sierra Camp, at 5 miles. A few more steep and somewhat slippery switchbacks lead down to a bridge back to the other side of the river. To your right is the lovely White Cascade falling into a pool in front of Glen Aulin High Sierra Camp, at 5.2 miles.

To reach the camp, cross a second bridge to the right over Cold Creek. Northward up Cold Creek, behind the High Sierra camp, is a backpackers' campground with bear-proof boxes and a solar composting toilet. If you prefer, you can remain on the west side of Cold Creek, cross a rocky, red, iron-stained granite shoulder alongside a rushing cascade to reach the Glen itself about a half mile farther on. The area was burned a few years ago, but there are still good camping areas near the river. Be sure to stay at least 100 feet away from the shore. You'll need a bear canister here. Return the way you came.

22 Sunrise High Sierra Camp

General description:	Out-and-back day hike or backpack.
Total distance:	10.4 miles.
Difficulty:	Moderate.
Elevation gain:	1,420 feet.
Trail traffic:	Moderately heavy.
Best months:	July–mid-September.
Maps:	USGS Tenaya Lake quad.
Permits:	None as a day hike; available for backpackers in advance or from the Tuolumne Meadows Wilderness Center.

Finding the trailhead: Drive to the southwest end of Tenaya Lake on Tioga Road (California 120). The trailhead is across the street from the lake on the south side. You can also ride the Tuolumne Meadows shuttle to Stop 10, Sunrise Lakes Trailhead. Be sure to leave food and ice chests in the bear-proof boxes provided.

Sunrise High Sierra Camp

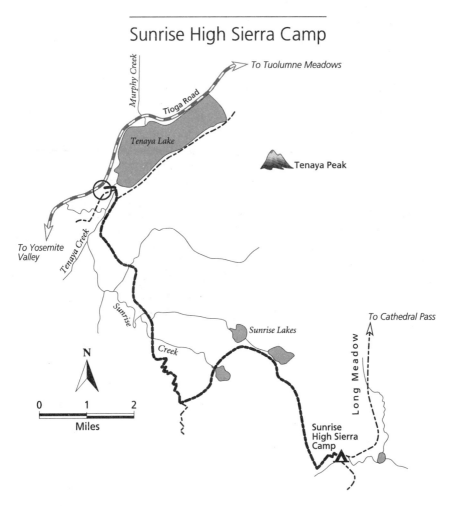

Trailhead facilities: Toilets only. Water, toilets, and snacks at Sunrise High Sierra Camp.

Key points:
- 0.0   Trailhead.
- 0.2   Tuolumne Lodge cutoff.
- 2.5   Clouds Rest/Half Dome junction.
- 5.1   John Muir Trail junction.
- 5.2   Sunrise High Sierra Camp.

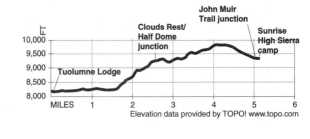

The hike: A paved trail begins behind the parking area. Turn left (east). Tenaya Lake can be glimpsed through the trees. Soon the pavement ends. Cross a sandy-bottomed creek draining Tenaya Lake that you'll probably have to wade early in the year. The trail swings right (south) just across the creek at 0.1 mile. A sign incorrectly says "Sunrise: 5 miles." At 0.2 mile, a trail leading back to Tuolumne Meadows Lodge goes off to the left. Just a little farther on, a second (also incorrect) sign says "Sunrise: 5.1 miles." The trail dips and rises now and then as it crosses several little streams, then it begins to climb the east slope above Tenaya Canyon. The switchbacking climb is relieved by views of Mount Hoffman and Tioga Road across the canyon.

At the crest of the ridge (2.5 miles), the trail splits. The right (south) fork leads back to Clouds Rest and Half Dome, the left (east) leads to Sunrise Lakes. Follow along the ridgeline for a short time, then drop into the bowl containing the first of the Sunrise Lakes. Its depth makes it a deep, almost improbable, blue. Camping is not recommended here. The sides of the bowl slope too steeply and the immediate lakeside is much too fragile (not to mention illegal) for camping. The trail now climbs up out of the bowl and follows its south rim. The second Sunrise Lake lies somewhat below the trail to the north and offers better camping.

The route crosses a smooth, round lump of classic exfoliating Yosemite granite to reach the uppermost, and largest, of the lakes. There are plenty of camping spaces here along the north shore, but the area is showing signs of overuse. Continue up a moderate hill alongside a wildflower-lined creek until reaching a wide, sandy saddle with scattered hemlock and pine. The jagged Clark Range defines the horizon to the south. The trail eases gently down to the backpackers' camping area behind the High Sierra camp, where there is a toilet, piped water, and bear boxes.

Just beyond and downhill at 5.1 miles, the trail meets a junction with the John Muir Trail. Turn left and follow the deeply worn ruts along the edge of the meadow to the High Sierra camp. From the camp's front door, the view of an emerald-green meadow backed by Merced Peak to the southeast and Mount Clark to the southwest invites contemplation and rest. The High Sierra Camp sells snacks and emergency supplies for a limited number of hours during the day.

If you are not following the HSC loop, return the way you came.

23 The High Sierra Camp Loop

General description: Overnight loop hike with great views and a lot of lakes.

Total distance: 46.6 miles.

Difficulty: Moderate.

Elevation gain: 2,380 feet.

Trail traffic: Moderately heavy.

Best months: All summer whenever Tioga Road is open.

Maps: USGS Falls Ridge, Tioga Pass, Tenaya Lake, Merced Peak, Vogelsang Peak, and Mount Lyell quads.

Permits: Available in advance or from the Tuolumne Meadows Wilderness Center.

Finding the trailhead: From the Lembert Dome parking lot on Tioga Road (California 120), just west of the turnoff to the wilderness center and Tuolumne Meadows Lodge, drive down the secondary road that parallels Tioga Road and park along its south side.

Trailhead facilities: None; restrooms, emergency supplies, and water at all the High Sierra camps.

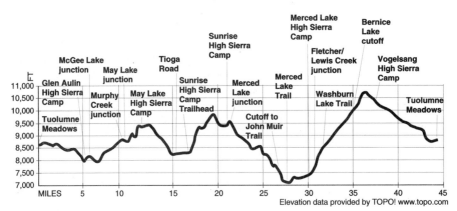

Elevation data provided by TOPO! www.topo.com

Key points:

- 0.0   Trailhead.
- 5.2   Glen Aulin High Sierra Camp.
- 5.4   McGee Lake junction.
- 9.6   Murphy Creek junction.
- 10.0 May Lake junction.
- 13.3 May Lake High Sierra Camp.
- 14.5 May Lake Trailhead.
- 15.0 Tioga Road.
- 15.9 Sunrise High Sierra Camp Trailhead at Tenaya Lake.
- 21.1 Sunrise High Sierra Camp.
- 22.0 Merced Lake junction.
- 28.1 Cutoff back to John Muir Trail.

The High Sierra Camp Loop

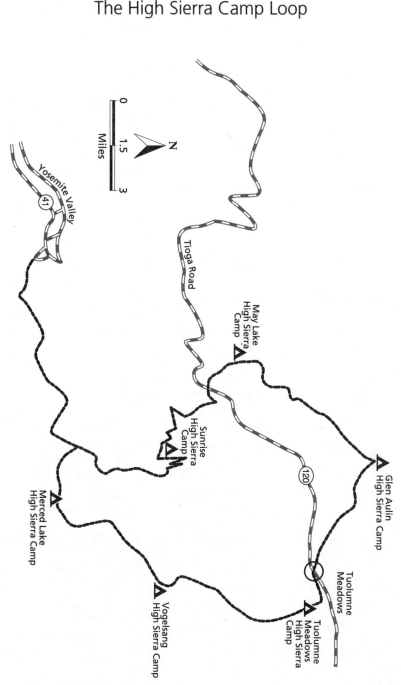

28.9	Merced Lake Trail.
31.0	Merced Lake High Sierra Camp.
31.3	Ranger station.
32.3	Fletcher/Lewis Creek junction.
33.3	Washburn Lake Trail.
36.3	Bernice Lake cutoff.
39.0	Vogelsang High Sierra Camp.

The hike: This loop is most commonly begun at Tuolumne Meadows and followed in a counterclockwise direction. Follow Hike 21, to 5.2 miles at Glen Aulin High Sierra Camp. After visiting the camp, retrace your steps back across the bridge over Conness Creek, turn left and cross the next bridge to the south side of the Tuolumne River, then climb the short slope to meet the McGee Lake junction at 5.4 miles. McGee Lake is oddly situated at the top of a narrow saddle, each side of which is topped by a dome. Skirt the north shore of the lake, looking straight down the canyon to Tuolumne Peak. There are a few campsites at the lakeside. Now descend mostly through forest to cross Cathedral Creek, then climb again to meet the trail at 9.6 miles that runs down to Tenaya Lake via Murphy Creek. Take the right fork here, and soon meet the May Lake junction at 10 miles. The trail begins a fairly steep, beautiful climb up an open slope down which little creeks trickle, each watering a miniature garden. Enjoy the views across the canyon to Mount Conness, then drop briefly down the west side of the rocky ridge.

When you reenter the forest and swing west, keep an eye out for Raisin Lake through gaps in the rocks. This warm lake is a great place for a swim after your long, hot climb. May Lake is not far away, but swimming there is prohibited. Beyond Raisin Lake, another short set of switchbacks takes you up past a meadow with an ephemeral pond, then meets the northeast end of May Lake and skirts its shore to the High Sierra camp at 13.3 miles. The backpackers' camping area is beyond the camp at the lake's southern end. Mount Hoffman makes a great day hike, if you have time, because it is at the geographic center of the park and offers a 360-degree sweep. There is no official trail to the top, but it is so frequently climbed that the way up is obvious.

From May Lake, follow the heavily traveled trail down to the May Lake trailhead at the end of a road, at 14.5 miles. Cross the road, then descend through forest to cross Tioga Road at 15 miles. There is a complicated set of junctions here, but it's easy to see where to go. Just head north toward Tenaya Lake to the Sunrise trailhead at 15.9 miles. (The topo shows a campground here, but it was dismantled years ago.)

Now follow Hike 22, to Sunrise, at 21.1 miles.

From the High Sierra Camp, head north on the John Muir Trail alongside a meadow to a junction at 22 miles. Turn right (east), cross the creek and the meadow, and climb to the Cathedral Fork of Echo Creek. The trail swings south and descends, crossing a couple of tributaries of the Cathedral Fork, to meet the main branch, which you cross on a bridge to the south side, then cross back to the northeast side again on another bridge. There are good views up the Merced River Canyon from here.

A marmot watches passers-by on the High Sierra camp loop.

In about half a mile, meet a cutoff back to the John Muir Trail to the west, at 28.1 miles. Continue ahead (south) to reach the Merced Lake Trail in Echo Valley, at 28.9 miles. There is space for camping here, but the area was burned in 1966 and it is still not very attractive. Turn left (east). Just past the junction, cross several little branches of Echo Creek yet again and follow the Merced River upstream along its north shore. Pass through a gate, and arrive at Merced Lake, whose edge you skirt very closely, pass the marshy meadow at the lake's upper end, then the backpackers' campground, then the High Sierra camp, at 31 miles. Continue east through lodgepole and fir forest, crossing several little creeks on footbridges. At 31.3 miles, the Merced Lake Ranger Station and corral appear on the right. Turn left (north) at the junction here, and switchback steeply up above Lewis Creek to meet the Fletcher Creek Trail at 32.3 miles. There are good views up the Fletcher Creek drainage and back down to Merced Lake.

You have two options for reaching Vogelsang from here. The Fletcher Creek Trail passes to the west of Vogelsang Peak and is shorter by about a mile. The Lewis Creek passes to the east. The longer trail, Lewis Creek, is described here because it is much more scenic and less frequently used. Follow the right fork to 33.3 miles, where you pass the turnoff to the trail leading to Isberg Pass. Continue northeast past the confluence with Florence Creek with its beautiful little waterfall, past the turnoff to Bernice Lake at 36.3 miles, and toil up the open, rocky grade to Vogelsang Pass, the highest point on the loop at almost 11,000 feet. The view back down Lewis Creek is spectacular, with the entire Clark Range spread out to the south. Across the drainage, lonely Gallison and Bernice lakes nestle in their barren cirques. Round a corner at the top of the pass, skirt some tiny ponds, then descend the bouldery slope to Vogelsang Lake, at the base of Vogelsang Peak, where fat marmot sentries watch from (almost) every few rocks. Cross the lake's outlet on logs and wind down the partly rocky, partly muddy slope toward the huddle of white tents of the High Sierra camp below. The outlet stream comes from unseen Fletcher Lake around the corner; cross it on logs and make your way around to the front of the camp at a junction, at 39 miles. The backpackers' camping area with toilets and bear boxes is on the north side of Fletcher Lake, east of the High Sierra camp.

From the junction in front of the camp, follow Hike 19, back down to Tuolumne Meadows.

The Southern Park

The Southern Park

The trails into the southern park begin from Wawona, Glacier Point Road, or the short spur road off California 41 to the Mariposa Grove of Big Trees. Most trailheads start at around 4,000 feet, and offer hiking opportunities earlier in the season than in other parts of Yosemite. You'll find more solitude in this part of the park, too, perhaps because there is less water in high summer, the time when most people come to Yosemite. The crown of the southern park is Mount Clark, whose distinctive, narrow summit can be seen from many miles away.

Many of the southern trails begin near Wawona, the site of a historical overnight stage stop on the way to Yosemite Valley. The beautiful old Wawona Hotel, built in the 1870s, is still in operation. You can visit the Pioneer Yosemite History Center to learn about the early days of Yosemite, or even play a round of golf. There is a campground, gas station, gift shop, grocery store, and stables. Wawona is about 4 miles inside the park from the California 41 entrance to Yosemite. Just past "town," a new bridge crosses the Merced River, and just past that is Chilnualna Fall Road on the right. The Wawona Ranger Station,which issues wilderness permits, is a short distance up the road. Almost all the trailheads out of Wawona are off this road, all are clearly marked, and all have parking areas. The road ends just past North Wawona, a little settlement with a store and a few cottages for rent. It is part of an inholding (private property surrounded by a national park).

The remaining trails into the southern park depart from Glacier Point Road to the south and east.

24 Mariposa Grove of Big Trees

General description: A loop hike through the giant sequoias.
Total distance: 5.9 miles.
Difficulty: Moderate.
Elevation gain: 1,000 feet.
Trail traffic: Heavy in the lower grove, moderate in the upper grove.
Best months: Spring, summer, or fall, or until snow closes the road.
Maps: USGS Mariposa Grove quad and "Mariposa Grove of Giant Sequoias Guide and Map" by Jon Kinney, available at the trailhead for fifty cents.
Permits: None.

Finding the trailhead: From the entrance station to Yosemite on Wawona Road (California 41), head right (east) for 2 miles to the Mariposa Grove. There is limited parking at the trailhead, so it is suggested that you park at

Mariposa Grove of Big Trees

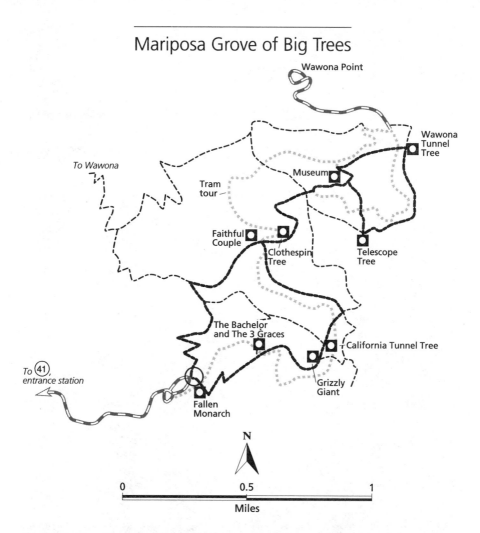

the lot across the street from the entrance station or in front of the store at Wawona and take the free shuttle bus to the grove. The buses run every 20 minutes. Open-air tram tours are available here. They take 50 minutes and cost $7.50. The trailhead is marked by a sign at the northeast end of the parking lot.

Trailhead facilities: Restrooms, water, snacks, and a gift shop are at the parking lot near where the tram tours begin; pit toilets are at the museum and along trails. Carry your own water.

Key Points:

0.0	Trailhead.
0.8	Grizzly Giant.
1.6	The Faithful Couple.
2.0	Four-way junction.
2.2	Museum.
2.7	Telescope Tree.

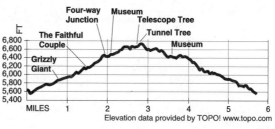

Elevation data provided by TOPO! www.topo.com

The Clothespin Tree in Mariposa Grove. JANE MAGID PHOTO

3.1   Fallen Tunnel Tree.
3.6   Return to museum.
5.9   Return to parking lot.

The hike: The giant sequoias are the largest living things on earth and are among the oldest, up to 3,000 years. The bristlecone pines in the White Mountains to the east are older, and the coast redwoods are taller, but these are certainly the most massive and arguably the most awe inspiring. The trail is marked by a series of interpretive panels with fascinating tidbits of information about the trees, among them the fact that these huge organisms have very shallow root systems, tiny seeds, and depend upon fire to maintain their health and reproduction.

The area is divided into upper and lower groves. A veritable maze of trails, all well marked, runs through both, so you can easily design your own hike to be longer or shorter than the one described here. This hike takes you past all the highlights of both the upper and lower groves with a minimum amount of backtracking.

From the busy parking lot follow the signed trail and the crowds eastward to a beautiful grouping of trees called The Bachelor and The Three Graces, then climb to the massive, beheaded Grizzly Giant at 0.8 mile, probably the largest tree in the grove. Just beyond is the California Tunnel Tree. The tunnel was cut in 1895 for stagecoaches full of tourists to pass through. Some things never change. Climb northwest to the Faithful Couple at 1.6 miles, two trees that have grown so closely together that they appear to be one at the base. Pass the aptly named Clothespin Tree, and at 2 miles, reach a confusing four-way trail junction near a tour bus road. Just follow the signs there to the museum, at 2.2 miles, in a lovely little meadow with a nature trail. The museum has exhibits and books about the trees, as well as restrooms and water.

From the museum head south, following the signs again to the Telescope Tree at 2.7 miles. It's off the trail a few yards to the left. Don't miss the experience of standing inside and gazing up and out the top of a still-living tree.

You are in the upper grove now; the crowds will have all but disappeared, the gabble of the tram tours has faded away, and the still, solemn dignity of the forest begins to settle over you . . . unless you are joined by a noisy, chattering, scolding chickaree, or Douglas squirrel. These are not to be confused with the chickadee, a small bird that also resides here. Chickarees are some of the most entertaining creatures of sequoia and fir forests; they're lively and quick and very vocal. Their backs are gray-brown, their undersides buffy white. A black racing stripe running horizontally along the body separates top from bottom. They ensure reproduction of the trees by cutting down the cones, which would otherwise remain on the branches for many years.

At 3.1 miles look left, downhill, to find the Fallen Tunnel Tree. This is the highest point on the hike, at 6,600 feet. There's not much to see now, but from 1881 when the tunnel was cut through the standing Big Tree, the Fallen Tunnel Tree was one of the most popular tourist attractions in California. In

1969, a heavy snowfall finally toppled it. Continue on downhill back to the museum at 3.6 miles, then follow the signs back to the parking lot.

Option: This hike may be extended by 1 mile and a 200-foot gain in elevation by taking the old road that begins about 0.3 mile north of the Fallen Tunnel Tree and following it to its end at Wawona Point Vista. Enjoy the view of Wawona and the Merced River, then return to the main trail. Another trail from the museum leads to Wawona itself, 6.5 miles to the southeast.

25 Alder Creek

General description:	An isolated out-and-back day hike or backpack for wildflower enthusiasts.
Total distance:	12.2 miles.
Difficulty:	Moderate as a day hike, easy as a backpack.
Elevation gain:	1,500 feet.
Trail traffic:	Light.
Best months:	April–June.
Maps:	USGS Wawona quad.
Permits:	None required for a day hike; for overnight, pick up a wilderness permit at the Wawona Information Station.

Finding the trailhead: From the California 41 entrance to Yosemite, drive 4 miles north to the village of Wawona. Cross the new bridge over the Merced River and turn right on Chilnualna Fall Road. Just past the stables, about a quarter mile up the road on the right, is a parking area and sign indicating the Alder Creek Trailhead.

Trailhead facilities: The ranger station just behind the trailhead parking area has restrooms and water. Gas and other supplies are available in Wawona.

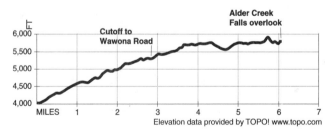

Elevation data provided by TOPO! www.topo.com

Key points:
- 0.0   Alder Creek Trailhead.
- 2.9   Cutoff trail to Wawona Road.
- 6.1   Alder Creek Falls overlook.

Alder Creek

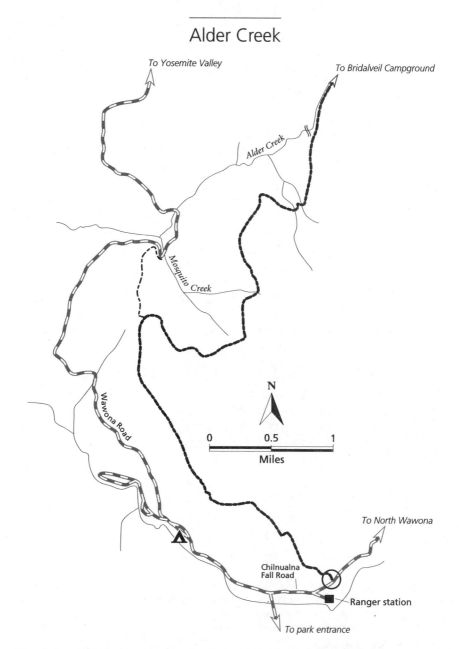

To Yosemite Valley

To Bridalveil Campground

Alder Creek

Mosquito Creek

Wawona Road

N

0   0.5   1
Miles

To North Wawona

Chilnualna
Fall Road

Ranger station

To park entrance

The hike: This is a perfect early season hike for wildflower lovers in a quiet and infrequently traveled section of the park. The trail climbs gently but steadily along what used to be an old railroad bed, through a forest of ponderosa pine, some truly monumental in size, along with black oak, incense-cedar, and some tree-sized manzanita. The spectacular pink and magenta harlequin lupine grows here in spring, along with some very showy Mariposa lilies and countless other species. The trail climbs along a ridge high above the Merced River and the highway, though neither is visible or audible. At 2.9 miles, a short spur trail descends abruptly to the left (north) to meet Wawona Road, in 0.7 mile. You could begin or end your hike at Wawona Road at the end of this spur, but the trailhead is unmarked and there is little space to park on the road. Continue along the right fork, which turns southeast and continues upward with a few short, steep sections, then swings north again.

Pause a moment here to notice a subtle change in the atmosphere. You are still in a conifer forest, but are now on the north-facing slope. The air has all at once become cooler, damper, even quieter. The ground is covered with ferns and berries, the canopy is darker and denser with white fir and sugar pine, unlike the warmer, sunnier, more open ponderosa forest just a few paces around the corner. Soon the path levels out and at 6.1 miles the trail widens and the prospect opens to reveal the gorge of Alder Creek that pours over a cliff as a 60-foot waterfall. Beside you on the trail are several seeps and springs with tiny hanging gardens and lots of big comfortable sitting rocks, a perfect place for lunch. If you are day hiking, return the way you came. If you plan to spend the night (or several), continue upstream past the falls, where the canyon narrows and the trail is squeezed in close to the creek, which is now lined with willow, chokecherry, and alder. Between here and a three-way junction a mile ahead, there are a few campsites. Several different backpacking loops are possible from this point. You can continue north to the Bridalveil Creek Campground 5.6 miles away or turn east to Deer Camp, then south to Chilnualna Fall, finishing back on Chilnualna Fall Road, less than 2 miles from the Alder Creek Trailhead. The distance for this semiloop is 18 miles.

Note: Watch for rattlesnakes in this low-elevation area, especially in the morning and evening hours. They are not aggressive, but they do not like to be handled or stepped on.

26 Chilnualna Fall

General description:	An all-uphill out-and-back day hike to the tumbling and spectacular Chilnualna Fall.
Total distance:	8.2 miles.
Difficulty:	Moderately strenuous.
Elevation gain:	2,100 feet.
Trail traffic:	Moderate.
Best months:	Early summer and early fall. Mid-July–August can be very hot.
Maps:	USGS Wawona and Mariposa Grove quads.
Permits:	None required for a day hike; wilderness permit required to camp at the top of the falls or beyond, available at the Wawona Ranger Station.

Chilnualna Fall

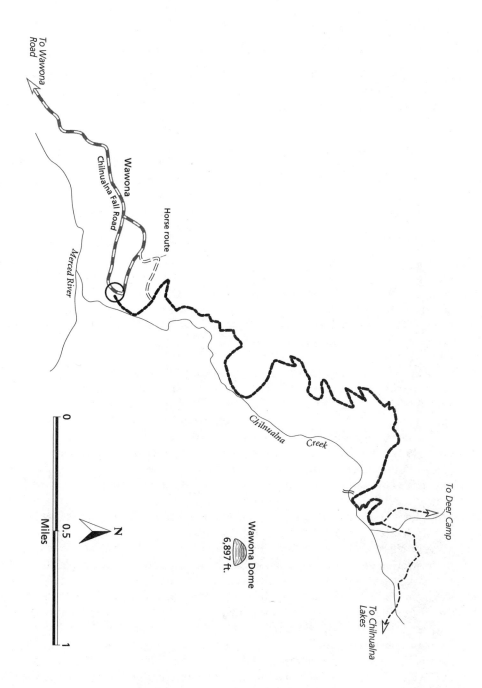

Finding the trailhead: Follow Chilnualna Fall Road from Wawona through the little village of North Wawona for 2 miles to a signed parking lot on the right. Do not leave food in your car. There are no bear boxes here, but there are bears.

Trailhead facilities: Food, gas, supplies, and telephones in North Wawona.

Key points:
  0.0   Trailhead.
  0.2   Junction horse trail and foot trail.
  4.1   Chilnualna Fall.

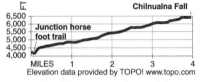

Elevation data provided by TOPO! www.topo.com

The hike: Chilnualna Creek seldom flows slowly, but instead tumbles in cascades and waterfalls almost constantly for most of its length. The most spectacular sections and highest waterfalls are found at the beginning and end of the hike, and the trail has been built so that it comes closest to the river at the beginning and end. This route would be much more heavily used if it were not tucked away in a little corner of Yosemite. The waterfall is as exciting as any in Yosemite Valley, but few tourists know about it.

Follow the trail signs from the parking lot and cross the paved road. A sign there routes horse traffic to the left and foot traffic to the right. The footpath, much too rugged for horses, heads steeply up, sometimes on big granite stairsteps right beside the roaring water, then cuts away from the stream where the horse and foot trails rejoin at a big trail sign, at 0.2 mile. Wide, long switchbacks make the northward climb almost painless. The forest floor is covered with a solid carpet of the little white shrub called kit-kit-dizze under oak, pine, and incense-cedar. At about a mile, the trail switchbacks near to the creek, then climbs out of reach of water until very near the end of the hike, except for little tributary streams that are reliable only in early season. Views of the sensuous rounded curve of Wawona Dome to the southeast come and go. As you gain height, more of Chilnualna's upper falls comes into view, with its clouds of mist rising. When the trail is almost at the height of the falls, it rounds a ridge blasted out of the rock by dynamite and deposits the hiker right beside the thundering cataract. Brilliant, magenta, mountain pride penstemon lines the cracks in the rocks. From here you can see all the way back down to the Wawona meadow.

Climb a few more hot and brushy switchbacks until the trail emerges on slabs of classic, smooth, exfoliating Yosemite granite, to an even more dramatic section of the falls. The smooth rock near the falls invites exploration, but move carefully—the wet rocks are slippery and it's a long way down. A sign at a trail junction tells you it is 5.6 miles back to Wawona, but that is the distance to the ranger station, which used to be the trailhead, not to the current trailhead at the parking lot. This is the end of your day hike; just return the way you came.

It is possible to make this the first leg of a multiday outing. The left fork of the trail continues northwest on to Deer Camp and to Glacier Point. The right fork leads to Chilnualna Lakes to the northeast. Campsites can be found a short distance up either fork.

Note: Watch for rattlesnakes in this low-elevation area, especially in the morning and evening hours. They are not aggressive, but they do not like to be handled or stepped on.

27 Buena Vista Crest

General description:	Lollipop loop, overnight hike to several lakes, and views of Cathedral Range.
Total distance:	28.2 miles.
Difficulty:	Easy.
Elevation gain:	2,320 feet.
Trail traffic:	Light to moderate.
Best months:	Early summer and fall. Glacier Point road is open only as far as Badger Pass Ski Area in winter.
Maps:	USGS Half Dome and Mariposa Grove quads.
Permits:	Wilderness permits available at the Wawona Ranger Station.

Finding the trailhead: Drive up Glacier Point Road 9 miles to the Bridalveil Creek Campground on the right. Continue straight through the campground to its south end. Just as the road begins to curve left, signs on the right say "Campfire Circle" and "Horse Camp 0.2 mile." The trailhead is just beyond the signs. Because parking space is somewhat cramped here, the trailhead sign will probably be hidden behind parked cars.

Trailhead facilities: Bridalveil Creek Campground has restrooms, a telephone, and water, but no food or hiking supplies.

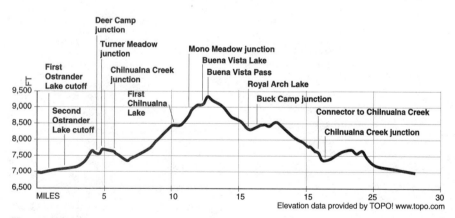

Elevation data provided by TOPO! www.topo.com

Key points:
- 0.0   Trailhead.
- 1.4   First Ostrander Lake cutoff.
- 2.2   Second Ostrander Lake cutoff.
- 4.7   Deer Camp junction.

Buena Vista Crest

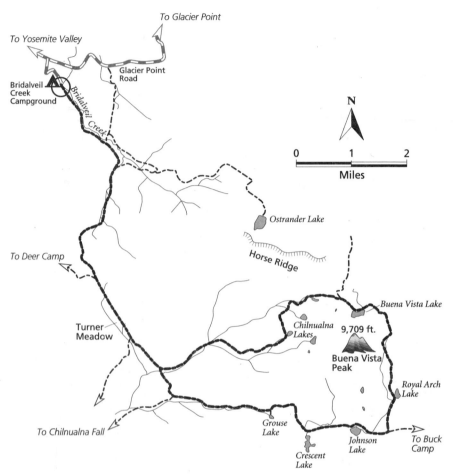

4.8	Turner Meadow junction.
6.7	Chilnualna Creek junction.
10.2	First Chilnualna lake.
11.9	Mono Meadow junction.
12.2	Buena Vista Lake.
15.0	Royal Arch Lake.
15.7	Buck Camp junction.
20.7	Connecting trail to Chilnualna Creek.
21.5	Chilnualna Creek junction (closing the loop).

The hike: This area returns lots of rewards for little effort. Elevations are low, so it is accessible when the higher country is still under snow, yet there is plenty of classic glacially sculpted Yosemite granite and lakes and an exceptionally rich variety of wildflowers. You can hike the loop in either direction, but the elevation gain is more gradual if you travel clockwise.

The hike begins in a southeasterly direction along Bridalveil Creek. Yellow metal signs high up in the lodgepole pine mark cross-country ski trails.

Graceful arches of granite crown Royal Arch Lake.

The trail rambles through forests and dazzling meadows filled with wild-flowers. At 1.4 miles, a side trail cuts back toward Glacier Point Road to connect with the Ostrander Lake Trail. This junction lies in a ghost forest of lodgepole pines that was burned in 1987, leaving ideal conditions for a spectacular wildflower display. Pass a packer campsite (arguably illegal; too near the stream and the trail), hop a branch of the creek, and, at 2.2 miles, meet a second trail that angles back to the northwest to meet the Ostrander Lake Trail again. Your trail crosses a couple of small streams that may be dry by midsummer, then climbs moderately up a slope under both white and red fir, glowing with brilliant chartreuse lichens.

The way becomes steeper and warmer as the forest cover thins to brush, then opens up in a sunny ridgetop clearing carpeted in pastels: yellow sulfur flower buckwheat, pink pussy paws, and blue Brewer lupine. Then it dips back down into forest. Just past a boggy meadow you reach another trail junction at 4.7 miles, where the Deer Camp Trail takes off to the right (west). Continue south past Turner Meadow, waist-deep in corn lilies, to yet another trail junction at 6 miles, beyond which there is a good campsite. Continue along the left (southeast) fork until, at 6.7 miles, you reach the junction that marks the beginning of the loop. Follow the trail sign left (east) toward Chilnualna and Buena Vista lakes and climb along Chilnualna Creek until you reach the first of the lakes, at 10.2 miles. There is plenty of good camping here. The lake is shallow, small, tranquil, and lovely in early season, but it is rapidly becoming a meadow. It loses much of its appeal by August, though by that time the blueberry bushes surrounding the lake are loaded with fruit.

Leaving the first lake, pass over a low rise, hop over the outlet of the second Chilnualna lake, about a half mile off the trail to the east, then skirt the third lake, which also offers some camping, though it can be swampy and mosquito-ridden early in the year. In fact, a section of the trail may be completely underwater in early season. Watch your map carefully here to stay on course. Climb up out of the lake basin along a rubbly granite slope that opens out at the top to unveil a fabulous vista all the way to the Cathedral Range, to the north. To the east, dramatic Mount Clark pulls the colorful Clark Range—Red Peak, Gray Peak, Merced Peak—behind it on a collision course with Half Dome and Mount Starr King, to the north. Here, at 11.9 miles, a trail heads northward toward Mono Meadow on Glacier Point Road, but your trail continues straight ahead to Buena Vista Lake, sparkling in its glacial cirque, at 12.2 miles. The high point at the top of the ridge is Buena Vista Peak (9,709 feet). There is plenty of good camping here.

Climb out of the lake basin, top Buena Vista Pass—the highest point on this loop at 9,300 feet—then descend, first through flowery meadows, then over exfoliating granite slabs, and finally through forest. You'll emerge at the small but stunning Royal Arch Lake, at 15 miles. Huge granite slabs have popped free and peeled away from the surrounding or underlying rock like layers of onion, leaving graceful arches framing the lake. There is limited camping at the south end of the lake. Be sure to camp at least 100 feet from the fragile lakeshore.

Proceeding downhill, the Buck Creek Trail cuts off to the east at 15.7 miles. Turn right (west) and descend past grassy Johnson Lake; it's almost hidden by lodgepoles and it offers little in the way of camping. Crescent Lake, about a half mile farther, has campsites (and blueberries!). Leaving the lake, rock-hop your way across the outlet stream, cross a glacial moraine dotted with red fir, pass Grouse Lake (hidden in the trees to your left), and continue down, down, down to the junction at 20.7 miles, where you turn right (north). The left fork leads back to Wawona via Chilnualna Fall. Very soon, at 21.5 miles, you rock-hop Chilnualna Creek to meet the junction closing the loop section of your hike. From here, retrace the "stick" portion of the lollipop back to the trailhead at Bridalveil Creek Campground.

28 Wawona Meadow

General description: A flat, low-elevation, a loop day hike through diverse vegetation.

Total distance: 3.5 miles.

Difficulty: Easy.

Elevation gain: 200 feet.

Trail traffic: Light.

Best months: April–June for wildflowers, though the trail is open all year.

Maps: USGS Wawona quad.

Permits: None.

Finding the trailhead: Drive to the little village of Wawona on Wawona Road (California 41). The Wawona Hotel is on the north side of the road, the golf course is on the south. Just across from the hotel, a road cuts through the middle of the golf course to a parking area and trailhead marked with a big signboard with photos and information about the area.

Trailhead facilities: Lodging, store, gas, phones, restrooms at Wawona. Pit toilets at the trailhead.

Key points:

0.0 Trailhead.
1.7 Creek crossing and trail junction.
3.2 Wawona Road (California 41) first crossing.
3.4 Wawona Road, second crossing.

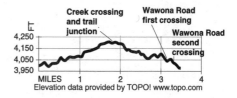

The hike: This is one of Yosemite's often-overlooked gems, especially for wildflower lovers, who will find some rare and unusual species blooming in early season. Except for an occasional group of equestrians, you'll have this little piece of the park to yourself.

You can follow the route in either direction, but it will be described here counterclockwise. It follows an old, mostly dirt road no longer used by vehicles except at the spots where it crosses Wawona Road. Start by skirting the south side of the golf course under a cover of incense-cedar and ponderosa pine. Very soon the manicured lawn is left behind and the meadow begins. This border zone between forest and meadow is called the ecotone, and it's usually the richest in living organisms. You are almost guaranteed a cluster of mule deer. They are very tame, but do not attempt to pet or feed them. Deer account for more serious injuries in Yosemite than bears.

Now and then a little spur trail leads out into the meadow. It can be boggy and muddy toward the center and the vegetation is fragile, so step with care. Down among the grasses and sedges, look for little three-petaled white star tulips in May. The tall cabbage-like stalks growing in clumps are

Shady forest floor is home to many species of flowers like this lady's slipper orchid.

Wawona Meadow

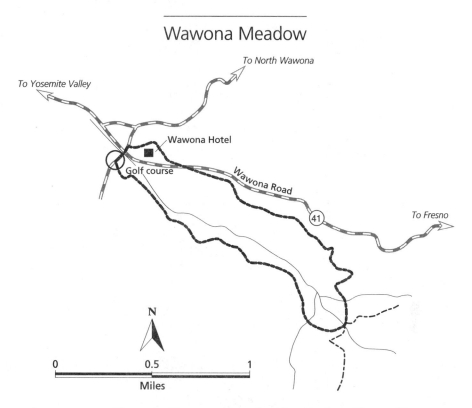

poisonous corn lily, sometimes confused with skunk cabbage. There are islands of willow and chokecherry, usually broadcasting birdsong selections from warblers and blackbirds.

On the shady forest floor watch for saprophytes (leafless plants that live on decaying material in the soil) like the scarlet snow plant, the knobby brown spikes of pinedrops, and the odd little orchids, like coral root. You can even find lady's slipper orchids in damp patches. In June, great fragrant clumps of western azalea burst into bloom, along with several kinds of lilies.

At 1.7 miles another trail comes in from the right (east) alongside a little creek. Continue along the road and step across another little chokecherry-lined rivulet flowing around little rock islands crowded with monkey flowers. The road becomes partly eroded asphalt and runs through a section of forest in which the bases of the trees are slightly blackened from a management-set fire.

At 3.2 miles, reach a closed gate, and just beyond it cross Wawona Road. The trail continues on to the Wawona Hotel, where, at 3.4 miles, it crosses the road to the south side again and cuts back through the golf course to the trailhead.

29 Ostrander Lake

General description: An out-and-back day hike or overnighter to a rustic stone cabin.

Total distance: 12.4 miles.

Difficulty: Strenuous as a day hike, easy to moderate as a backpack.

Elevation gain: 1,600 feet.

Trail traffic: Moderate.

Best months: Late June–September.

Maps: USGS Half Dome and Mariposa Grove quads.

Permits: A wilderness permit, available at Yosemite Valley or Wawona is required for an overnight stay. No permit is necessary for a day hike.

Finding the trailhead: Drive up Glacier Point Road about 9 miles from Chinquapin to a marked parking area and trailhead on the right, about a mile past the turnoff to the Bridalveil Creek Campground.

Trailhead facilities: Pit toilet.

Key points:
- 0.0 Trailhead.
- 1.7 Connector trail to Bridalveil Creek Campground.
- 2.3 Second connector to Bridalveil Creek Trail.
- 6.2 Ostrander Lake hut.

Ostrander Lake from the ski hut.

Ostrander Lake

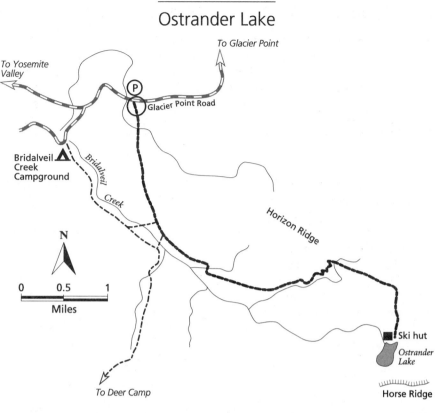

To Glacier Point

To Yosemite Valley

P

Glacier Point Road

Bridalveil Creek Campground

Bridalveil Creek

N

0   0.5   1
Miles

Horizon Ridge

Ski hut

Ostrander Lake

Horse Ridge

To Deer Camp

The hike: Ostrander Lake hut is a favorite winter destination for skiers. In summer there is good camping near the lakeside and lots of wildflowers along the way. The trail is

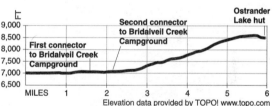

relatively flat at the beginning but it undulates a bit in the middle. Most of the serious elevation gain comes toward the end. It begins in a ghost forest of lodgepole pine, a good place to watch for brown creepers and mountain chickadees harvesting insects in the decaying wood. The forest was burned in 1987, opening the ground to sunshine, and wildflowers now flourish. In the drier places grow yarrow, paintbrush, lupine, goldenrod, and tall, purple, appropriately named fireweed in a riot of color. In the marshier areas are willow, lilies, yampah, and Bigelow sneezeweed—nature renewing itself in a flamboyant explosion of color and new life.

At 1.7 miles is a junction with a trail on the right that cuts back to join the Bridalveil Creek Trail leading to Bridalveil Creek Campground. Keep left and continue on through alternating sun and shade to a second fork where in a little clearing another connector trail turns right again to join Bridalveil Creek in another place.

115

You'll probably notice that the mileage on the trail signs at this junction do not agree. Don't let it confuse you. They don't differ by much, and the route is the same. Past this point there is only an occasionally burned snag among the flourishing white fir and ponderosa pine. This is fortunate for the hiker, because now the trail begins to climb. Traces of old asphalt appear underfoot, evidence that the trail used to be a road. It occasionally leaves the forest and passes over open rock slabs skirting the base of domelike Horizon Ridge. In the open places are patches of low-growing manzanita and silvery sagebrush. The trail swings northward to a saddle, abruptly turns southeast to climb straight up a smooth, rounded hill, and then makes one broader switchback before reaching the summit. A worn little path on the left leads to a view of Half Dome and Mount Starr King, and behind the trees to the right, the Clark Range.

The main trail now descends through a pure stand of red fir and drops into the rocky basin containing Ostrander Lake, at 6.2 miles. Horse Ridge, a wonderful example of exfoliating granite, bounds the lake on the south. Its overhanging brow makes it distinguishable from many miles away, even though it is not very high. The ski hut overlooks the lake on the north; campsites are found to the west. A sign on the hut warns winter visitors not to attempt to cross Horse Ridge due to avalanche danger. Northern flickers (a kind of woodpecker) tap at the trees. Enjoy lunch or set up camp, then return the way you came.

30 Ottoway Lakes

General description:	Out-and-back or overnight backpack into a remote and rugged area of the park.
Total distance:	30.4 miles.
Difficulty:	Moderate.
Elevation gain:	2,400 feet.
Trail traffic:	Light.
Best months:	July–September.
Maps:	USGS Half Dome and Merced Peak quads.
Permits:	Available in advance or from the wilderness center in Yosemite Valley.

Finding the trailhead: From Wawona Road (California 41), drive 10 miles up Glacier Point Road from Chinquapin. Parking and the marked trailhead are on the right.

Trailhead facilities: None.

Key points:
0.0 Mono Meadow Trailhead.
0.6 Mono Meadow.

Ottoway Lakes and The Clark Range

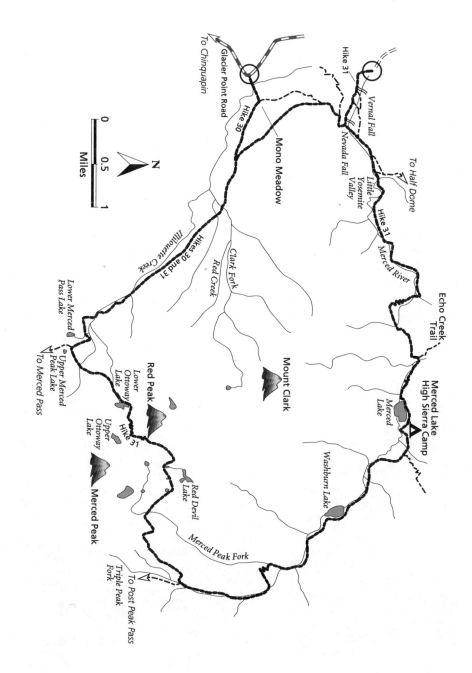

2.9   Illilouette Creek and Glacier Point junction.
3.0   First Nevada Fall junction.
4.6   Second Nevada Fall junction.
12.1 Merced Pass junction.
15.2 Lower Ottoway Lake.

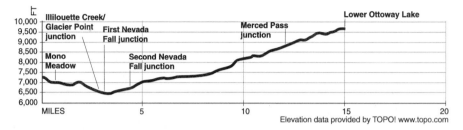

FT

| | | | Lower Ottoway Lake |
10,000 — Illilouette Creek/
9,500 — Glacier Point   First Nevada   Merced Pass
9,000 — junction   Fall junction   junction
8,500 — Mono   Second Nevada
8,000 — Meadow   Fall junction
7,500
7,000
6,500
6,000

MILES   5   10   15   20

Elevation data provided by TOPO! www.topo.com

The hike: This is the shortest route into the Clark Range. The first part of the hike is through a recent burn, but the colorful and dramatic Ottoway Lakes basin more than makes up for the less interesting beginning. The trail drops down from Glacier Point Road into soggy Mono Meadow at 0.6 mile. The numerous creeklets through the meadow support a dense growth of tall wildflowers of all kinds and colors, but they can make route-finding difficult. Watch for the yellow markers on the trees to find the trail on the far side of the meadow. Back in the dense lodgepole forest, the trail soon offers a log-crossing over a tributary of Illilouette Creek. A little later, after some fairly steep downhill hiking, arrive at a junction, at 2.9 miles. Follow the sign directing you to Nevada Fall and Ottoway Lakes.

Lower Ottoway Lake.

In just a few yards, find the main branch of Illilouette Creek. Turn upstream for a few yards to where a row of boulders indicate the ford. The creek can be deep and dangerous at high water, so you might have to use the log-crossing a short distance upstream. Pick out the place where the trail resumes on the other side before you cross, so you can find it again. On the north side of the creek is a sandy flat and another junction at 3 miles. Turn right (east) toward Merced Pass. Mount Starr King lies directly ahead.

Climb a gravelly slope with limited patches of shade on a trail that is sometimes obscure. Back in the forest again, another trail cuts back toward Nevada Fall, at 4.6 miles. Continue straight ahead and cross the Clark Fork of Illilouette Creek above a pretty waterfall. Nearby there are several good campsites. Shortly thereafter, cross Red Creek, then climb steadily, listening for the music of Illilouette Creek as the trail draws nearer and nearer to its northeast bank. The path crosses dozens of little trickles flowing down to the creek over smooth rocks; the trickles are all lined with miniature gardens of monkey flowers, ferns, and lilies. In about a mile you'll come to the first of a number of tributaries that flow together to join the main stream. None are deep enough to pose any problem in crossing, but they do inundate the trail in early season. Make sure to keep an eye on the tree blazes to keep on track.

At 12.1 miles, reach the Merced Pass junction. The right fork leads to timbered Merced Pass and to Fernandez Pass on the eastern boundary of the park. Follow the left fork toward Ottoway Lakes. This junction lies between Upper and Lower Merced pass lakes, neither of which is visible from the trail. The lower lake is down in a bowl to the west of the junction. The upper one is more scenic and has some camping. Follow an unmarked trail to the east about midway between the Merced Pass and Ottoway Lake trails for a few hundred yards to find it.

As you draw nearer to Ottoway Lakes, more of the red metamorphic rock of parts of the Clark Range comes into view. Finally, at 15.2 miles, Lower Ottoway Lake appears right at the contact between the young gray granite and the ancient red slate. The setting of this lake is stunning, with the sharp point of Merced Peak behind the cascading creek connecting the upper and lower lakes. The irregular rocky shoreline of the lake has dozens of little bays and inlets trimmed with white Labrador tea and red mountain heather that invite many hours of exploration. There are several small campsites among the rocks and whitebark pines.

If you plan to continue on over Red Peak Pass, Lower Ottoway Lake is the last timber for many miles. If a thunderstorm is brewing, wait it out here. If this is your final destination, return the way you came.

31 The Clark Range

See map on page 117

General description:	Overnight backpacking ascent to an awe-inspiring panorama of the southern park.
Total distance:	50.6 miles.
Difficulty:	Strenuous.
Elevation gain:	7,200 feet.
Trail traffic:	Light, except for the first and last few miles.
Best months:	July–September, but check first about trail conditions, since Red Peak Pass is frequently buried deep under snow until late in the season.
Maps:	USGS Half Dome, Merced Peak, and Mount Lyell quads.
Permits:	Available in advance or from the wilderness center in Yosemite Valley.

Finding the trailhead: Park in the backpackers' parking lot next to Curry Village and follow the well-marked path to Happy Isles, or ride the Yosemite Valley shuttle bus from anyplace in the valley and get off at Stop 16, Happy Isles.

Trailhead facilities: Snacks, toilets, water, and phones at Happy Isles.

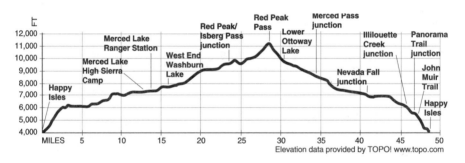

Elevation data provided by TOPO! www.topo.com

Key points:

0.0	Happy Isles.
24.2	Red Peak/Isberg Pass junction.
28.5	Red Peak Pass.
31.4	Lower Ottoway Lake.
34.5	Merced Pass junction.
42.0	Nevada Fall junction.
45.2	Illilouette Creek junction.
45.6	Panorama Trail junction.
46.7	John Muir Trail.

The hike: You can begin and end this loop at any one of several points, including Glacier Point and via Mono Meadow off Glacier Point Road. If wilderness permits are not available for one trailhead, you can try another. Follow Hike 32, Merced River High Trail, to 24.2 miles at the Red Peak/Isberg Pass junction on the Triple Peak Fork of the Merced River. Turn right (west) heading up to Red Peak Pass, climbing at first moderately, then more steeply as you cross a ridge coming down from Triple Divide Peak. The timber becomes more scattered and more stunted and there are numerous lakelets where it is possible to find small, sheltered campsites. The trail over the smooth rock is sometimes indistinct, so watch for ducks to keep you on track. You lose a little elevation descending into a lake-dotted bowl. As you climb out of it, you can see Red Devil Lake off the trail to the north. It is more heavily timbered than the topo indicates, and is the last good sheltered place to camp this side of the pass. The peaks beyond it include Mounts Florence, Maclure, and Lyell, highest in the park at 13,114 feet. The trail makes a dogleg to the left before beginning its final ascent to the pass. The hike becomes more spectacular with every step, as Mounts Ritter and Banner and the spiky Minarets appear to the east. On a different scale, dozens of snowmelt rivulets at your feet nourish miniature gardens of alpine flowers. Toil your way up the last few short, steep, rocky switchbacks to the top of the pass at 28.5 miles, between two pointed rock towers at about 11,200 feet. Stay long enough to get your fill of the awe-inspiring panorama. The route down the other side of the pass is just as steep and rocky as the ascent, and it will require all your attention.

Your descent begins almost straight down toward intensely blue Upper Ottoway Lake and its neighboring tarns, then swings west to reach the north shore of Lower Ottoway Lake, at 31.4 miles. Now follow Hike 30, Ottoway Lakes, in reverse until you reach the Nevada Fall junction at 42 miles, where you take the right fork. Contour around the ridge above Illilouette Creek through brush, over open rock, and through burned forest to 45.6 miles, where you meet the Panorama Trail heading back to Glacier Point. Continue toward Nevada Fall, descending on switchbacks to meet the John Muir Trail at 43.1 miles, where you turn left and join the crowds returning to Happy Isles.

32 Merced River High Trail

General description: A little-used lollipop loop to some of the park's best-kept secrets.
Total distance: 50.8 miles.
Difficulty: Moderate to strenuous.
Elevation gain: 6,000 feet.
Trail traffic: Almost none except at the beginning and end.
Best months: Late June–September.
Maps: USGS Half Dome, Merced Peak, Mount Lyell quads.
Permits: Available in advance or from the wilderness center in Yosemite Valley.

Finding the trailhead: Park in the backpackers' parking lot next to Curry Village and follow the well-marked path to Happy Isles, or ride the Yosemite Valley shuttle bus from anyplace in the valley and get off at Stop 16, Happy Isles.

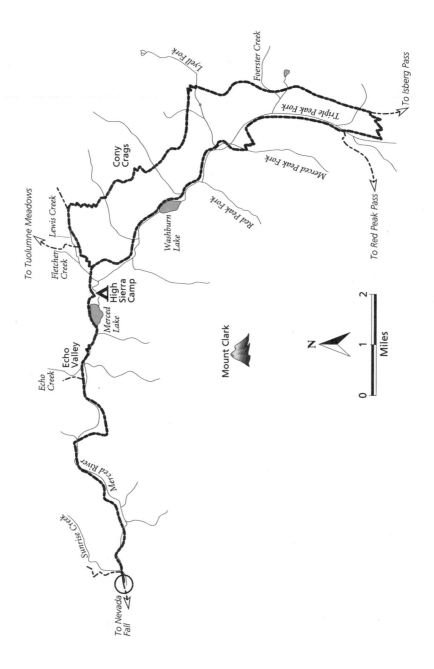

Trailhead facilities: Water, phones, restrooms, and snacks at Happy Isles; water, restrooms, and snacks at Merced Lake.

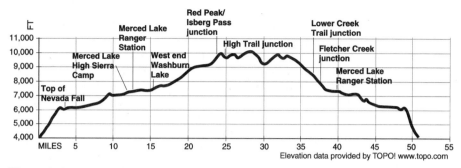

Elevation data provided by TOPO! www.topo.com

Key points:

0.0	Happy Isles Trailhead.
13.4	Merced Lake High Sierra Camp.
13.7	Merced Lake Ranger Station.
15.8	West end Washburn Lake.
24.2	Red Peak/Isberg Pass junction.
25.4	High Trail junction.
35.3	Lewis Creek junction.
36.4	Fletcher Creek junction.
37.4	Merced Lake Ranger Station.

The hike: This trail is one of Yosemite's best kept secrets, passing one spectacular viewpoint after another. You'll have plenty of solitude for most of the way because it's roughly 2 miles longer and a thousand feet higher than the parallel Merced Lake/Washburn Lake/Triple Peak Fork route. It is well worth the extra effort.

Follow Hike 16 to Merced Lake High Sierra Camp at 13.4 miles, then continue east through lodgepole and fir forest, crossing several little creeks on footbridges. At 13.7 miles, the Merced Lake Ranger Station and corral appear on the right. This is manned all summer and the ranger there is happy to provide current local trail conditions. The Lewis Creek Trail switchbacks steeply northward from here and is the route by which you will return. For now, walk about 100 feet past the junction and ranger station to a solitary fencepost. Stand beside it and look up. Whose face do you see in the rock?

Continue southeast, climbing gradually at first, then more steeply until you reach the west end of pretty Washburn Lake, at 15.8 miles. Three tributary streams flow into the lake from the north, and the third of these can be deep enough to wade, in early season. Past the lake, the trail rambles along the river, which never ceases to change or entertain, now cascading from one pool to another, now sliding on slowly through sensuous curves. The trail crosses the river to a perfect viewpoint for watching the Lyell Fork pour down the cliff to the east, then begins to climb in earnest. A little farther on, the Triple Peak Fork tumbles over a wall in a spectacular waterfall. Very soon the Merced Peak Fork is crossed on another bridge, and the trail climbs over steep, open rock to join the Triple Peak Fork above the falls. The climb tops out at about 8,800 feet before leveling off to wander through flowery meadows for many miles. This long section of trail is so idyllic that you're bound to want to camp, but camping is marginal on your side of the river; there is not much level ground and it's often marshy. If the river is low enough to wade, however, there are plenty of good dry sites on the other side. At 24.2 miles, meet the Isberg/Red Peak Pass junction. The right fork leads to Red Peak Pass and the Clark Range.

Your route follows the left fork. Immediately rock-hop or wade the river, then plod steadily upward, first toward the south, then toward the northeast, following a giant switchback. At 25.4 miles, reach another trail junction where you turn left (north). The right fork leads to Isberg Pass on the border of the park. You are now on the High Trail. At first it dips and climbs along the east side of the ridge with only a few frustrating glimpses of the open, lake-filled country to the east, but hold on to your hat! In about a mile, the vegetation thins and you cross to the west side of the crest where a stupendous panorama of the multicolored Clark Range unfolds, stretching from Triple Divide Peak to Mount Clark. Far below the Merced River flows through the valley, fed by dozens of cascades and waterfalls rushing down the slickrock on the opposite side. Your trail drops about 400 feet to cross Foerster Creek, climbs again, then passes a small pond and proceeds over fairly level ground. There are many excellent campsites between Foerster Creek and the pond with flat sitting-rocks for phenomenal sunset viewing. Shortly thereafter the trail tops out at 10,000 feet. Just beyond the crest another stunning view of the Merced River canyon and Washburn Lake opens out. Beyond, lie the highest peaks in Yosemite, including Mount Lyell, highest in the park, at 13,114 feet.

Now the trail plunges downward almost 1,000 feet on steep switchbacks to meet and cross the Lyell Fork. This crossing can be dangerous in early season. The safest way across is on a big fallen log about 200 yards downstream. The climb back out of this canyon is fortunately more gradual than the trail into it.

The trail continues to follow the ridge, at one point passing through a broad crack in the cliff, occasionally affording more stunning views of the Clark Range. It dips to ford two forks of the stream that feeds Washburn Lake, climbs, then contours around the base of Cony Crags, a distinctively rugged rock outcrop, and at last drops steeply down into the gorge cut by Lewis Creek. Here, at 35.3 miles, it meets the trail that heads northeast to Vogelsang High Sierra Camp before continuing to descend to another junction at 36.4 miles, where another trail heads back northward to reach Vogelsang by a different route. This is the end of your solitude. Just ahead lies Merced Lake High Sierra Camp. If you want one more night away from the crowds, you can detour about a quarter mile up the Fletcher Creek Trail to a well-developed campsite. Upon returning to the main trail, continue to descend on steep switchbacks until you reach the Merced Lake Ranger Station at the junction with the Merced Lake Trail, at 37.4 miles, closing the lollipop loop. Return to Merced Lake and back to Happy Isles the way you came.

South of Tuolumne Meadows

South of Tuolumne Meadows

California 120, Tioga Road, is the only automobile route that runs all the way across Yosemite. It leaves the park on its northeastern border at Tioga Pass at 9,945 feet, the highest automobile pass in California. Tuolumne Meadows is the only developed area on this side of Yosemite with a visitor center, store, café, mountaineering shop, campground, lodge, and gas. This is the largest high-elevation meadow in the Sierra Nevada, and its beauty is stunning. The land to the south contains some of the most sensational peaks and passes in the park, especially the Cathedral Range, with its crowning glory, Cathedral Peak, and Mount Lyell with its associated glacier. Dozens of day hikes and backpacks begin from Tioga Road between Tenaya Lake and Tioga Pass, as well as a number of trails connecting Tuolumne Meadows with Yosemite Valley, including the John Muir and Pacific Crest trails.

A free shuttle bus runs between Tuolumne Lodge and Olmstead Point every hour, and from Tuolumne Lodge to Tioga Pass four times each day. A schedule and map of shuttle stops is available at the visitor center.

The only camping is at the Tuolumne Meadows Campground (part reservation, part first-come, first-served) and there is a walk-in camping area for backpackers limited to a one-night stay. Tuolumne Lodge has tent cabins and meals, available by reservation far in advance, or sometimes by last-minute good luck.

You can get wilderness permits for overnight stays at the Tuolumne Meadows Wilderness Center if you have not applied in advance. The wilderness center is just off Tioga Road on the way to the Tuolumne Lodge east of the campground. This region is very popular with backpackers, so get there early and be flexible in your trip planning.

33 Tenaya Lake

General description:	Out-and-back or shuttle hike through gardens of flowers along one of the park's biggest and most beautiful lakes.
Total distance:	3 miles.
Difficulty:	Easy.
Elevation gain:	50 feet.
Trail traffic:	Heavy.
Best months:	All summer; whenever Tioga Road is open.
Maps:	USGS Tenaya Lake quad.
Permits:	None.

Tenaya Lake

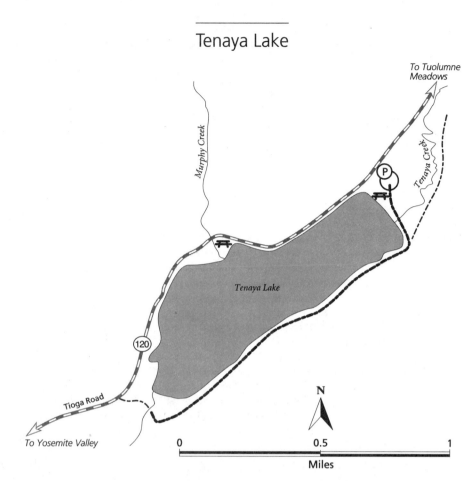

To Tuolumne Meadows

Murphy Creek

Tenaya Creek

P

Tenaya Lake

120

Tioga Road

To Yosemite Valley

N

0   0.5   1

Miles

Finding the trailhead: Ride the free shuttle bus from Tuolumne Meadows to Stop 9 at the northeast end of Tenaya Lake, or drive to the same spot on Tioga Road (California 120). Turn into the picnic area parking lot where

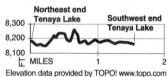

you will find toilets, bear boxes, and a sign directing you to the trail. There is another picnic area more than halfway along the length of the lake just off Tioga Road, but the trail begins at the one at the northeast end.

Trailhead facilities: Toilets.

The hike: Tenaya lake was named for Chief Tenaya, who, with all his people, was driven from his home in Yosemite by the U.S. Cavalry. It is a very big lake by Yosemite standards, and a very popular one, too, with its wide, sandy beach and proximity to the road. Follow the trail sign to the picnic tables on the beach and head south along the shore. Unless it is quite late in the summer, you will probably have to wade the inlet creek. The beach is a good vantage point from which to watch climbers clinging to the bare rock faces of the surrounding domes. Pick up the obvious trail that runs alongside the lake's south shore and stroll through garden after garden of wildflowers beside several trickling brooks and wander as far as you wish along the lakeside before returning to the trailhead. If you don't want to retrace your steps, when you meet the Sunrise Trail at the east end of the lake, turn right and follow it a short distance to Tioga Road, at Stop 10, then ride the shuttle back to Stop 9. The topo map shows a campground here, but this has been dismantled. You can circumnavigate the entire lake, but once you reach its north side, you must walk along the shoulder of the busy Tioga Road for the whole length of the lake to return to the parking lot.

34 Clouds Rest

General description:	Out-and-back day hike or overnighter to stunning views of Half Dome from its most dramatic angle.
Total distance:	14.4 miles.
Difficulty:	Strenuous.
Elevation gain:	1,770 feet.
Trail traffic:	Moderately heavy.
Best months:	All summer; whenever Tioga Road is open.
Maps:	USGS Tenaya Lake quad.
Permits:	None for a day hike. Available in advance or from the wilderness center in Tuolumne Meadows for an overnighter.

Finding the trailhead: Drive to the southwest end of Tenaya Lake on Tioga Road (California 120). The trailhead is across the street from the lake on the south side. You can also ride the Tuolumne Meadows shuttle to Stop 10, Sunrise Lakes Trailhead. Be sure to leave food and ice chests in the bear-proof boxes provided.

Trailhead facilities: Restrooms.

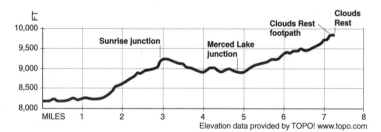

Elevation data provided by TOPO! www.topo.com

Key points:

0.0   Trailhead.
2.5   Sunrise junction.
4.7   Merced Lake junction.
7.0   Clouds Rest footpath.

Clouds Rest and Tenaya Lake to Half Dome

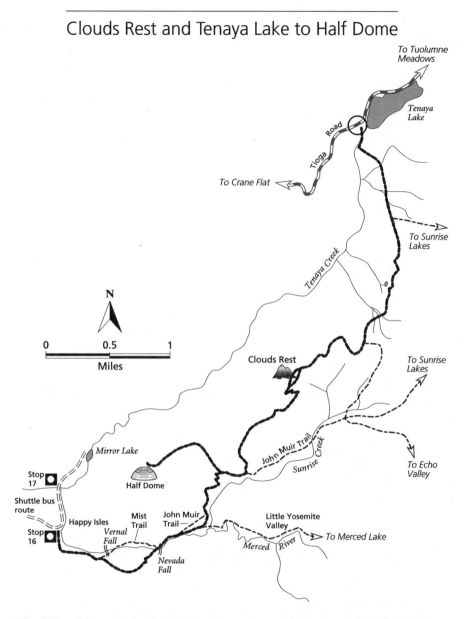

The hike: The very best views in Yosemite are from the top of Clouds Rest, but the actual summit is not advised for those who have no head for heights. It's a long and narrow knife-edged ridge, not at all dangerous if you watch your step, but very high and exposed. Fortunately, it is possible to bypass the scary part on a parallel horse trail that still offers good views.

To begin, follow Hike 22, to the first trail junction at 2.5 miles at the top of a saddle. Continue due south, following the sign to Clouds Rest, and descend to the base of Sunrise Peak, whose slickrock slabs swoop gracefully down to a little meadow. The trail skirts the meadow, then climbs a ridge of boulders shed from the peak on which some scraggly aspens are fighting for a foothold. As you descend into deeper forest you get one teasing glimpse partway down into Yosemite Valley before the trail levels out. Pass a small pond, then cross several little tributaries of Tenaya Creek. There are some small campsites nearby and these are your last source of water. Now climb easily to a junction at 4.7 miles and continue straight ahead (southwest), climbing more steeply through an open forest of western white pine. The thin slice of granite that is the summit gradually appears as you gain elevation. Follow the ridgetop as it swings around toward the peak and watch for Mount Clark protruding from the crest across Merced Canyon like a giant shark tooth. As the trail climbs, it crosses to the west side of the ridge and provides a taste of the view up Tenaya Canyon from the top.

At 7 miles you reach the base of the summit itself. To the right, slightly above you, watch for the sign that says "Footpath to Clouds Rest." It isn't very conspicuous, but if you should miss it, you can continue around the eastern flank of the peak on a horse trail to meet a more obvious signed junction, then double back up to the summit. On the footpath, scramble steeply over rocks weathered to the shapes of gigantic stacks of pancakes, with little bunches of purple rockfringe and pale buckwheat lining their edges. From here it becomes clear why the Sierra Nevada has been called the "Range of Light." The dazzling white granite rises in wave after wave of ridges to the horizon, with Tenaya Lake glowing like a jewel in the center, and Matterhorn Peak and the Sawtooth Ridge crowning it all. Down-canyon, you can look over the bulbous tops of North Dome and Basket Dome, and beyond them the long arm of Yosemite Valley stretching all the way to El Capitan. Directly ahead of you is Half Dome, seen from its most dramatic angle here. If you have binoculars or very sharp eyes you may be able to spot climbers struggling up the steel cables to the summit. To the east the Merced River canyon winds off into the distance below the park's highest peaks—Mounts Lyell, Maclure, and Florence. When you can tear yourself away, retrace your steps to your camp or the trailhead.

35 Tenaya Lake to Half Dome

See map on page 129

General description:	Shuttle; overnight hike to the summit of Half Dome.
Total distance:	20.5 miles.
Difficulty:	Difficult.
Elevation gain:	5,830 feet.
Trail traffic:	Moderately heavy.
Best months:	All summer; whenever Tioga Road is open and the Half Dome cables have been installed for the season.
Maps:	USGS Tenaya Lake, Yosemite Falls, and Half Dome quads.
Permits:	Available in advance or from the wilderness center in Tuolumne Meadows or Yosemite Valley.

A view of Half Dome from Clouds Rest.

Finding the trailhead: Drive to the southwest end of Tenaya Lake on Tioga Road (California 120). You can leave a car in Yosemite Valley and ride the shuttle up to the trailhead to begin, or leave a car at the top and ride the shuttle back up after your hike.

Trailhead facilities: Restrooms. Restrooms also at Little Yosemite Valley, Nevada Fall, and Vernal Fall. Snacks, water, phones, and restrooms at Happy Isles.

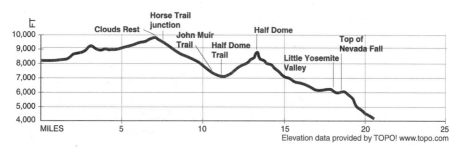

Elevation data provided by TOPO! www.topo.com

Key points:

0.0   Sunrise Lakes Trailhead.
7.2   Clouds Rest.
7.8   Horse trail junction.
10.1 John Muir Trail.
10.5 Half Dome Trail.
12.5 Half Dome summit.

The hike: Follow Hike 34, to the summit at 7.2 miles. Drop steeply down along the west side of the ridge over big boulders, then over granite stairsteps heading toward the pointed teeth along the ridge called the Pinnacles. The trail crosses back to the east side of the ridge and descends, less steeply now, on big switchbacks through manzanita and chinquapin, along with red fir and western white pine, to a junction at 7.8 miles. This is where the horse (and acrophobics') trail rejoins the summit footpath. Swing around to the west, passing beneath the Pinnacles that from this angle have lost their pointed look, then drop on steep switchbacks, heading south, to meet the John Muir Trail, at 10.1 miles. A short detour to the left (east) leads to a few campsites and the only water between Half Dome and Clouds Rest. If you don't need to stop, turn right (west) on the John Muir Trail, losing elevation less steeply now, and meet the Half Dome Trail, at 10.5 miles. From here, follow Hike 7, to the summit at 12.5 miles, then go in reverse back to Yosemite Valley at Happy Isles.

36 Cathedral Lakes

General description:	An out-and-back day hike or overnighter to both lakes and views of stunning Cathedral Peak.
Total distance:	8 miles (to visit both lakes).
Difficulty:	Moderate day hike; easy backpack.
Elevation gain:	1,040 feet.
Trail traffic:	Moderately heavy.
Best months:	July–September.
Maps:	USGS Tenaya Lake quad.
Permits:	None as a day hike; available in advance or from the Tuolumne Meadows wilderness center for overnighters.

Finding the trailhead: The busy trailhead is just west of the Tuolumne Meadows Visitor Center on Tioga Road (California 120.) The trail begins on the south side of the street. There is parking space on both sides. Be sure to leave all food and ice chests in the bear-proof boxes. You can also ride the Tuolumne Meadows shuttle to Stop 7, Cathedral Lakes Trailhead.

Trailhead facilities: None. Groceries, water, toilets, phones, and gas available nearby at Tuolumne Meadows Village.

Key points:
- 0.0 Trailhead.
- 0.1 Tuolumne Meadows High Sierra Camp/Tenaya Lake junction.
- 3.0 Cutoff to Lower Cathedral Lake.
- 4.0 Return to cutoff.
- 4.5 Upper Cathedral Lake.

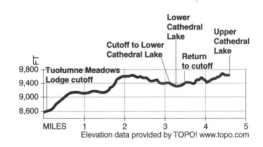

Cathedral Lakes

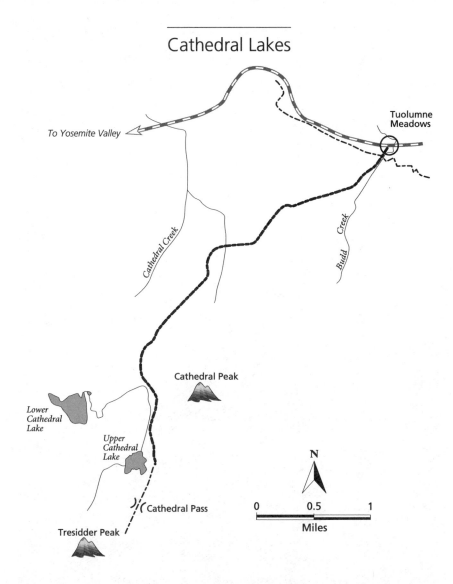

The hike: The scenery around the Cathedral Lakes is among the finest in Yosemite, it's easy to reach, it's part of the famous John Muir Trail, and it's a favorite route between Tuolumne Meadows and Yosemite Valley. For all these reasons, it is very popular and shows signs of overuse. The bears consider these lakes their local supermarket, and there are no bear-proof boxes. Do not even *consider* spending the night here without a bear canister.

Start hiking southwest on a wide flat path 0.1 mile to a junction marked by a big sign with maps and trail information. Your route lies straight ahead. It climbs easily through lodgepole pine forest, gaining about 500 feet in elevation. As it levels out, the rounded rear end of the ridge on which Cathedral Peak is perched looms on the left. The trail curves left to skirt the base beside a flowery meadow, crosses several little branches of Cathedral

133

The needle-like spire of Cathedral Peak.

Creek, then continues to climb, more steeply now. When it levels out again, the pointed profile of the top of Cathedral Peak becomes visible. The wide, sandy trail descends a little, and the square, raggedy ridge of Tresidder Peak shows briefly to the south. Continue curving left through a lovely, but often buggy, dell. At 3 miles is the junction to Lower Cathedral Lake. To visit this one first, turn right (southwest) and descend through more exquisite flower gardens to the lower lake, at 3.5 miles. The lake lies at the end of a meadow enclosed by a classic glacial cirque. Cathedral Peak seen head-on from here seems a single, needle-like spire piercing the heavens. The lake is surrounded by warm, flat rock slabs, perfect for sunbathing. There is plenty of overused camping toward the northwest shore. Wood fires are prohibited.

To reach the higher lake, return to the trail junction at 4 miles, then turn right and continue to climb southeast up a rocky trail to the beautiful subalpine bowl containing Upper Cathedral Lake; it's surrounded by Cathedral, Echo, and Tresidder peaks. The low saddle to the south is Cathedral Pass. There are plenty of campsites in the area.

A short climb to the top of the pass before returning to the trailhead is worth the effort. The view of the upper lake flanked by Cathedral Peak in craggy profile is stunning.

37 Elizabeth Lake

General description:	Out-and-back day hike to a sparkling lake at the foot of Unicorn Peak.
Total distance:	4.6 miles.
Difficulty:	Moderate.
Elevation gain:	780 feet.
Best months:	All summer; whenever the road is open.
Maps:	USGS Vogelsang Peak quad.
Permits:	None.

Finding the trailhead: Drive to the Tuolumne Meadows Campground, about 9 miles west of the Tioga Pass Entrance Station on Tioga Road (California 120). At the kiosk at the campground entrance, pick up a map of the campground and a parking permit. Follow the map through the campground, turn left between Loops B and C, and pass the group campsites to where the road is barred by a locked gate. Park here and look for the clearly marked trailhead. Store all food and ice chests in the bear-proof boxes provided.

Trailhead facilities: Toilets and water.

Key points:

0.0   Elizabeth Lake Trailhead.
0.1   Trail junction.
2.3   Elizabeth Lake.

Elevation data provided by TOPO! www.topo.com

Elizabeth Lake

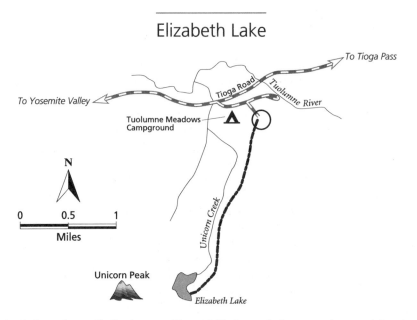

The hike: The trail climbs steadily uphill through forest, going straight ahead at a junction at 0.1 mile. As the route ascends, it draws nearer and nearer to Unicorn Creek, which drains Elizabeth Lake. A little beyond the halfway point, the slope becomes gentler and finally levels out at the end of a meadow dotted with young lodgepole pines that have been forced into contorted shapes by the weight of winter snows. The trail curves to the right and crosses Unicorn Creek, and soon, Elizabeth Lake appears, sparkling at the foot of Unicorn Peak. A number of trails have been worn around the lake, so you can wander its shores as long as you like before retracing your steps to the trailhead. Because of the lake's fragility and proximity to the campground and the road, overnight camping is prohibited.

38 Lyell Fork

General description:	An out-and-back day hike or overnighter along a section of the famous John Muir Trail.
Total distance:	11.2 miles.
Difficulty:	Moderate day hike; easy backpack.
Elevation gain:	100 feet.
Trail traffic:	Moderate.
Best months:	All summer; whenever Tioga Road is open.
Maps:	USGS Tioga Pass and Vogelsang Peak quads.
Permits:	None required for a day hike; available in advance or at the Tuolumne Meadows Wilderness Center if you are backpacking.

Lyell Fork and Lyell Fork to Donahue Pass

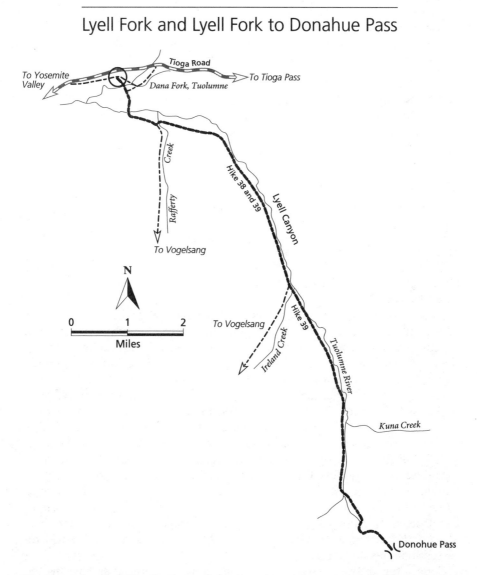

Finding the trailhead: From the west, drive Tioga Road (California 120) eastward past the Tuolumne Meadows Visitor Center, store, and campground, all on the right (south). Cross the bridge over the Tuolumne River. In about a mile, turn right at the entrance to the wilderness center. Follow the road as it curves round to the left for about a half mile to the Dog Lake parking lot on the left. Leave ice chests, food, and anything a bear might mistake for food in the boxes provided at the parking lot. You can also reach this trailhead by riding the Tuolumne Meadows shuttle to Stop 2, Dog Lake Trailhead.

Trailhead facilities: None. Groceries, café, and phones are available a mile west on Tioga Road.

Key points:

0.0   Trailhead.
0.2   Bridge over Dana Fork and junction with Tuolumne Meadows Lodge.
0.3   Junction with Gaylor Lakes Trail.
0.6   Twin bridges over Lyell Fork.
0.7   Cutoff to Tuolumne Meadows Campground.
1.3   Rafferty Creek Bridge junction.
5.6   John Muir Trail/Vogelsang junction.

The hike: This is a beautiful, easy ramble along a section of the famous John Muir Trail. To begin, cross the road south of the parking lot to the trailhead sign. Follow the trail southeast to a footbridge over the Dana Fork at 0.2 mile. Ignore the cutoff back to the Tuolumne

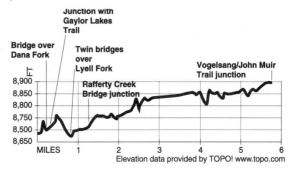

Meadows Lodge and cross the bridge, then turn left and follow the river upstream, pausing to enjoy the wildflower gardens along the shore, where dozens of different species vie for attention. At 0.3 mile is another cutoff to the left toward Gaylor Lakes. Keep right here, too. (You might have noticed that although the trailhead sign was marked "Vogelsang 6.7" and the sign in front of you says "Vogelsang 6.8" you haven't been walking backward. The trail signs have been erected at different times and are not always consistent.) The route now bends slightly to the right, crosses a low rise alongside a marshy area, and reaches the twin bridges over the Lyell Fork, at 0.6 mile. This is surely one of the most sublime vistas in Yosemite, with the clear turquoise river winding toward you through the green meadow. At your feet deep bowls have been gouged into the granite by the scouring force of silt carried from the mountains by spring runoff, and the water swirls in beautiful patterns over the rocks. The massive gray hulk on your left is Mammoth Peak (not to be confused with Mammoth Mountain, the ski resort, which lies farther south).

Soon after you leave the twin bridges, another path leads back to the Tuolumne Meadows Campground, at 0.7 mile. Continue left on the John Muir Trail through lodgepole forest and over open rock to 1.3 miles, where the Rafferty Creek Trail heads uphill to the right, a more direct route to Vogelsang. Cross the bridge over the creek on your left and continue through forest and meadows that, in early season, are a solid mass of pale lavender shooting stars (and mosquitoes). Soon the sound of the river becomes apparent—it's been hidden for a while behind a low ridge—and a glorious view of Lyell Canyon opens up before you. Sometimes the river flows deep and clear, sometimes it slides over slickrock into perfect bathing pools. Any one of a thousand spots along the bank invites lunch, a snack, a sunbath, a nap. The turquoise color of the water comes from glacial "flour," rock ground

138

The Lyell Fork along a portion of the John Muir Trail.

so finely by the Lyell Glacier upstream that it remains suspended in the current and reflects green light.

At 5.6 miles the John Muir Trail and the Vogelsang/Ireland Lake trails split. Good campsites are just uphill to the right of the trail sign. This is a notorious bear hangout, and the bears here are intelligent and resourceful. Consider the hanging of food to be a delaying tactic only. You will sleep more soundly if you carry a bear-proof canister. Return the way you came.

39 Lyell Fork to Donohue Pass

See map on page 137

General description:	Out-and-back, overnight hike to the headwaters of the Lyell Fork of the Tuolumne River.
Total distance:	24.8 miles.
Difficulty:	Moderate.
Elevation gain:	2,400 feet.
Trail traffic:	Heavy at first, moderate toward the pass.
Best months:	Mid-July–September.
Maps:	USGS Tioga Pass, Vogelsang Peak, and Koip Peak quads.
Permits:	Available in advance or from the Tuolumne Meadows Visitor Center.

Finding the trailhead: From the west, drive Tioga Road (California 120) eastward past the Tuolumne Meadows Visitor Center, store, and campground, all on the right (south). Cross the bridge over the Tuolumne River. In about a mile turn right at the entrance to the wilderness center. Follow the road as it curves around to the left for about a half mile to the Dog Lake parking area on the left. Leave ice chests, food, and anything a bear might mistake for food in the boxes provided in the parking lot. You can also reach this trailhead by riding the Tuolumne Meadows shuttle to Stop 2, Dog Lake Trailhead.

Trailhead facilities: Store, café, phones, campground, and lodge at Tuolumne Meadows.

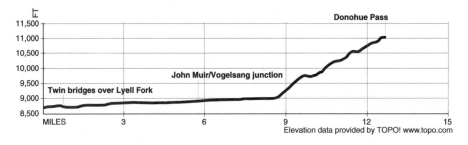

Elevation data provided by TOPO! www.topo.com

Key points:
  0.0   Trailhead.
  5.6   John Muir Trail/Vogelsang junction.
  12.4 Donohue Pass.

The hike: This route takes you to the headwaters of the Lyell Fork of the Tuolumne River. It passes just below the river's source, the Lyell Glacier, tucked beneath the shaded crest of Mount Lyell, the highest peak in Yosemite at 13,114 feet. Mount Maclure, only slightly lower and farther west along the same ridge, shelters its own glacier, which also feeds the Tuolumne River. The route follows the southernmost leg of the John Muir and Pacific Crest trails before they leave the park, so you're bound to encounter lots of through-hikers along the way. Follow Hike 38 to 5.6 miles, at the John Muir Trail/Vogelsang junction. Keep left, and accompany the meandering turquoise river upstream through the riotously blooming meadow. Just beyond the point where Kuna Creek drops down from the Kuna Crest to join the Lyell Fork from the east, the trail begins to climb, winding among avalanche debris. Views of the river snaking away to the north down the canyon get better and better as you gain elevation. Cross the river on a bridge and arrive at Lyell Base Camp. It's a busy place, used by climbers preparing to tackle the mountain. There are plenty of good campsites here, and plenty of bears.

The trees begin to disappear as you climb beyond the camp, and from here on you get superb views up the canyon to the peaks and glaciers. One of the finest of these is from the outlet of a little lake at the end of a flowery meadow. This outlet can be tricky to cross at high water. It's safer to wade than to hop across on the slippery rocks, but the water is extremely cold. Just past this crossing, there is a rocky little rise sheltered by whitebark

Mount Lyell and Lyell Glacier in the summer.

pine that could be used as a last, and simply exquisite, campsite before the pass. Climb another little rise, turn left (east), and cross the outlet of another tarn, not as difficult as the last one. Now work your way up over open granite, negotiating snow patches that often remain until midsummer to Donohue Pass and the Yosemite Park boundary at 11,000 feet. Beyond, the John Muir and Pacific Crest trails descend through an open rocky basin toward Rush Creek in the Ansel Adams Wilderness.

40 Mono Pass

General description:	Out-and-back day hike to a beautiful meadow ringed by red rocks of Mount Lewis and Mount Gibbs and sparkling blue lakes.
Total distance:	10.2 miles.
Difficulty:	Moderate.
Elevation gain:	910 feet.
Trail traffic:	Moderate.
Best months:	Summer and fall; whenever Tioga Road is open.
Maps:	USGS Koip Peak, Mount Dana, and Tioga Pass quads.
Permits:	None for a day hike; available in advance or at the Tuolumne Meadows Wilderness Center for overnighters.

Mono Pass

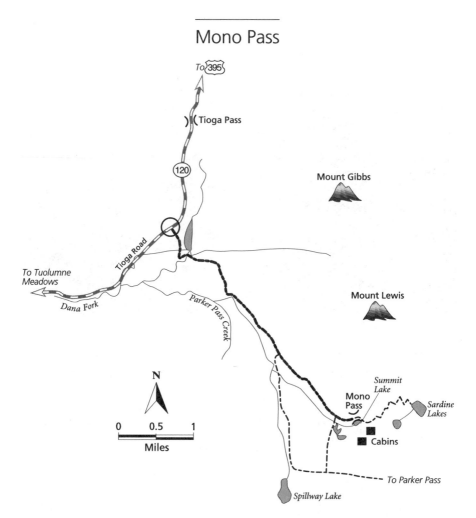

Finding the trailhead: On Tioga Road (California 120) drive about 6 miles east of Tuolumne Meadows, or a little more than a mile south of the Tioga Pass Entrance Station. The marked trailhead and parking lot are on the southeast side of the road.

Trailhead facilities: Toilets.

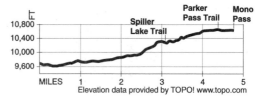

Key points:
- 0.0   Trailhead.
- 3.4   Spiller Lake Trail.
- 4.7   Parker Pass Trail.

The hike: Mono Pass was a major trade route across the Sierra between the Miwok people on the west side and the Piutes on the east. It was also the site of the Golden Crown Mine active in the early 1880s. Some of the old wooden structures built during that time are still standing.

The trail begins in lodgepole forest, now and then crossing narrow fingers of Dana Meadow and fording several little tributaries of the Dana Fork of the Tuolumne River. It climbs along a moraine past the first of several old miners' cabins, then joins and finally crosses Parker Pass Creek. At 3.4 miles, it meets a junction with the trail to Spiller Lake. Keep left and continue to climb through the forest past a second tumbledown cabin on the right. Shortly beyond this cabin, at 4.7 miles, the Parker Pass Trail cuts off to the right. There is no sign at the junction, but there are some large ducks, and the trail is visible on the other side of the meadow.

This meadow is one of the most beautiful in Yosemite. The red rocks of Mount Lewis ahead and Mount Gibbs on the north complement the green of the meadow and the deep, deep blue of the little lakes tastefully embellished with graceful arrangements of whitebark pine. Mono Pass marks the border between Yosemite and the Ansel Adams Wilderness. You can make a detour on down the other side of the pass to beautiful Sardine Lake, but the return trip is a steep climb. Across from the pass, beyond Summit Lake to the southeast, there a sandy bench covered with whitebark pine. Here you'll find several more miners' cabins in better condition than the earlier ones. This is the best place to camp, protected as it is by clumps of trees from the winds that blow through the pass. Return the way you came.

North of Tuolumne Meadows

North of Tuolumne Meadows

For general information about the Tuolumne Meadows area, including a discussion of facilities, services permits, camping, and shuttle buses, see South of Tuolumne Meadows section.

The Grand Canyon of the Tuolumne River dominates this region and defines its northern boundary. The Lyell Fork of the Tuolumne originates at the Lyell Glacier and the Dana Fork rises from the snowfields of Mount Dana, both to the south. The forks meet in Tuolumne Meadows and wander languorously northwest for a few miles, then begin their headlong rush toward the Pacific Ocean in an almost continuous series of cascades and waterfalls. The canyon they carved was gouged even deeper by glaciers, which produced a narrow slot in the granite with vertical walls that are in some places higher than those of Yosemite Valley.

All the hikes described here explore the country between Tuolumne Meadows and this Grand Canyon. Since every trailhead in this section originates from or near Tioga Road, there will be other hikers in the backcountry, and there will be some competition for wilderness permits. Still, the trails in this region are not as heavily used as are those south of the road. There are high peaks, passes, waterfalls, and sensationally beautiful scenery but overall, the terrain is slightly less rugged and the average elevation is a little lower than the country to the south. Furthermore, there are no trails heading directly to Yosemite Valley.

41 Waterwheel Falls and the Grand Canyon of the Tuolumne

General description:	Rugged, overnight shuttle hike following the Tuolumne River, with good views of waterfalls.
Total distance:	28.1 miles.
Difficulty:	Strenuous.
Elevation gain:	4,180 feet.
Trail traffic:	Moderate.
Best months:	Early July is best for cooler temperatures and full-flowing waterfalls.
Maps:	USGS Falls Ridge, Hetch Hetchy Reservoir, Tamarack Flat, Ten Lakes, and Tioga Pass quads.
Permits:	Available in advance or from the Tuolumne Meadows Wilderness Center.

Waterwheel Falls and the
Grand Canyon of the Tuolumne

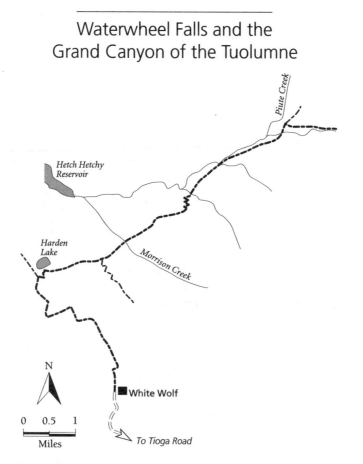

Finding the trailhead: From the west, follow Tioga Road (California 120) past the Tuolumne Meadows Visitor Center, store, café, and campground, all on the right. Just after crossing the bridge over the Tuolumne River, turn left (north) into the Lembert Dome parking area. From the east (Tioga Pass) follow Tioga Road past the turnoff to the wilderness center on the left and continue about a hundred yards to the Lembert Dome parking area on the right. You can also ride the Tuolumne Meadows shuttle to Stop 4, Lembert Dome. Overnight parking is prohibited in the parking lot, so if you are planning to backpack, park along the paved road parallel to Tioga Road. At a

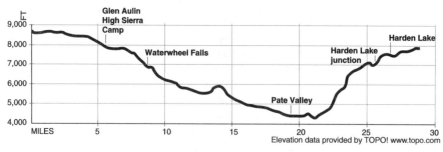

Elevation data provided by TOPO! www.topo.com

Waterwheel Falls and the
Grand Canyon of the Tuolumne

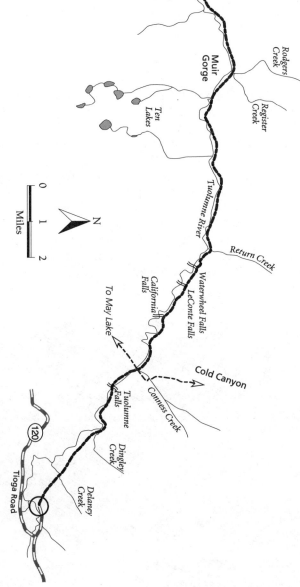

closed gate, this road turns sharply to the right and heads toward the stables. The trail begins at the gate.

Trailhead facilities: All amenities at Tuolumne Meadows; very small store, café, phones, and campground at White Wolf.

Key points:
- 0.0 Trailhead.
- 5.2 Glen Aulin High Sierra Camp.
- 7.8 Waterwheel Falls.
- 19.5 Pate Valley.
- 25.7 Harden Lake junction.
- 27.2 Harden Lake.

The hike: This is a rugged but fairly low-elevation backpack that begins at Tuolumne Meadows and follows the Tuolumne River through the Grand Canyon of the Tuolumne almost as far as the Hetch Hetchy Reservoir; one then climbs steeply out of the canyon up to White Wolf. To begin, follow Hike 21 to the High Sierra camp at 5.2 miles. From the camp, cross to the west side of Conness Creek, cross a ridge, and descend into the burned-over glen. Wander for a mile through a waist-high sea of lupines that have taken advantage of the open ground newly created by the fire. The river flows quiet and deep beside you for a while, then both trail and river drop over the first of a long series of stair-steps down past California Falls, LeConte Falls, and finally the famous Waterwheels, at 7.8 miles. These are best enjoyed in early season, when the roaring Tuolumne rushes down a smooth slope until it hits a series of grooves in the rocks that sometimes fling the water more than 20 feet into the air.

Waterwheel Falls in the Grand Canyon of the Tuolumne.

148

Watch for a little spur trail leading toward the riverside for a better view, but **do not** walk out onto the slippery rock beside the water, especially if it is wet. The combination of slimy algae on polished rock creates a surface as slick as glass, and a slip could be fatal.

Return to the main trail and continue to switchback down to a bridge over Return Creek. Soon the canyon walls narrow and eventually become so precipitous at Muir Gorge that the trail must make a detour over the top of a smooth polished shoulder. It then drops steeply into the drainage of Register Creek, which you cross on rocks below a pretty cascade.

A little farther on, cross Rodgers Creek on a bridge. Now that you are well into the zone of black oak and chaparral, the canyon can be very hot and the flies voracious. You must also stay alert for rattlesnakes. Fortunately, there are lots of inviting little pools alternating with lovely cascades for cooling off. At 19.5 miles, enter Pate Valley and pass the trail that takes off northward up Piute Creek. Continue straight ahead and cross the two branches of the river to its south side. There are plenty of good campsites in Pate Valley, and plenty of bears. This is a good place to spend the night no matter what time you arrive, because the climb up out of the canyon can be very hot and should be tackled early in the morning. Make sure you have plenty of water if it is past mid-July. Morrison Creek, the only stream you will meet on your way up, is sometimes dry later in the summer.

As you gain elevation, the Hetch Hetchy Reservoir comes into view down the canyon. After the first set of switchbacks, cross Morrison Creek in a cool aspen grove, then climb another set of switchbacks alongside the creek. At 25.7 miles, pass the first junction to Harden Lake and continue straight ahead (west), climbing less steeply at first, then mounting a last set of switchbacks to Harden Lake (no camping allowed) at 27.2 miles. From the lake, follow Hike 42, Harden Lake, in reverse, back up the fire road to White Wolf.

42 Harden Lake

General description:	Out-and-back day hike with an extravagantly profuse and varied array of wildflowers.
Total distance:	6 miles.
Difficulty:	Easy.
Elevation gain:	270 feet.
Trail traffic:	Moderate.
Best months:	All summer; whenever the road is open. The flower show continues all season and is at its most spectacular in July—when the mosquitoes are most voracious. Be prepared.
Maps:	USGS Tamarack Flat and Hetch Hetchy Reservoir quads.
Permits:	None.

Harden Lake

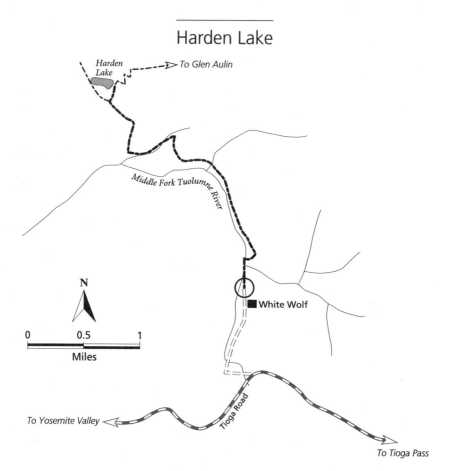

Finding the trailhead: Drive to the White Wolf turnoff on Tioga Road (California 120), 14 miles east of Crane Flat or 17 miles west of Tenaya Lake. Turn north on the White Wolf Road and drive about a mile to White Wolf, where there is a lodge with tent cabins and a campground. Park in front of the lodge.

Trailhead facilities: Food, water, toilets, and phones at White Wolf.

Key points:
- 0.0   Trailhead.
- 3.0   Harden Lake.

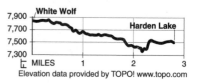

Elevation data provided by TOPO! www.topo.com

The hike: This is an easy stroll along a road now used only by service vehicles. Its appeal lies in its extravagantly profuse and varied array of wildflowers. The hike is all downhill until about the last half mile (which means it's uphill on the way back. Take water). From White Wolf Lodge, follow the road north past the campground on the right and the tent cabins on the left, past a sign that says "Road Closed," then past the employee housing and the ranger station. Here the paving ends. Go around another locked gate. The road crosses the Middle Fork of the Tuolumne River. The wildflower show begins at once. The river, really just a creek here, is lined with tall lupine, lilies, senecio, and many more, a riot of color, almost tropical in profusion. The drier areas along the roadside vie with the creekside with their own show of flowers: yarrow, Jacob's ladder, columbine. A special favorite is Lewis' monkey flower with its pastel stripes of pink and blue.

Ignore any side roads or trails branching off the main route. One goes to the sewage treatment plant, others go nowhere in particular or just return to the road. The Middle Fork and the road gradually part company and the road continues to descend until about the last half mile, where it swings right and climbs to a junction. Follow the right fork for just a few yards to reach the lake. It is a pleasant, but unspectacular spot. The sign at the lake reads "Harden Lake 7,600 feet" but the topo lists the elevation as 7,848 feet. Take your pick. Return the way you came.

43 Lukens Lake

General description:	Out-and-back day hike for wildflower lovers.
Total distance:	1.6 miles.
Difficulty:	Easy.
Elevation gain:	200 feet.
Trail traffic:	Moderately heavy.
Best months:	All summer; whenever Tioga Road is open.
Maps:	USGS Yosemite Falls quad.
Permits:	None.

Finding the trailhead: On Tioga Road (California 120) drive about 2 miles east of the White Wolf junction. The signed parking area is on the south side of the road, but the trail begins on the north side.

Trailhead facilities: None.

Key points:
    0.0   Trailhead.
    0.8   Lukens Lake.

The hike: Lukens Lake is a favorite of wildflower lovers. Cross Tioga Road carefully and head uphill through an almost pure-red fir forest. The cones underfoot come from the occasional western white pine or hemlock. Fir cones do not fall but decompose and release their seeds while still on the tree. Watch for odd

Lukens Lake is a favorite destination for wildflower lovers.

Lukens Lake

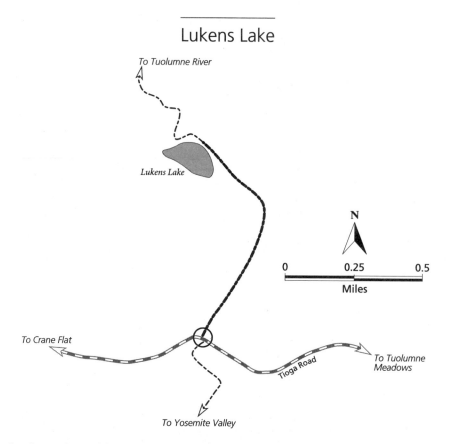

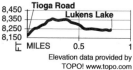

leaflessplants like pinedrops, brilliant red snow plant, and little saprophytic orchids on the forest floor. In the sunny spots are chinquapin, green-and-gold shrubs with spiny but delicious edible nuts.

The trail tops a rise, then descends to a creek filled with dozens of species of waist-high wildflowers, and turns to follow the creek left to Lukens Lake. The moisture that allows for the lush display of wildflowers means lots of mosquitoes, too. Take repellent. Retrace your steps to Tioga Road.

44 Ten Lakes

General description: Shuttle; overnight hike through diverse habitat to numerous lakes.
Total distance: 22.4 miles.
Difficulty: Moderate.
Elevation gain: 2,560 feet.
Trail traffic: Moderate.
Best months: All summer; whenever Tioga Road is open.
Maps: USGS Falls Ridge, Ten Lakes, Tenaya Lake, and Yosemite Falls quads.
Permits: Available in advance or from the wilderness center at Yosemite Valley or Tuolumne Meadows.

Finding the trailhead: On Tioga Road (California 120) drive about 20 miles east of Crane Flat or 26 miles west of Tuolumne Meadows. There is parking on both sides of the highway. The Ten Lakes Trail departs from the north side. You will need to leave another car or arrange to be picked up at the May Lake Trailhead, at the end of the spur road that heads north of Tioga Road along Snow Creek.

Trailhead facilities: None.

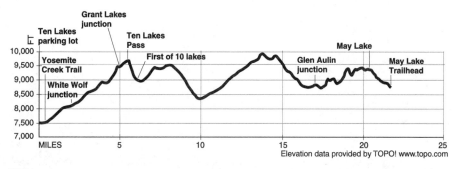

Key points:
- 0.0   Ten Lakes parking lot/Trailhead.
- 0.1   Yosemite Creek Trail.
- 2.1   White Wolf junction.
- 5.9   Grant Lakes junction.
- 6.3   Ten Lakes.
- 17.5 Glen Aulin junction.
- 21.1 May Lake.

The hike: From the parking area, follow the trail that parallels the road west to the junction with the Yosemite Creek trail at 0.1 mile. The trail heads northward through the forest over level ground, then emerges into sunshine. Soon it begins to climb along the western slope above Yosemite Creek amid ceanothus and manzanita, sometimes you'll need to hop little mossy (and slippery) rivulets. A foaming white cascade tumbles down a

Ten Lakes

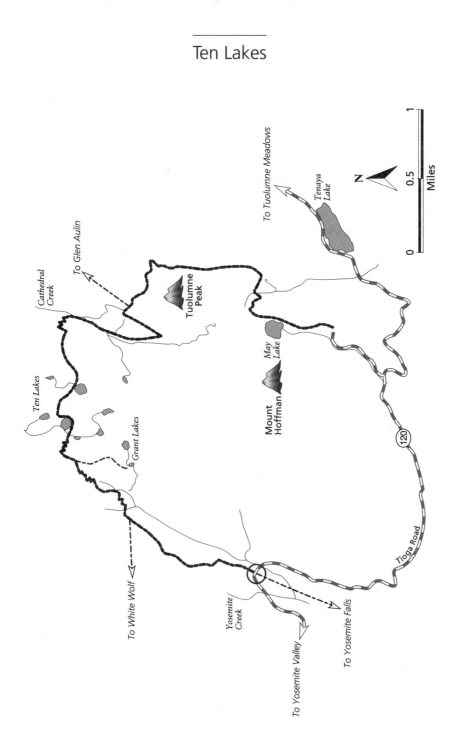

shallow notch across the canyon to the east below Mount Hoffman. The trail reenters the forest and crosses several little creeks, then meets the White Wolf Trail at 2.1 miles. Continue straight ahead (north) and cross a branch of Yosemite Creek that can present a challenge early in the year. Alongside grow some truly gigantic lupines. The trail now climbs relentlessly, working its way northeast to reach Half Moon Meadow at the base of an open granite ridge. There are a few marginal campsites at the northern end. Now the trail climbs very steeply between two little creeks and wonderful wildflower gardens. The grade lessens as the trail passes through a moist patch of sedges, until it reaches the top of the ridge above Half Moon Meadow at the Grant Lakes junction at 5.9 miles. The Grant Lakes lie at the bottom of a flowery bowl and offer more solitude than you will find at Ten Lakes.

To continue on to Ten Lakes, cross over the open ridge called Ten Lakes Pass and pause to gasp at a stupendous panorama that extends from Mount Conness, past the great red Tioga Crest, across to Matterhorn Peak and the Sawtooth Ridge all the way to Tower Peak. The Grand Canyon of the Tuolumne River cuts a deep gash between the ridge just in front of you and the peaks behind. Now the trail drops down off the pass to the west, but don't put away your camera yet, for another grand vista soon appears. Here, four of the (approximately) ten lakes descend from bowl to bowl, north to south down toward the Grand Canyon of the Tuolumne against a backdrop of more dramatic high peaks. These strings of glacial lakes are sometimes called paternoster lakes, since they resemble beads strung together on a rosary.

The trail now descends steeply through willows and more flowers, then sloshes through a marshy spot to reach a stream connecting two of the lakes. This crossing can be dangerous early in the year. Just beyond it is the southern shore of one of the larger Ten Lakes, at 6.3 miles. There is plenty of camping here, but you will have lots of neighbors, and you will probably have bears. This is a popular spot for a layover, providing an opportunity to visit several of the other lakes above and below this one without a pack.

The route between this lake and the next one along the main trail is obscure. Watch carefully for tree blazes and keep an eye on the topo to find the spot where the trail makes a steep rocky climb to a ridge high above the east side of the lake you just left. Now the trail swings southeast and passes fairly close to the shoreline of the next lake. This one also has good camping and is not usually as crowded as the first. Now descend through a forested gully, round a corner, and begin a steep drop down spectacular granite slabs decorated with some very picturesque old junipers into the beautiful basin of the south fork of Cathedral Creek. There are a few campsites back off the trail where you can rest your aching knees and cool your feet after the long descent.

The south fork presents another challenging crossing because the creek is quite deep and you can't see the bottom. A walking stick is handy here if you can't find a log. The trail follows the east side of the creek for almost 2 miles before it switchbacks up the hillside, then climbs northward to cross a shoulder of Tuolumne Peak, rising and falling over lots of little pockets where snow patches linger late into the summer. It drops through a narrow slot and rounds a corner, where it follows a narrow ridge alongside a couple of tiny tarns on the south and an open panorama of the Cathedral Range to the north. Now the trail makes a long descent down the forested mountainside until it levels out in a boggy hollow filled with avalanche debris. There it meets a junction with the trail to Glen Aulin, at 17.5 miles.

Turn right (south), cross a wide saddle, then begin a steep but beautiful climb up a mostly open slope down which little creeks trickle through miniature gardens. Across the Murphy Creek drainage to the east are Polly Dome, Mount Conness, and the northern crest on the skyline. The path then drops briefly down the west side of the rocky ridge. When it enters the forest again, watch to the left for a glimpse of Raisin Lake, almost hidden behind the rocks. This is a welcome stop for a swim after your long, hot climb. May Lake is not too much farther, but it is closed to swimming. Beyond Raisin Lake another short, steep set of switchbacks takes you up a slope, past a meadow with an ephemeral pond, then meets the northeast end of May Lake and skirts its shore to the High Sierra camp, at 21.2 miles. From here, follow Hike 20 in reverse, to the trailhead at the end of the Snow Flat Road.

45 Soda Springs and Parsons Lodge

General description:	Out-and-back day hike leading to the wildflower-filled heart of Tuolumne Meadows.
Total distance:	1.2 miles.
Difficulty:	Easy.
Elevation gain:	40 feet.
Trail traffic:	Heavy.
Best months:	All summer; whenever Tioga Road is open.
Maps:	USGS Tioga Pass and Vogelsang Peak quads.
Permits:	None.

Finding the trailhead: From the visitor center in Tuolumne Meadows, drive a few hundred yards east on Tioga Road to the signed trailhead on the left (north) side of the road.

Trailhead facilities: Food, water, gas, post office, and telephone are all available in Tuolumne Meadows.

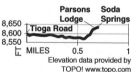

Key points:
- 0.0   Trailhead.
- 0.6   Soda Springs.

The hike: A wide, sandy trail heads right into the heart of enormous Tuolumne Meadows amid a riot of wildflowers: purple meadow penstemon,

Soda Springs and Parsons Lodge

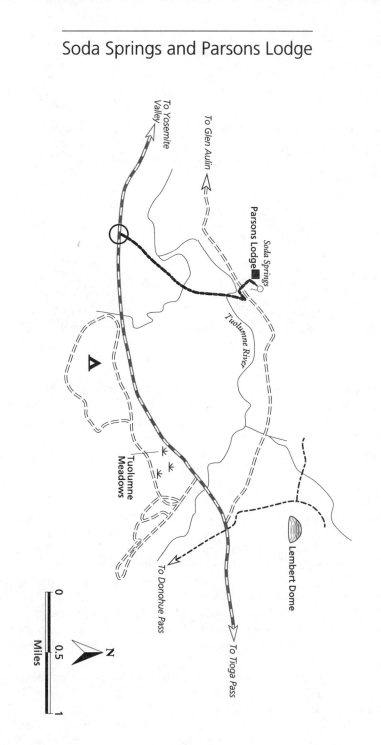

To Yosemite Valley

To Glen Aulin

Parsons Lodge

Soda Springs

Tuolumne River

Tuolumne Meadows

Lembert Dome

To Donohue Pass

To Tioga Pass

N

0   0.5   1
Miles

The ground bubbles with naturally carbonated soda springs.

shooting stars, white pussytoes, and yellow goldenrod. Off to the right (east) is long, sloping Lembert Dome, and farther beyond, the two red hulks of Mount Dana and Mount Gibbs. To their right is gray granite Mammoth Peak (not to be confused with Mammoth Mountain, the ski area, farther to the south). Ahead, across the main channel of the river winding its sinuous way through the meadow, the path crosses a wood-and-stone footbridge. Pause here and turn around for a panoramic view of the Cathedral Range, with the spires of Cathedral Peak itself, then Echo Peak and the Cockscomb rising behind rounded Fairview Dome. To continue ahead, just beyond the bridge the trail intersects a gravel road on which you turn left (west) and proceed a few yards to another sign directing you to Soda Springs and Parsons Lodge to the right (north), up a little slope. Parsons Lodge, built of local stone by the Sierra Club in 1915 and sold to the National park service in 1973, is open daily during the summer and contains exhibits about the history of the area. Next door, the log-built McCauley Cabin houses park service volunteers who are eager to share local lore. Rest for a while on the rocks in front of the lodge to watch the activities of the marmot families who live in burrows nearby.

Now head toward the tumbledown, roofless log structure clearly visible to the east. Here, naturally carbonated soda springs bubble out of the ground in dozens of places, staining the soil red-brown. This is a good place to see mule deer, especially mornings and evenings, as they come to lick the minerals deposited by the springs. You can spend a whole day wandering these meadows, using the well-marked trails to create your own loop, or you can return the way you came to Tioga Road.

46 Dog Lake

General description: Out-and-back day hike to a lovely lake, with an optional loop.
Total distance: 3.2 miles.
Difficulty: Easy.
Elevation gain: 570 feet.
Trail traffic: Moderate.
Best months: Late spring to fall; whenever Tioga Road is open.
Maps: USGS Tioga Pass quad.
Permits: None for day hike; available for backpacking at wilderness center.

Finding the trailhead: From the west, drive Tioga Road (California 120 eastward past the Tuolumne Meadows Visitor Center, store, and campground, all on the right. Just after crossing the bridge over the Tuolumne River, turn left into the Lembert Dome parking area. From the east (Tioga Pass) on Tioga Road, pass the turnoff to the wilderness center and Tuolumne Meadows Lodge on the left, then turn right into the Lembert Dome parking lot a few hundred yards beyond.

Trailhead facilities: Toilets, no water.

Key points:
0.0   Trailhead.
0.1   Dog Lake/Lembert Dome split.
0.2   Trail to stables.
1.1   Trail to Lembert Dome.
1.5   Dog Lake cutoff.
1.6   Dog Lake.

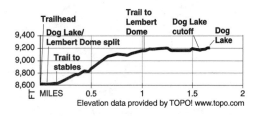

The hike: Set out northward from the Lembert Dome Trailhead sign through lodgepole pines, cross an open rocky slab polished to a high sheen in places by glacial ice, then reenter the forest. The trail forks at 0.1 mile. (This split is not shown on the topo map.) Take the left fork. At 0.2 mile another trail comes in from the stables to the left. This time, take the right fork. Just a few yards after that, another trail comes in from the same place. Keep right again. Climb steeply alongside the sheer face of Lembert Dome, then cross a little creek. The grade now becomes gentler. At 1.1 miles a trail cuts off to the right around the back side of Lembert Dome; continue straight ahead toward Dog Lake. At 1.5 miles, turn right onto the Dog Lake Trail and at 1.6 miles, reach an opening in the forest that perfectly frames the lake. The sign in front of you says the water level of the lake is 9,240 feet, while it is marked 9,170 feet on the topo map. Take your pick. Dog Lake is surrounded on three sides by lodgepole pine, but at the far east end, a green meadow provides the foreground for the huge red bulks of Mount Dana and Mount Gibbs.

The official mapped trail continues for about a half mile along the south shore of the lake, but it is possible to circumnavigate the lake, adding about

Dog Lake and Lembert Dome

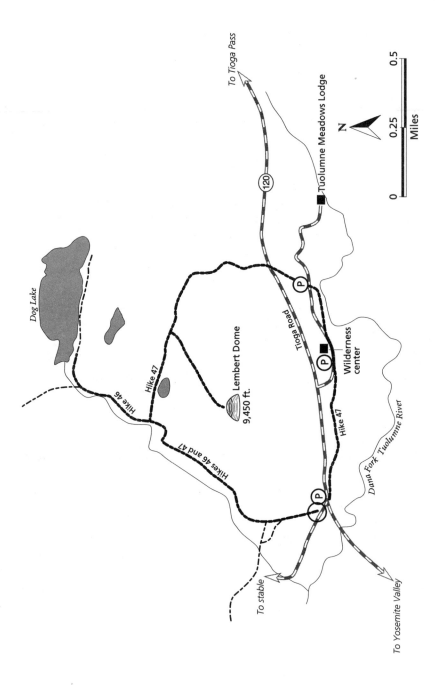

1.5 miles to your hike. The meadow around the lakeshore, especially at the east and north ends, can be boggy, and it is very fragile, so travel with care. From the northeast end of the lake, there's a good view of Cathedral Peak poking up through the forest. Camping is not permitted here because the area is too delicate and too close to the road. Return the way you came.

47 Lembert Dome

See map on page 160

General description: Loop hike with a side trip to the top of Lembert Dome.
Total distance: 3.7 miles.
Difficulty: Moderate.
Elevation gain: 870 feet.
Trail traffic: Moderately heavy.
Best months: Late June–mid-September; when Tioga Road is open.
Maps: USGS Tioga Pass quad.
Permits: None.

Finding the trailhead: From the west, follow Tioga Road (California 120) past the Tuolumne Meadows Visitor Center, store, café, and campground, all on the right. Just after crossing the bridge over the Tuolumne River, turn left into the Lembert Dome parking area. From the east (Tioga Pass) on Tioga Road, pass the turnoff to the wilderness center on the left, continue about a hundred yards, then turn right into the Lembert Dome parking area.

Trailhead facilities: Picnic tables and restrooms. Groceries, telephone, and supplies a half mile to the west.

Key points:
0.0   Trailhead.
0.1   Trail fork.
0.2   Trail from stables.
1.3   Lembert Dome/Dog Lake junction.
1.7   Trail to top of Lembert Dome.
2.0   Top of Lembert Dome.
2.3   Return to trail junction.
3.1   Tioga Road.
3.2   John Muir Trail sign.

Elevation data provided by TOPO! www.topo.com

The hike: Lembert Dome, among the premiere features of Tuolumne Meadows, is the huge, lopsided, smoothly polished mound of granite just north of Tioga Road. This hike takes you to the top of the dome, approaching from the west and returning to the east. Near the top, the going is steep and the rock is slick and smooth. You'll need good boots with lug soles, and if you're bothered by heights, don't try it. If you have doubts, remember that coming down a steep slope is more difficult than going up.

Set out northward, past the picnic tables and restrooms from the Dog Lake/Lembert Dome Trailhead sign beneath the lodgepoles, then cross an open rocky slab, where the route is marked by big boulders. The granite has patches polished to a high sheen by glaciers. If you look carefully you can see the striations or scratches in the rock showing the direction in which the rivers of ice flowed.

The trail forks at 0.1 mile. Continue straight ahead toward Dog Lake. (This split is not shown on the topo map.) At 0.2 mile, another trail comes in from the stables to the left (west). This time, take the right fork. Just a few yards after that, yet another trail comes in from the same place. Keep right again. Climb fairly steeply alongside the sheer face of Lembert Dome, then cross a little creek. The grade becomes more gradual now. At 1.3 miles turn right (east) at another signed junction. The other fork goes on uphill to Dog Lake. Saunter along an almost flat path, passing a little pond at the base of the dome. At 1.7 miles is another junction not shown on the topo. You'll return to this point after visiting the summit.

Turn right here and climb westward up a wooded ridge to a rocky saddle between Lembert Dome itself and a smaller bump known as Dog Dome. Follow the layered exfoliating granite slabs that form a natural stairway straight up the slope, then pick the easiest way to the top, at 2 miles. The slope is a little less steep toward the left (south) side of the dome. When you

Lembert Dome from Tuolumne Meadows.

have caught your breath, stroll around on top, where the footing is more level, to take in the view. You can see the high peaks of the north boundary country, the warm red rocks of Mount Dana and Mount Gibbs on the eastern crest, and the Lyell Fork of the Tuolumne River flowing down from the Lyell Glacier to meet the Dana Fork in the broad green meadow. To the south, the spires of the Cathedral Range pierce the sky, and to the west, a series of rounded domes extend into the distance toward Yosemite Valley.

When you are ready, return to the last trail junction (2.3 miles) and follow the fairly steep switchbacks downhill to Tioga Road. Cross the road at 2.5 miles and continue another tenth mile to a parking lot on a small side road (the one that leads to Tuolumne Meadows High Sierra Camp). Cross this road (south) and find a trail marking the John Muir Trail, at 2.6 miles. Turn right and follow this alongside the road, then re-cross the road to the Lembert Dome parking area.

48 Young Lakes

General description: An out-and-back day hike or overnighter, with stunning vistas and meadows.
Total distance: 13.4 miles.
Difficulty: Easy to moderate as a backpack, strenuous as a day hike.
Elevation gain: 1,460 feet.
Trail traffic: Moderate.
Best months: Late spring–early fall; whenever Tioga Road is open.
Maps: USGS Tioga Pass quad.
Permits: Wilderness permits are required if the hike is done as a backpack; available in advance or at the Tuolumne Wilderness Center. Permits are not necessary for day hikers.

Finding the trailhead: From the west, drive Tioga Road (California 120) eastward past the Tuolumne Meadows Visitor Center, store, and campground, all on the right (south). Just after crossing the bridge over the Tuolumne River, turn left into the Lembert Dome parking area. From the east (Tioga Pass) on Tioga Road, pass the turnoff to the wilderness center on the left. The sign says "Wilderness Permits, Pacific Crest, John Muir." A few hundred yards beyond, turn right into the Lembert Dome parking lot and picnic area. You can also ride the Tuolumne Meadows shuttle to Stop 4, Lembert Dome. If you plan to spend the night at Young Lakes, park along the road that roughly parallels the highway; it leads to the stables. Leave any food in the bear-proof boxes. Overnight parking is not permitted in the Lembert Dome lot.

Young Lakes

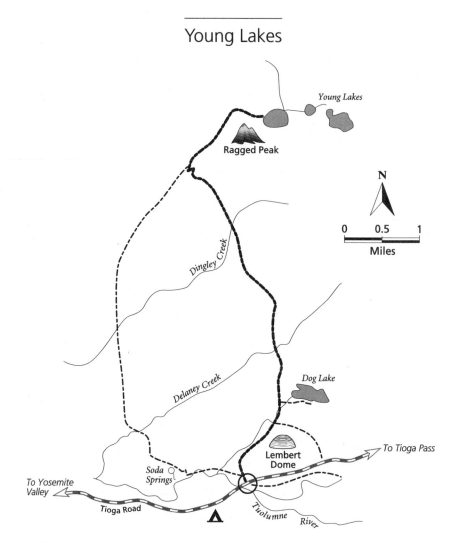

Young Lakes

Ragged Peak

Dingley Creek

Delaney Creek

Dog Lake

Soda Springs

Lembert Dome

To Tioga Pass

To Yosemite Valley

Tioga Road

Tuolumne River

N

0   0.5   1
Miles

Trailhead facilities: Toilets. Store, café, and telephones on Tioga Road less than a half mile to the right (west) of the trailhead.

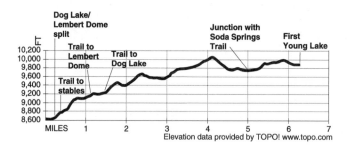

Dog Lake/
Lembert Dome
split

Trail to
Lembert
Dome

Trail to
Dog Lake

Junction with
Soda Springs
Trail

First
Young Lake

Trail to
stables

FT
10,200
10,000
9,800
9,600
9,400
9,200
9,000
8,800
8,600

MILES   1   2   3   4   5   6   7

Elevation data provided by TOPO! www.topo.com

Key points:
- 0.0 Trailhead.
- 0.1 Dog Lake/Lembert Dome split.
- 0.2 Trail to stables.
- 1.3 Trail to Lembert Dome.
- 1.5 Trail to Dog Lake.
- 5.2 Junction with Soda Springs Trail.
- 6.7 First Young Lake.

The hike: Set out northward from the Lembert Dome/Dog Lake Trailhead sign through lodgepole pines, then cross an open rocky slab, polished to a high sheen in spots by glaciers, then reenter the forest. The trail forks here at 0.1 mile. Take the left fork toward Dog Lake. At 0.2 mile, a trail comes in from the stables to the left (west). Shortly after that, yet another trail comes in from the same place. Keep right at both junctions. Continue climbing steeply alongside the sheer face of Lembert Dome, then cross a little creek. The grade becomes less extreme now. At 1.1 miles, a trail cuts off to the right (east) to skirt the back side of Lembert Dome. Continue straight ahead toward Dog Lake. At 1.5 miles, the Dog Lake Trail turns right. Your trail continues straight ahead again, crossing the outlet stream from the lake and ascending a moderate slope for about a half mile to a lovely meadow, where you will be sure to want to stop awhile.

Hop across or wade Delaney Creek and look eastward up the meadow at the red bulks of Mount Gibbs and Mount Dana on the skyline. Cross the meadow and continue the easy climb up a forested little ridge around the west side of another unnamed but beautifully rounded dome, then emerge into another meadow. Pause to gasp at one of the most stunning vistas in the entire Sierra Nevada.

The whole Cathedral Range lies before you. The spectacular skyline to the south is punctuated by the spires of Unicorn, Echo, and Cathedral peaks. To the right (west) is Mount Hoffman, at the geographic center of Yosemite; to the left (southwest) is Mount Lyell, highest peak in the park (13,114 feet), and it shelters Lyell glacier, largest in the park. Equally beautiful, but on a different scale, are the flower gardens along Dingley Creek, right at your feet.

The trail now climbs a short distance to cross a shoulder of the Ragged Peak ridge, the highest point on this hike, then descends to a junction, at 5.2 miles. Here, another trail comes up from Tuolumne Meadows farther to the southwest. Your trail continues northward and curves gradually to the east, goes around Ragged Peak, and at last dips into the basin containing the lowest of the three Young Lakes, at 6.7 miles.

There is plenty of good camping along the western side of the lake. Use extra care in practicing minimum impact techniques here. These lakes are so easily accessible and lie in a setting of such staggering beauty that they have become a popular destination. Carry a bear canister. There are few good trees for hanging food out of the reach of the area's numerous and active bears.

The higher lakes are well worth exploration. An unofficial use trail is worn alongside the next two lakes. From above, you can look down to see all three lakes at once, with snaggle-toothed Ragged Peak jutting into the sky beyond them to the south. On your return to Tuolumne Meadows, after you have descended the first 1.5 miles to the trail junction, you can, for a change of scene, take the right (west) fork leading down to Soda Springs, where you turn left (east) to follow a dirt road back to your car. The trail you came in on, however, is more scenic.

49 Polly Dome Lakes

General description:	Out-and-back day hike, exposing a wealth of interesting geologic features.
Total distance:	5 miles.
Difficulty:	Easy.
Elevation gain:	520 feet.
Trail traffic:	Moderate.
Best months:	All summer; whenever Tioga Road is open.
Maps:	USGS Tenaya Lake quad.
Permits:	None.

Finding the trailhead: Park in the picnic area on the south side of Tioga Road, about halfway along Tenaya Lake. Cross the road to the signed trailhead.

Trailhead facilities: Pit toilets.

Key points:
   0.0   Trailhead.
   2.5   Polly Dome Lakes.

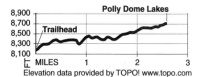

The hike: This trail exhibits a wealth of classic glacial features, including house-sized erratics, or boulders transported from their place of origin by ice and deposited wherever the ice could no longer carry them. There is shiny glacial polish and striations on the rocks showing the direction of the flow, sometimes interrupted by a series of crescent-shaped gouges called chatter marks, produced when the ice dragged big boulders, bounding and shuddering, across the surface.

The trail climbs gently northward alongside Murphy Creek, first through lodgepole pine

Polly Dome Lakes with Polly Dome in background.

Crescent-shaped gouges called chatter marks from big boulders dragged by glaciers.

Polly Dome Lakes

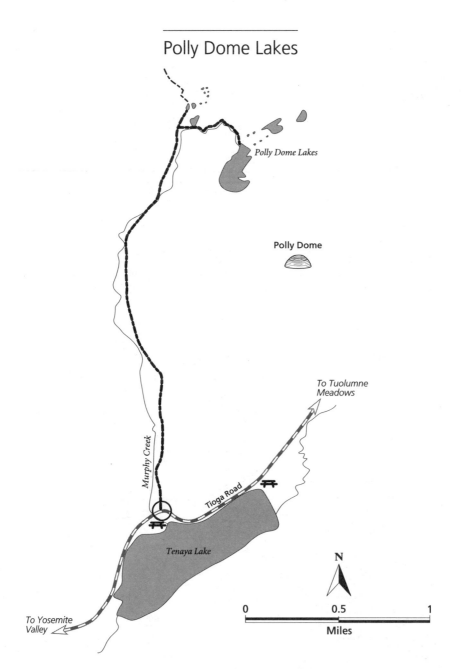

forest, then over open rock slabs marked by ducks. At the beginning, you can see Mount Hoffman off to the left, but very soon it disappears behind a lighter-colored ridge. The largest of the Polly Dome Lakes is a bit off the trail, but easy to find. As soon as you reach the first little pond off to the right with Polly Dome in the background, turn off the trail and follow its inlet a short distance upstream to the lake. When you are ready, retrace your steps to Tenaya Lake.

50 Gaylor Lakes

General description:	Out-and-back day hike through alpine country, with good wildlife viewing.
Total distance:	3 miles.
Difficulty:	Moderately strenuous.
Elevation gain:	560 feet.
Trail traffic:	Moderate.
Best months:	July–August
Maps:	USGS Tioga Pass quad.
Permits:	None, since camping is prohibited here.

Finding the trailhead: On Tioga Road (California 120) immediately inside (and to the south of) the eastern park entrance, you'll find the trailhead and parking area on the west side of the road.

Trailhead facilities: Toilets.

Key points:

   0.0   Trailhead.
   1.5   Gaylor Lakes.

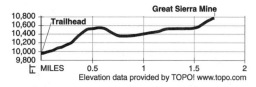

The hike: This is grand, high, wide alpine country reached by a short but steep climb. Follow the well-used trail uphill through subalpine forest. The trail tops out on a broad, open saddle on broken metamorphic rock. Behind you, massive red Mount Dana thrusts upward above lake-dotted Dana Meadows. Beyond a few clumps of windblown whitebark pine, the trail drops as steeply as it rose to the first of the Gaylor Lakes. It skirts the north edge of the lake, which seems to reach to the very lip of the shallow dish in which it sits. Beyond it, the spiky tops of the Cathedral Range seem to be emerging from the surface of the lake itself.

The trail climbs gradually north past Gaylor Peak, skirts the west end of another lake, swings around a ridge to the left, then climbs to another ridgetop at the border of the park. There you'll find the old Great Sierra Mine, a failed silver-mining operation that commands another grand view. The plateau is so high and exposed that permanent snowfields lie in the shady folds of the mountains, and even in July you might have to cross some snow patches or wade through some slush. You can explore this broad basin all day, examining tiny alpine belly flowers and watching the activities of the pikas, marmots, and Belding ground squirrels. You can also cross the low rise immediately west of Gaylor Peak to discover the Granite Lakes in another shallow bowl at the base of a classic glacial cirque.

There is a second route leading to the lakes that begins a few miles farther west on Tioga Road, but the trailhead is not obvious and the distance to the first lake is longer. The two trails do not meet in the lake basin, so if you

Gaylor Lakes

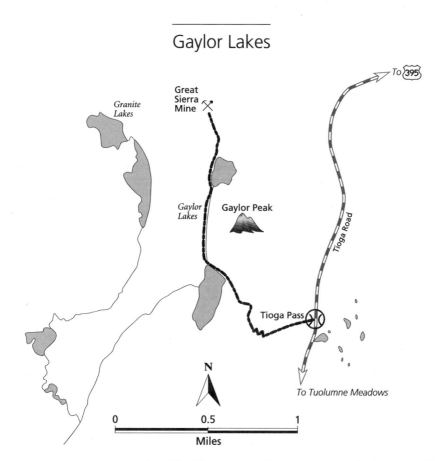

want to make a longer shuttle hike, you will have to travel about a mile cross-country between the trails, or return the way you came.

Hetch Hetchy

Hetch Hetchy

Hetch Hetchy Reservoir, begun in 1914, completed in 1923, then expanded in 1938, provides water and power for the city of San Francisco. Before the dam captured and tamed the Tuolumne River, the Hetch Hetchy Valley was said to rival Yosemite itself in scenic beauty. John Muir's famous, if fruitless, battle against the dam brought the need to preserve such wilderness treasures to the attention of the public and gave impetus to the growth of the National Park Service and to the conservation movement as a whole. Even now, a campaign is under way to convince legislators to raze the dam, drain the reservoir, and allow Hetch Hetchy to return to its original state. The area around the lake has the best display of springtime wildflowers in the park. It's a great place to hike in early season when the higher country is still under snow, and is pleasant in October when the black oaks change color. In midsummer, it's dry and hot. No swimming or boating is allowed in the reservoir.

There are no overnight accommodations at Hetch Hetchy, except for a walk-in, backpackers' campground. You must have a wilderness permit to use it, and you are limited to a one-night stay. The Hodgden Meadow Campground near the Big Oak Flat entrance is the closest park campground and requires reservations. There is also a Forest Service campground on Evergreen Road open on a first-come, first-served basis, and other accommodations in nearby Groveland.

To reach the main Hetch Hetchy trailhead at O'Shaughnessy Dam, you must leave Yosemite Park at the Big Oak Flat Entrance Station if you are coming from the east, then re-enter it at the Hetch Hetchy Entrance Station about 8 miles up a side road. From the west, turn off the highway before you reach the main entrance station. (See directions at the beginning of each hike.) Wilderness permits are available at the Hetch Hetchy Entrance Station and at the Big Oak Flat Entrance Station. It's a good idea to ask about the condition of the road before you start out because the road washes out regularly and is frequently closed for repairs.

51 Wapama Falls

General description: Out-and-back day hike to the refreshing spray of a
beautiful falls.
Total distance: 5 miles.
Difficulty: Easy.
Elevation gain: 200 feet.
Trail traffic: Heavy.
Best months: Mid April–June.
Maps: USGS Lake Eleanor quad.
Permits: None.

Finding the trailhead: Drive 1 mile west of the Big Oak Flat Entrance
Station to Yosemite on California 120. Turn right (north) on Evergreen Road
and drive about 7 miles. At Camp Mather, turn right (northeast) on Hetch
Hetchy Road. Pass through the park entrance station in about a mile, then
continue on for 8 miles more to where the road ends in a one-way loop.
Partway around is the dam, and just beyond it, a parking area.

Trailhead facilities: Water, restrooms, and phone on the right side of the
road just before you reach the dam and parking area on the one-way loop
road.

Key points:

0.0   O'Shaughnessy Dam Trailhead.
0.1   Tunnel.
0.9   Trail/road junction.
2.5   Wapama Falls.

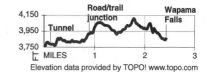
Elevation data provided by TOPO! www.topo.com

The hike: Walk across the dam past some historical markers. On the far side at
0.1 mile, enjoy the troupe of acrobatic swallows swooping and diving before
the entrance to a dark and dripping tunnel. Pass through the tunnel and continue along the level
road skirting the lake;
it's lined with live oak,
bay trees, and poison
oak, along with dozens
of species of wildflow-
ers, among them the
unusual pink-and-yel-
low harlequin lupine,
which grows in open,
sunny places. Little
trickles of water seep
from cracks in the
rocks to nourish but-
tercups, monkey-flow-
ers, and columbines. In

Hetch Hetchy Reservoir.

173

Wapama Falls, Rancheria Falls, and Lake Vernon

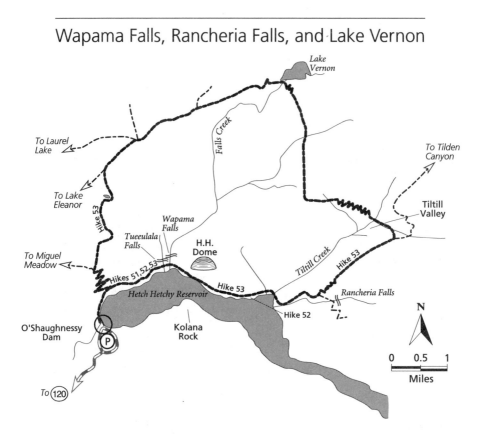

May, if you're lucky, you'll catch the spring migration of the little brown-and-orange California newts crossing the trail in such numbers that you must step carefully to avoid crushing them. The low elevation here also makes this a likely spot for snakes of several kinds, including rattlers. They are not aggressive, but they do not like to be handled or stepped on.

The road climbs fairly gently for a while, then at 0.9 mile, it continues on to the left, while the trail to the falls cuts toward the lake to the right. The route rises and falls and curves back and forth past more delicate little gardens, waterfalls, and pools while Kolana Rock broods darkly over the reservoir on the other side.

Farther along, Tueeulala Falls tumbles down over the trail. Early in the season you'll probably get your feet wet as you pass, but by mid-June the creek that feeds it is often dry. The trail continues along the cliff above the lake, climbing and descending for a short distance more until at last, at 2.5 miles, the spray and thunder of Wapama Falls make themselves felt. Toward the bottom, the fall splits into several sections, each of which is crossed on a separate footbridge. Sometimes the bridges are shin-deep underwater, though safe to wade; at other times the force of the falling torrent is so great that it is risky to cross. You can enjoy the falls from either side, or from the middle—if you crave a refreshing shower.

Return the way you came.

52 Rancheria Falls

See map on page 174

General description:	Out-and-back day hike with a good, early season display of wildflowers.
Total distance:	14.4 miles.
Difficulty:	Moderate.
Elevation gain:	660 feet.
Trail traffic:	Heavy.
Best months:	Mid-April–June.
Maps:	USGS Hetch Hetchy Reservoir and Lake Eleanor quads.
Permits:	None for a day hike; available at the Hetch Hetchy Entrance Station for backpackers.

Finding the trailhead: Drive 1 mile west of the Big Oak Flat Entrance Station to Yosemite on California 120. Turn right (north) on Evergreen Road for about 7 miles. At Camp Mather turn right (northeast) on Hetch Hetchy Road. Pass through the park entrance station in about a mile, then continue on for 8 miles to where the road ends in a one-way loop. Partway around is the dam, and just beyond it, a parking area.

Trailhead facilities: Water, restrooms, and phone on the right side of the road just before you reach the dam and parking area on the one-way loop road.

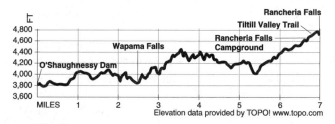

Elevation data provided by TOPO! www.topo.com

Key points:
- 0.0   O'Shaughnessy Dam Trailhead.
- 2.5   Wapama Falls.
- 6.9   Rancheria Falls campground.
- 7.1   Tiltill Valley Trail.
- 7.2   Rancheria Falls.

The hike: This is a good early season backpack with the best springtime wildflower display in the park. The Rancheria Falls camping area is notorious for its panhandling bears, so be sure to carry a canister. To begin, follow Hike 51 to 2.5 miles. After crossing the bridges at the base of the falls, the trail gains some elevation above the lake and passes along the base of Hetch Hetchy Dome. Now and then it climbs or drops on switchbacks to avoid various obstacles, then descends to cross a shady, unnamed creek on a bridge, rounds a corner, and crosses more substantial Tiltill Creek on another bridge. Finally, after one last hot climb, it tops out on a shoulder from which there

Rancheria Falls before Hetch Hetchy Reservoir.

is a good view of Rancheria Creek roaring down a series of water slides to the reservoir. After about a quarter mile, watch for ducks marking the turn-off to the camping area toward the river to the right, at 6.9 miles. There is no sign. This is such a popular spot that it is especially important to pitch your tent at least 100 feet from the creekside and practice Zero Impact camping.

To visit the top of the falls, continue on up the trail, keeping to the right at a junction with the trail to Tiltill Valley, at 7.1 miles. The bridge over the creek is just around a rocky corner. Above the bridge, the creek is squeezed into the neck of a deep, narrow funnel that opens out just downstream and releases water in a boiling, foaming rush down past the campground.

When you are ready, retrace your steps to the dam and the parking lot.

53 Lake Vernon

See map on page 174

General description: Overnight loop hike for the early season and a high-country feel.
Total distance: 26.9 miles.
Difficulty: Moderate.
Elevation gain: 3,680 feet.
Trail traffic: Heavy at beginning and end, light in the middle.
Best months: Late April–June.
Maps: USGS Hetch Hetchy Reservoir, Kibbie Lake, Lake Eleanor, and Tiltill Mountain quads.
Permits: Available in advance or from the Hetch Hetchy Entrance Station.

Finding the trailhead: Drive 1 mile west of the Big Oak Flat Entrance Station to Yosemite on California 120. Turn right (north) onto Evergreen Road and drive about seven miles. At Camp Mather turn right (northeast) onto Hetch Hetchy Road. Pass through the park entrance station in about a mile, then continue on for 8 miles to where the road ends in a one-way loop at O'Shaughnessy Dam and the parking area.

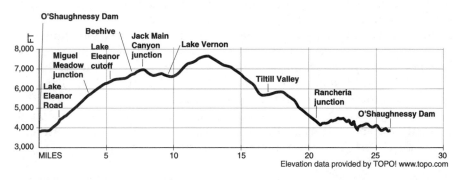

Key points:

0.0	O'Shaughnessy Dam trailhead.
1.0	Lake Eleanor Road/trail junction.
3.6	Miguel Meadow junction.
6.0	Lake Eleanor cutoff.
6.8	Beehive.
8.1	Jack Main Canyon junction.
10.3	Vernon Lake junction.
17.1	Tiltill Valley.
19.8	Rancheria junction.

The hike: The Lake Vernon region offers a real subalpine feeling at a relatively low elevation, so this loop is a good way to have a true High Sierra backpack when the higher country is still under snow. Follow Hike 51 to 1 mile, where the Lake Eleanor Road parts company with the trail that goes along the reservoir toward Rancheria Falls. Stay on the road (left) and follow the long, mostly shaded switchbacks to a junction with the trail to Miguel Meadow, at 3.6 miles. Keep right (north) and ascend beneath pines and incense-cedars to a more level stretch that winds through an open, rocky area lined with manzanita. Stay alert and watch the ducks to avoid losing the trail.

Reenter burned-over forest and continue climbing, passing a couple of tiny emerald-green meadows carpeted with white meadow foam and yellow monkey flowers. Arrive at another junction heading back to Lake Eleanor, at 6 miles, and keep right (north) again. Very soon you reach Beehive, at 6.8 miles. It is a soggy meadow with a piped spring protected by some wood planks. This water must be purified. There is some camping here. There is another trail that goes west to Laurel Lake from here, but it has not yet recovered from a severe burn and is not very attractive. Keep right, heading northeast out of Beehive, gaining elevation steadily to reach yet another junction, at 8.1 miles, heading northeast to the top of Moraine Ridge toward Wilmer Lake. Follow the right fork for a time, then drop down an open rocky slope and cross over a low hump to enter Lake Vernon basin. At 10.3 miles, a faint trail appears heading around to the right to the lake's northwest shore, where it soon ends. There is beautiful camping to be found on this side of the lake, mostly on broad flat rock slabs.

To continue, retrace your steps to the main trail, which can be a little obscure for a few dozen yards, and cross Falls Creek on a bridge. The route now climbs above the lake basin and looks out over splendid High Sierra scenery—wild and open glacier-scoured white granite, dotted with junipers. In springtime, this section of trail reeks with the smell of onions. So many tiny, low-growing, almost transparent little flowers sprout in the sandy soil at your feet that it's impossible to avoid stepping on some of them. The trail crosses over the top of this ridge, reenters forest, and hops a creek. It follows the ridge for a time, passes alongside a meadow, then swings left around its south end and crosses another creek. The route swings to the east and drops down the hot, south-facing slope through scratchy, overgrown ceanothus and manzanita for what seems like a long time before it once again reaches forest cover. Listen for the booming of male blue grouse announcing their territorial claims along this stretch. You are almost guaranteed to hear them in spring.

Continue the knee-jarring descent into Tiltill Valley and cross a creek. The trail sloshes alongside the north side of the soggy meadow, then rather abruptly turns south. A detour of a few yards eastward takes you to the only area near the meadow high and dry enough for camping. A big boulder at the upper end of the campsite has several bedrock mortars, smooth hollows in the rock where the native Miwok ground their acorn meal.

Back in the meadow's center, a trail to Tilden Lake and beyond cuts off to the east at 17.1 miles. The path is extremely mushy at the south side of the meadow and there is no convenient way to get around it. Your boots will dry on the climb to the top of the ridge above the meadow. Pass through a notch and skirt a lovely little pond lined with azaleas and blooming with yellow pond lilies. There may be lots of mosquitoes, too. Now you'll drop down hot dry switchbacks to meet the trail junction just above Rancheria Falls, at 19.8 miles. Turn right (north) and follow Hike 52 in reverse to the trailhead at the dam.

54 Jack Main Canyon and Tilden Lake

General description:	Overnight loop hike that extends into the remote North Boundary country.
Total distance:	44.8 miles.
Difficulty:	Moderately strenuous.
Elevation gain:	5,100 feet.
Trail traffic:	Heavy at beginning and end, light in the middle.
Best months:	Mid July–September.
Maps:	USGS Hetch Hetchy Reservoir, Kibbie Lake, Lake Eleanor, Tiltill Mountain and Piute Mountain quads.
Permits:	Available in advance or from the Hetch Hetchy Entrance Station.

Finding the trailhead: Drive 1 mile west of the Big Oak Flat Entrance Station to Yosemite on California 120. Turn right (north) onto Evergreen Road and drive about 7 miles. At Camp Mather turn right (northeast) onto Hetch Hetchy Road. Pass through the park entrance station in about a mile, then continue on for 8 miles to where the road ends in a one-way loop. Partway around is the dam, and just beyond it, a parking area.

Trailhead facilities: Water, restrooms, and phones on the right side of the Hetch Hetchy Road, just before the dam and the parking area on the one-way loop.

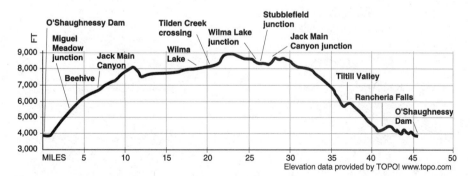

Elevation data provided by TOPO! www.topo.com

Key points:

    0.0   O'Shaughnessy Dam Trailhead.

    8.1   Jack Main Canyon junction.

Jack Main Canyon and Tilden Lake

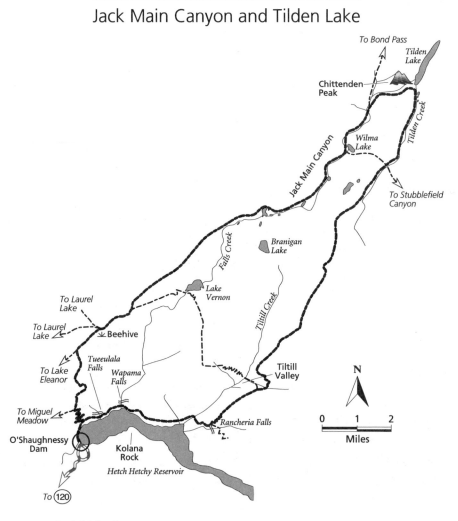

15.1   Jack Main Canyon.
18.1   Wilma or Wilmer Lake.
20.0   Tilden Creek Crossing.
21.7   Tilden Lake outlet.
25.4   Wilma Lake junction.
25.5   Stubblefield junction.
28.1   Jack Main Canyon junction.
35.9   Tiltill Valley.

The hike: This hike has been included in the Hetch Hetchy section because it begins and ends there, but part of it extends into the remote north boundary country where spring runoff in early season makes some sections of trail completely impassable and many creek crossings extremely dangerous. Be sure to check with the park service about trail conditions before beginning this hike.

Follow Hike 53 to the Jack Main Canyon junction at 8.1 miles, where you keep left and climb Moraine Ridge. This stretch of trail can be tiring. Part of it is shaded, part is open, grassy, and waterless, with heavy sand underfoot that makes uphill progress tedious. Drop down off the toe of Moraine Ridge on a section of trail known as the Golden Stairs into Jack Main Canyon, and along the way enjoy a glimpse of one of the Branigan Lakes to the east. At the base of the stairs, meet Falls Creek, which drops into Hetch Hetchy Reservoir as Wapama Falls far below. It must be one of the most interesting and beautiful streams in Yosemite. It winds its way along the floor of Jack Main Canyon, cascading from pool to pool, widening out in lazy meanders through blooming meadows, and roaring through narrow gaps in the canyon walls. There are plenty of good places to camp, the finest being on sunny rock slabs above one of the many small, unnamed lakes. The trail undulates over uneven ground that is sometimes very rocky, sometimes very sloppy, sometimes completely underwater. At 15.1 miles, a trail heads off to the east to connect with the Pacific Crest Trail (PCT) in a little more than 2 miles. You can make a shorter loop using this route if you don't have time for the longer one, or if the trail farther north at Wilma Lake is flooded.

To continue, keep left and continue to ascend very gradually, passing through interesting, narrow slots that have trapped snowmelt lakes that have no inlets or outlets. Pass to the west of a long, wide meadow just below Wilma Lake. You can't reach the lake directly from here, but must continue north to the junction with the Pacific Crest Trail, at 18.1 miles, then cut back along the PCT to the south to reach the lakeshore. If the water is high, this section may be too deep and wide to negotiate.

Return to the main trail. Your trail and the Pacific Crest Trail now coincide and continue north. Pass through a gate and wander along the flat valley floor to 20 miles, where you leave the PCT again and turn right (east). Climb a ridge to meet the southern end of Tilden Lake at its outlet at 21.7 miles, where Chittenden Peak squats beside the outlet. Tilden Lake is a classic glacial finger lake that has plenty of good camping on its southeast side. There are great views up the lake canyon, with Tower Peak at the far end. The trail follows the irregular shore for a while, then swings south through meadows and pools and climbs to meet the PCT at 25.4 miles. Keep left here. The right fork goes back to Wilma Lake.

In a very short time, at 25.5 miles, leave the PCT as it goes east toward Stubblefield Canyon. Your trail goes right (southwest), dropping into a valley just west of main Tilden Canyon through more grassy, marshy meadows and ponds, then climbs to a junction with the trail back over to Jack Main Canyon, at 28.1 miles. Just beyond this are good views back to Tower Peak and the surrounding wilderness. Descend very gradually now through the forest to the south until you reach a ridge where you descend more steeply over rocks through hot, open brush toward Tiltill Valley, which is now visible below with the Hetch Hetchy Reservoir beyond. At the end of a knee-knocking drop, splash through the meadow at Tiltill Valley to meet the trail back down to Rancheria Falls, at 35.9 miles. Now follow Hike 52 in reverse back to the dam.

The North Boundary Country

The North Boundary Country

This is Yosemite at its wildest. It is part of the largest roadless area in California, and one of the largest in the United States. The average elevation here is lower than in other parts of Yosemite, though the northeastern crest has some high peaks. The topography away from the crest appears to be more rolling, too, but the hiking is no less strenuous. The glaciers that shaped the land have gouged a series of parallel canyons that make east-west hiking exhausting. There is more open rock and fewer extensive stands of forest because the recent (in geologic terms) glaciers have scoured away most of the soil. When the snow melts in spring these rocky canyons carry enormous volumes of water, at least partly because there is little soil to absorb it. Early in the year, even well into July, big sections of the trails may be completely submerged, and many stream crossings are high and very dangerous. Trails are not as frequently patrolled or maintained, so you must be well prepared, must be skilled at route finding, and must take special pains to find out about trail conditions before you start.

The shorter hikes that begin near U.S. Highway 395 on the eastern border of the park are popular, since most pass through part of the Hoover Wilderness, part of the Toiyabe and Inyo national forests, which allow more commercial development than the park service does. The forest service also stocks the hundreds of lakes with trout and permits hunting, so day hikers will meet lots of fishermen, and in fall, a few hunters. Hikers who have penetrated farther than a day's journey into the park from any of its borders, or those who have entered from one of the more remote trailheads to the north, however, will only meet other hardy souls like themselves and a few through-hikers on the Pacific Crest Trail.

All the hikes in this section except Hike 61 begin off U.S. Highway 395, or Tioga Road, California 120. Supplies and gas can be found in Lee Vining or Bridgeport on U.S. Highway 395, and in Tuolumne Meadows. Trailheads with small resorts like Mono Village, Saddlebag Lake, Lundy Lake, Virginia Pass, and Tioga Pass have cafés and limited groceries.

For hikes beginning outside Yosemite, get permits at the Mono Basin or Bridgeport USDA Forest Service ranger stations. They are good inside the park, and are also subject to trailhead quotas.

55 Saddlebag Lake and 20 Lakes Basin

General description:	A day-hike loop that is a favorite among Yosemite's hikers.
Total distance:	8.3 miles.
Difficulty:	Moderate.
Elevation gain:	310 feet.
Trail traffic:	Moderately heavy.
Best months:	All summer; whenever Tioga Road is open; however, high water, wet meadows, and deep snow sometimes make travel difficult early in the season.
Maps:	USGS Dunderberg Peak and Tioga Pass quads.
Permits:	None for a day hike. Available at the kiosk in the backpackers' parking lot at Saddlebag Lake, or from the Mono Basin Visitor Center just outside Lee Vining at Mono Lake.

Finding the trailhead: From Tioga Road (California 120) drive about a mile east of the Yosemite Park entrance and turn west onto Saddlebag Lake Road. Drive 2.5 miles over partly paved road to the south end of the lake. Follow the signs to the backpackers' parking lot near the wilderness permit kiosk or to the day-use parking area at the end of the road.

Trailhead facilities: None; café, store, and nearby campground at Saddlebag Lake Resort.

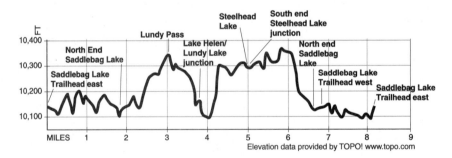

Key points:
- 0.0   Saddlebag Lake Trailhead east.
- 2.2   North end of Saddlebag Lake.
- 3.1   Lundy Pass.
- 3.9   Helen Lake/Lundy Lake junction.
- 4.9   Steelhead Lake.
- 5.4   South Steelhead Lake junction.
- 6.6   North end Saddlebag Lake.
- 6.7   Saddlebag Lake Trailhead west.

Saddlebag Lake and 20 Lakes Basin

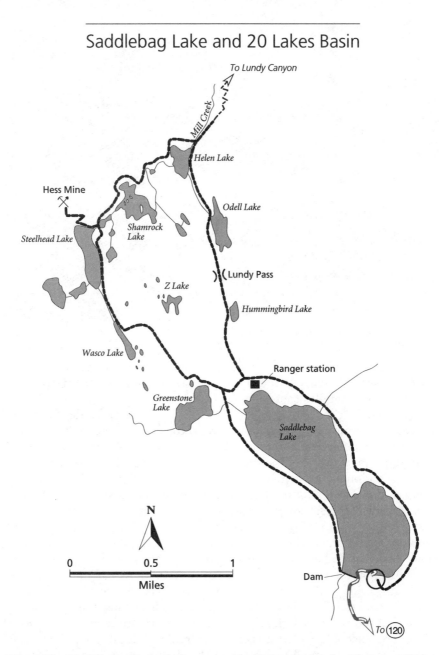

To Lundy Canyon

Mill Creek

Helen Lake

Hess Mine

Odell Lake

Shamrock Lake

Steelhead Lake

Z Lake

)(*Lundy Pass*

Hummingbird Lake

Wasco Lake

Ranger station

Greenstone Lake

Saddlebag Lake

N

| 0 | 0.5 | 1 |

Miles

Dam

To (120)

The hike: Saddlebag Lake is just outside Yosemite in the Hoover Wilderness and, like Lundy Canyon, is a favorite of Yosemite hikers. It is also a backdoor cross-country entrance into the park by way of McCabe Lakes. The region behind and including Saddlebag Lake is known as the 20 Lakes Basin, but is not identified by that name (or any other) name on the topo. The loop can be hiked in either direction but the views are better if you proceed counterclockwise. The lakes are stocked with trout and are simply swarming with fishermen. The little resort near the trailhead operates a

Shamrock Lake and North Peak in the 20 Lakes Basin.

shuttle boat that will drop you off at the far end of the lake and pick you up later at whatever time you specify, if you are in a hurry. It is inexpensive and saves you 1.5 miles each way.

Begin at the closed gate near the sign welcoming hikers to the basin and warning that campfires are prohibited. Skirt the eastern shore of the lake on broken red and black rock. While this entire basin is a veritable wonderland of wildflowers, this part of the trail is lined with sagebrush and pennyroyal and is exceptionally aromatic. Directly ahead is the Shepherd Crest culminating in the sharp point of Sheep Peak, surprisingly white among the adjoining rusty peaks. As you progress along Saddlebag's eastern shore, North Peak gradually appears from behind a nearby ridge, then, even bigger Mount Conness, among the highest peaks in the park at 13,053 feet. It shelters a small glacier at its base. A ranger station that looks like a little dollhouse surrounded by the round white heads of flowers known as ranger buttons stands at the end of the lake above the shuttle boat landing.

Just beyond the cabin, at 2.2 miles, the trail splits. Follow the right (north) fork and climb easily past the sign announcing the entrance to the Hoover Wilderness. Just beyond, to the right of the trail, is little Hummingbird Lake. Above it are a few small campsites in the shelter of the whitebark pine. Cross the outlet from the lake over rather flimsy logs and continue climbing to Lundy Pass, at 3.1 miles. Below soaring, rusty red-and-black cliffs lies Odell Lake, with an odd little round island in the middle. Descend to the northwestern shore of the lake, then follow its outlet down a steep, narrow, rocky gorge, crossing the creek partway down, to Helen Lake. This gorge holds some snow for most of the year, and in early season it may be too steep, icy, and dangerous to attempt.

The path around the eastern side of Helen Lake goes along a rocky and precipitous slope to the outlet where a sign at 3.9 miles points the way to Lundy Canyon, straight ahead (the end point of Hike 53). Your route is to the left (west). Follow a use-trail not shown on the topo map, around the west side of the lake. It's quite distinct, and passes several little ponds, waterfalls, and meadows spangled with alpine wildflowers. Climb a beautifully ice-polished ridge and follow ducks to look out upon one of the prettiest views in the Sierra. Shamrock Lake below has an irregular rocky shoreline and several picturesque islands, all trimmed with perfect arrangements of gnarled whitebark pine and brilliant, magenta mountain pride pentstemon. Beyond, North Peak provides a majestic backdrop. The trail descends around the west side of Shamrock to another small unnamed lake. Here, a very short steep path drops down to the right to meet an old mining road running past Steelhead Lake, at 4.9 miles. The road ends about 100 yards to the right at the abandoned Hess Mine.

The flat ridge above the mine between North and Sheep peaks is a fairly easy cross-country route into Yosemite via McCabe Lakes. Your present route turns left, crossing an outlet from the lake on a log, and follows the road southward along the main outlet from Steelhead Lake. At 5.4 miles, a trail cuts off from the road to the right toward the western shore. Stay on the road, which swings left just above Wasco Lake, then turns right again to parallel Greenstone Lake. A low, flat isthmus separates Wasco from Saddlebag Lake, and several use-trails leave the road to cross to the west side of the basin, at 6.6 miles. Some of these fade out partway across the meadow and some arrive at the creek connecting the two lakes, at a place where it is impossible to cross. Follow any (or none) of these paths to wherever you can ford easily and pick up the trail on the other side heading south along the western shore of Saddlebag Lake. Follow the rough, rocky path along the mountainside to the dam, at 6.7 miles. You can cross on the top of the dam if the spillway is closed, or if it is open, follow a trail downstream and over a bridge to meet Saddlebag Lake Road, on which you turn left and proceed to your car.

56 Lundy Canyon

General description:	Out-and-back day hike or shuttle to a beautiful canyon full of wildflowers and waterfalls.
Total distance:	10.8 miles.
Difficulty:	Strenuous.
Elevation gain:	1,940 feet.
Trail traffic:	Moderate.
Best months:	July–October.
Maps:	USGS Dunderberg Peak quad.
Permits:	None for a day hike. Backpacker permits at the Mono Basin Visitor Center, just outside Lee Vining at Mono Lake.

Finding the trailhead: From U.S. Highway 395 take the Lundy Lake turn-off 7 miles north of Lee Vining. Drive west 5 miles to the far end of Lundy Lake. When the road forks just below the lake, keep right. The left fork ends at the dam. Pass the tiny general store and continue for about a mile on a narrow bumpy road through a campground to where the road makes a one-way loop.

Trailhead facilities: Parking, pit toilet; snacks, toilets, and water at Lundy Lake Resort.

Key points:

0.0   Trailhead.

5.0   Helen Lake.

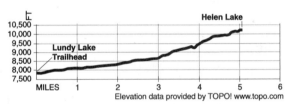

The hike: Lundy Canyon is part of the Hoover Wilderness. It does not actually belong to Yosemite, but it can be used as a route into the park via a short cross-country connection. At any rate, it is well known to those who love Yosemite and is included here because it is the most beautiful canyon in the area, with the finest wildflower display, the most brilliant fall colors, and the greatest number of waterfalls.

Begin along the northeast slope of Lundy Canyon above Mill Creek on colorful red, black, and white rock. A very active population of beavers has dammed the lower part of the creek in several places, but eventually the slope becomes too steep and the stream too rapid for the dams as it drops over the first of several sets of waterfalls. The trail crosses the creek amid riotously blooming flower gardens under dense quaking aspen, whose brilliant golden foliage more than compensates for the lack of blooms in late September. Cross another branch of the creek on logs and come to the remains of an old trapper's cabin. Out in the open again, waterfalls fall down the cliffs on all sides of the canyon above the aspen groves. The low contorted shapes of these trees hint of the violence of snow and rockfall that occur here during winter.

Lundy Canyon

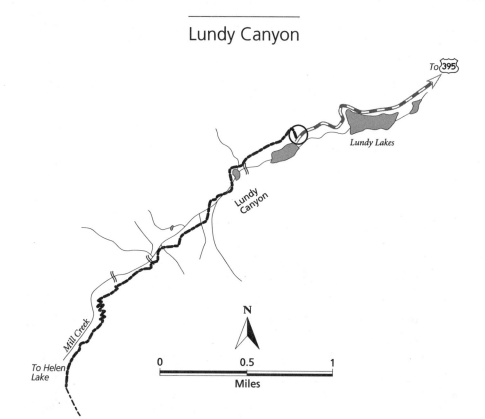

The trail now begins to climb the slope above the canyon. Ignore any apparent trails that cut away from the main route, and continue upward southwest, then due south, zigzagging up a very steep and rough, slatey slope. Partway to the top of the ridge, the trail meets Mill Creek and climbs close alongside it, as it tumbles down a gully. The top of this gully holds snow until quite late in the year. If the trail is mostly snow covered or icy, do not continue upward without crampons or an ice axe. At last, the trail tops a rise and enters the 20 Lakes Basin. A very short distance farther, Mill Creek rushes through a narrow slot, beyond which lies Helen Lake. Beyond, North Peak rises above a permanent snowfield, and just behind it Mount Conness shades the Conness Glacier. This is the 20 Lakes Basin, though it is not named on the map.

You can return this way, descending the rocky gully very cautiously, or you can continue on down into the basin, exploring the lakes and skirting big Saddlebag Lake, where you can leave a car or arrange to be picked up. (See Hike 54.) There is camping in the Upper part of Lundy Canyon as well as in the 20 Lakes Basin, but no fires are allowed.

57 Green Creek

General description: Out-and-back day hike or overnighter to a drainage rich with interesting geology, lakes, forests, and aspen, golden in the fall.

Total distance: 11.6 miles.

Difficulty: Moderate as a backpack, strenuous as a day hike.

Elevation gain: 1,720 feet.

Trail traffic: Moderate.

Best months: Late September–mid-October for fall foliage; fine hiking and fishing all summer.

Maps: USGS Dunderberg Peak quad.

Permits: Required for an overnight stay, available from the USDA Forest Service ranger station in Bridgeport. No permit required for a day hike.

Finding the trailhead: From U.S. Highway 395, turn west on Green Creek Road 21 miles north of Lee Vining, 4.7 miles south of Bridgeport. Follow the dirt road for about 10 miles, just past the Green Creek Campground to the parking area.

Trailhead facilities: Drinking water and toilets at the Green Creek Campground.

Key points:

0.0   Green Creek Trailhead.

2.0   Green Creek Trail/ West Lake Trail junction.

3.5   East Lake.

4.5   Gilman Lake.

5.8   Hoover Lake.

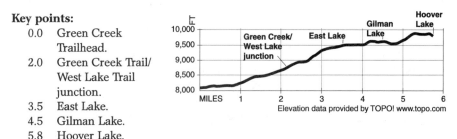

Elevation data provided by TOPO! www.topo.com

The hike: The Green Creek drainage offers high drama and great photos because of its vivid, red-and-white metamorphic rocks, intensely blue lakes, green forests, and, in fall, golden aspen. From the parking area, the trail rambles alongside Green Creek through dense quaking aspen groves and lots of water-loving wildflowers, then climbs steeply beside a series of noisy cascades. A sign marks the entrance to the Hoover Wilderness. Continue to climb steadily to a junction with the West Lake Trail, at 2 miles. Take the left fork south past the northwest corner of Green Lake, usually lined with anglers. The USDA Forest Service stocks these lakes but the park service does not stock its lakes, so the fishing is more challenging beyond the Yosemite Park border. There are plenty of good campsites around this lake, but you will have lots of neighbors.

Cross the stream and climb the steep switchbacks alongside, crossing again at the outlet from East Lake, largest in the basin, at 3.5 miles. There is a small,

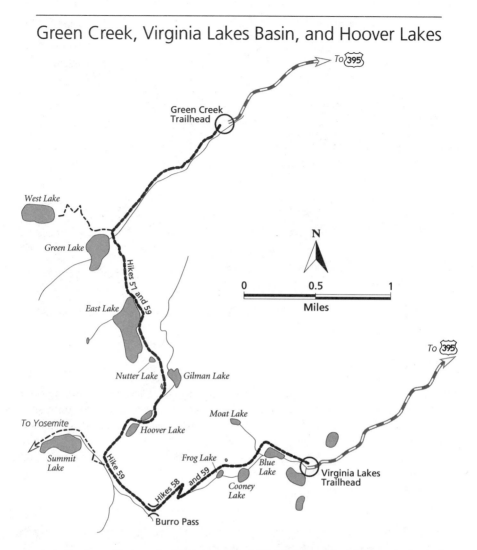

Green Creek, Virginia Lakes Basin, and Hoover Lakes

To (395)

Green Creek
Trailhead

West Lake

Green Lake

Hikes 51 and 59

East Lake

N

0   0.5   1
Miles

To (395)

Nutter Lake   Gilman Lake

Moat Lake

To Yosemite

Hoover Lake

Summit
Lake

Frog Lake

Blue
Lake

Virginia Lakes
Trailhead

Hike 59

Hikes 58 and 59

Cooney
Lake

Burro Pass

manmade dam that probably made the lake bigger than it was originally. There is plenty of camping near the dam. The trail follows the shoreline very closely for a time, then clambers over more open rocky ridges above the lake. Just beyond, beautiful little Nutter Lake appears below the trail at the base of a smooth rock outcrop, trimmed with red mountain heather in summer and bright red Sierra bilberry in fall. After passing a small, unnamed pond, Gilman Lake appears down in a pocket to the left (east), at 4.5 miles. A faint, unmarked spur trail leads down to the lakeside. You will find more solitude here than at some of the other lakes, since it is off the trail.

Cross the Gilman Lake inlet very carefully. The rocks are smooth and slimy here, and have soaked many a backpacker and pack. Ascend through a subalpine forest of lodgepole, whitebark pine, graceful, droopy mountain hemlock, and tall, straight, dignified silver pines. These last, with their reddish bark in more-or-less regular square plates, are widely scattered and

East Lake, the largest in the Green Creek drainage.

relatively uncommon.

All but small patches of trees are left behind as the rocky path skirts the lakeshore of the lower Hoover Lake on one side and the steep, shaley base of the ridge on the other, at 5.8 miles. There are a few isolated camping sites in clumps of trees near the lakes, but for the most part, camping here is bleak and exposed. The two Hoover lakes are separated by a narrow strip of broken rock, beneath which you can hear water flowing from the upper to the lower lake. Return the way you came.

58 Virginia Lakes Basin

See map on page 191

General description: An out-and-back high-elevation hike through a cluster of timberline lakes.
Total distance: 6.6 miles.
Difficulty: Moderately strenuous.
Elevation gain: 1,260 feet.
Trail traffic: Moderate.
Best months: July–September.
Maps: USGS Dunderberg Peak quad.
Permits: None for a day hike; for a backpack, they're available from the USDA Forest Service ranger station in Bridgeport.

Finding the trailhead: From U.S. Highway 395 at Conway Summit north of Mono Lake, take Virginia Lakes Road west for 6 miles. Beyond the pack station, the road forks. To the left is a small lodge, store, and café. To the right is the USDA Forest Service Trumbull Campground, and beyond that, the marked trailhead and hikers' parking lot.

Trailhead facilities: Store, café, lodge, and telephone at the largest of the Virginia lakes.

Key points:

  0.0 Trailhead.
  1.8 Frog Lakes.
  3.3 "Burro" Pass.

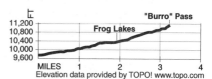

The hike: This hike is actually outside the Yosemite Park boundary in the Hoover Wilderness of the Toiyabe National Forest, but it is a convenient and very scenic route to many more hikes in the north boundary country of the park and beyond.

The trail begins climbing gradually around the north shore of Blue Lake. A long, cascading waterfall flowing from Cooney and Moat lakes above feeds the far end of the lake. There is nothing subtle about this scenery. While most of the basin containing the brilliant sapphire of the lake is gray granite, Dunderberg Peak to your right (north) is red, and Black Mountain to the left (south) is . . . you guessed it . . . black. White snow patches and green clumps of forest make this basin a favorite with color photographers.

The rocky slope beside Blue Lake is home to a colony of pikas, busy little earth-colored creatures related to rabbits, which scamper over the rocks of the high country all summer, cutting plant material to store in their burrows under the rubble for winter use. The bundles of grass they carry as they scurry over the talus makes them appear to have huge green mustaches. You can hear their sharp chirps of alarm as you approach, but they become invisible when immobile. If you stand quietly for a few minutes until they decide you are not dangerous, they will resume their activities.

As the trail climbs, it passes an old miner's log cabin, crosses the outlet from Moat Lake, then ascends through forest to the north shore of Cooney Lake. After gaining the shelf above the lake, it flattens out as it crosses a creek and winds through the open meadow basin containing the Frog Lakes, at 1.8 miles. The gnarled whitebark pines that mark timberline are left behind now as you climb toward the head of the canyon, passing one last stark unnamed lake before puffing up the few remaining steep switchbacks, sometimes through late-lying snowfields, to the pass, at 3.3 miles. This pass is unnamed on the USGS topos, but is known as "Burro Pass" to locals. There is another "real" officially-named Burro Pass to the west near Matterhorn Peak, so don't get the two confused. Whatever its name, it is actually just a broad, flat bench. Make sure to cross over to the west side before turning around or you will miss the dramatic multicolored panorama that includes the Sawtooth Range to the north behind Summit Lake. If you have come for only a day hike, return the way you came.

59 Hoover Lakes

See map on page 191

General description: Shuttle hike with a moderate climb to great views.
Total distance: 10.8 miles.
Difficulty: Strenuous.
Elevation gain: 1,380 feet.
Trail traffic: Moderate.
Best months: July–September
Maps: USGS Dunderberg Peak quad.
Permits: Available from the USDA Forest Service ranger station in Bridgeport.

Finding the trailhead: From U.S. Highway 395, turn west onto the Green Creek Road 21 miles north of Lee Vining, or 4.7 miles south of Bridgeport. Follow the dirt road for about 10 miles, just past the Green Creek Campground to the parking area. Leave another car or arrange to be picked up at the Virginia Lakes Trailhead (see Hike 55). The two trailheads are about 25 miles apart.

Trailhead facilities: Store, café, phones at Virginia Lakes Trailhead; pit toilets and water only at Green Creek.

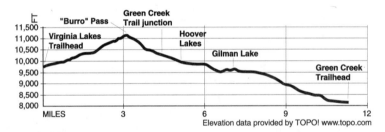

Elevation data provided by TOPO! www.topo.com

Key points:
- 0.0   Virginia Lakes Trailhead.
- 3.3   "Burro" Pass.
- 4.3   Green Creek Trail junction.
- 5.0   Hoover Lakes.

The hike: Follow Hike 55 to the ridge at the head of the canyon known locally as Burro Pass, at 3.3 miles, the highest point on this hike. When you have recovered from both the climb and the awe-inspiring vista of the Virginia and Camaica peaks to the north and the desolate, wildly beautiful country in between, head down on black, slatey slabs along a gully that usually holds snow well into summer. It is hard to watch your step over the steep rocky path, with so much to see. Dozens of species of pastel alpine wildflowers like the pale pinkish alpine columbines, are especially attractive growing out of cracks in the black rock.

At 4.3 miles you'll reach the junction with the Green Creek Trail. If you have time, you might make a half-mile detour up a gully to the wild, windblown shore of Summit Lake. The Yosemite Park boundary is at the far

Pikas, or rock rabbits, are abundant in the high country.

end. Back at the junction, follow the right (east) fork and descend to Hoover Lakes, at 5 miles. From here follow Hike 54 down to the trailhead.

60 Matterhorn Canyon

General description:	Shuttle hike to Upper Hoover Lake.
Total distance:	39.1 miles.
Difficulty:	Moderately strenuous.
Elevation gain:	3,410 feet.
Trail traffic:	Light, except at beginning and end.
Best months:	All summer; especially beautiful in September when the aspens turn gold and the bilberry ground cover is brilliant red.
Maps:	USGS Buckeye Ridge, Dunderberg Peak, Falls Ridge, Matterhorn Peak, and Twin Lakes quads.
Permits:	Required. Available from the USDA Forest Service ranger station in Bridgeport.

Finding the trailhead: From Bridgeport turn west off U.S. Highway 395 onto Twin Lakes Road and follow it about 13 miles to its end at Mono Village. Supervised overnight parking is available for a flat rate of $5. Drive to the kiosk in front of the campground for a parking permit and directions to the backpackers' lot. Behind the kiosk look for the sign that reads "Barney

Matterhorn Canyon

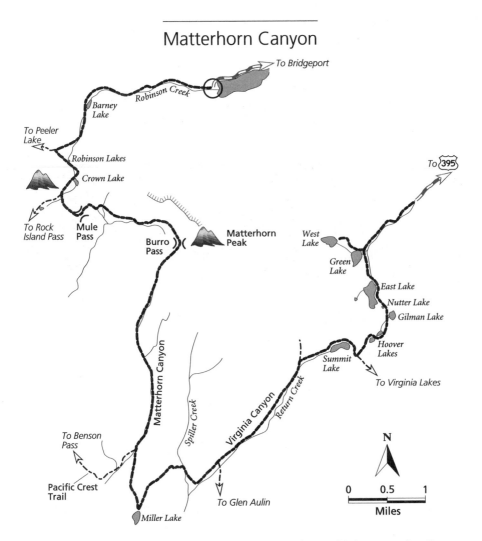

Lake Trail." Leave a second car (or arrange to be picked up) at the Green Creek Trailhead, 4.7 miles south of Bridgeport, 10 miles southeast of U.S. Highway 395.

Trailhead facilities: Water and restrooms at Green Creek; groceries, café, water, and phones at Mono Village.

Key points:
- 0.0   Mono Village.
- 4.0   Barney Lake.
- 6.3   Peeler Lake junction.
- 8.0   Crown Lake.
- 8.7   Rock Island Pass junction.
- 10.1   Mule Pass (Yosemite Park boundary).
- 12.8   Burro Pass.
- 19.0   Benson Pass Trail junction.
- 20.5   Miller Lake.
- 24.8   Return Creek.
- 28.8   Virginia Pass junction.
- 29.9   Summit Pass (Yosemite Park boundary).
- 31.9   Green Creek Trail.
- 32.9   Upper Hoover Lake.

The hike: The trail goes directly through the campground on a road until it reaches a meadow. Climb over a chain blocking the way, then turn right at another sign and leave the road. Pass through a forest of Jeffrey pine, then an aspen grove, then into the open, where you'll see a glorious panorama of Robinson, Eagle, Victoria, and Hunewell peaks and the Sawtooth Ridge. In the foreground is a field of mule ears, lupine, and in early season, irises. After passing the mouth of Little Slide Canyon coming in from the south, enter another grove of aspen and climb moderate switchbacks up through flowery gardens and cross a couple of little runnels until you reach Barney Lake, at 4 miles. It is overused around the edge, but if you cross the outlet stream on logs, you will find beautiful campsites among junipers above the lake's east side.

Skirt Barney Lake's west shore, watching for pikas in the rock piles and signs of beavers at the upper end of the swampy area above the lake. Cross Robinson Creek and begin switchbacking uphill, sometimes through a forest of graceful mountain hemlocks, sometimes through open rocky areas. At 6.3 miles, meet the junction with the Peeler Lake Trail, which goes off to the northwest. Your trail turns south, winds around a few big rocky outcrops, then drops into a basin, first passing a little pond with water improbably blue-green, then past the north edge of lower Robinson Lake. Camping at Robinson Lakes is usually too damp and buggy for comfort. The trail crosses an isthmus between the two lakes, climbs a few switchbacks, cuts through a gap where snow often lingers until late in the season, then reaches Crown Lake, at 8 miles. Backed by Crown Point, the lake is stunning, but the only camping nearby is at the lake's north end on sandy spaces among the rocks.

The trail skirts Crown Lake for a short distance before switchbacking up the slope to the west, past little pocket meadows with little lakes and miniature gardens to a junction with the Rock Island Pass Trail, at 8.5 miles. Keep left as your trail curves gently southward and continue up a narrowing gully,

Matterhorn Canyon and Sawtooth Ridge.

often partly snow filled. Just below the top is another sparkling little lake. The trail flattens out a bit just before reaching 10,400-foot Mule Pass, at 10.1 miles. This is the entrance to Yosemite.

The Sawtooth Ridge spreads out along the horizon with Matterhorn Peak at its far end. The trail descends, then rises to cross a little saddle, then drops down a gulch into the Piute Creek drainage, bottoming out at 9,400 feet. Follow the creek, climbing gently past numerous cascades and a small waterfall through a carpet of dwarf bilberry, brilliant green in summer, rich red in fall. There are several good campsites here along the creek.

Continue climbing moderately, heading straight for Matterhorn Peak until the sparse whitebark pine gives out altogether; the route curves south, and you easily cross Burro Pass, at 12.8 miles. At 10,600 feet, this is the highest point on the route.

The trail descends along the west side of the big bowl at the head of Matterhorn Canyon, then eases down very gently alongside Matterhorn Creek past some spectacular avalanche areas—the velocity of the snow was so great here that trees were flattened all the way down one side of the canyon and halfway up the other. Be sure to glance backward now and then as you descend. The jagged Sawtooth Ridge on the horizon back at the head of the canyon is spectacular. There are small campsites for the first couple of miles in the canyon, but after you have passed Quarry Peak, the walls narrow and camping becomes more difficult.

Cross Matterhorn Creek three times before reaching the junction with the Pacific Crest Trail, at 19 miles, then follow it almost due south, leaving the stream and climbing fairly steeply out of the canyon. The trail levels out just before a big meadow, at the far end of which lies Miller Lake, at 20.5

miles. This is a good, shallow, warm lake for swimming, and there is good camping across the meadow from the trail in the timber.

From the lake the route gently undulates, passing a couple more little ponds, goes through a gate, and makes a last steep, sandy climb out of the basin. Then it drops steeply on dusty switchbacks, down to cross Spiller Creek just before its confluence with Return Creek in Virginia Canyon, at 24.8 miles. Now you leave the Pacific Crest Trail and walk up Virginia Canyon, gaining elevation very gradually, passing more avalanche chutes on the way. Cross to the east side of Return Creek one last time to find the Virginia Pass junction on the far side, at 28.8 miles. There is a small, mediocre campsite just upstream.

Now climb the steep, forested slope to Summit Pass at 29.9 miles, leaving Yosemite at the top. Skirt the northern shore of Summit Lake, which is very beautiful but often very windy. Since it is also quite fragile, camping is discouraged near the lake, though there are a few small, protected sites past its east end. The trail drops below the lake along a flowery creek, rock-hops over another shallow stream, and turns left (north), climbing a little until it meets the Green Creek Trail junction, at 31.9 miles. Continue on down Green Creek to Hoover Lakes, at 32.9 miles. From here, follow Hike 55 in reverse to the Green Creek Trailhead.

61 Benson Pass

General description: A challenging overnight loop hike through diverse habitats.

Total distance: 59 miles.

Difficulty: Strenuous.

Elevation gain: 1,520 feet.

Trail traffic: Light to moderate.

Best months: July–September. Early in July the Grand Canyon of the Tuolumne is at its finest, but the creeks in the higher country may be too high to cross safely. Later in the year the lower section can be hot and dry. Be sure to check on trail conditions before beginning this hike.

Maps: USGS Dunderberg Peak, Falls Ridge, Matterhorn Peak, Ten Lakes, and Tioga Pass quads.

Permits: Available in advance or from the visitor center in Tuolumne Meadows.

Finding the trailhead: From the west, follow Tioga Road (California 120) past the Tuolumne Meadows Visitor Center, store, café, and campground, all on the right. Just after crossing the bridge over the Tuolumne River, turn left (north) into the Lembert Dome parking area. From the east (Tioga Pass), follow Tioga Road past the turnoff to the wilderness center on the left and

Benson Pass

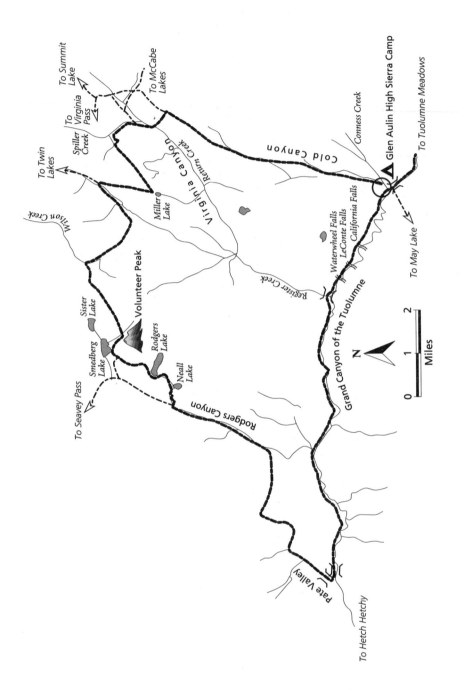

continue about a hundred yards to the Lembert Dome parking area on the right. You can also ride the Tuolumne Meadows shuttle bus to Stop 4, Lembert Dome. Overnight parking is prohibited in the parking lot, so park along the paved road parallel to Tioga Road. At a closed gate, this road turns sharply to the right and heads toward the stables. The trail begins at the gate.

Trailhead facilities: Store, café, phones, and campground at Tuolumne Meadows.

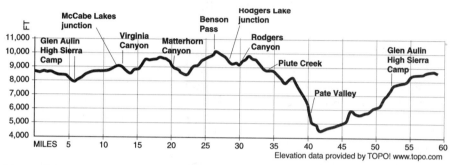

Elevation data provided by TOPO! www.topo.com

Key points:

0.0	Trailhead.
5.2	Glen Aulin High Sierra Camp.
12.2	McCabe Lakes junction.
13.2	Virginia Canyon.
19.0	Matterhorn Canyon.
26.5	Rodgers Lake junction.
27.1	Seavey Pass junction.
30.1	Rodgers Canyon.
34.9	Piute Creek.
39.5	Pate Valley.

The hike: Follow Hike 21 to the High Sierra camp at 5.2 miles, then head northward, still on the Pacific Crest Trail, partly through open forest, partly through meadow, up Cold Canyon, with Mount Conness at its head. The McCabe Lakes junction, at 12.2 miles, is not shown correctly on the topo, but if you stay left, following the PCT, you'll be on track. At 13.2 miles keep left again, dropping to cross Spiller Creek, then climbing fairly steeply on dusty switchbacks. Pass through a gate, and make another sandy descent, cross a low rise, pass a couple of shallow ponds, then emerge into the meadow bordering Miller Lake. It's a nice warm lake for swimming and there is good camping in the timber across the meadow from the trail. Leaving the lake, the trail swings back northward, crossing a shoulder with views to the Sawtooth Ridge, then drops steeply into Matterhorn Canyon, at 19 miles, in a flowery meadow where there is more good camping. The Pacific Crest Trail makes a sharp dogleg here cutting back southwest, crossing Matterhorn Creek, and following alongside its broad, meandering course downstream for more than a mile. The trail swings northwest, climbing along Wilson Creek, which it crosses several times before it turns west and climbs switchbacks to wide, grassy Benson Pass, decorated with whitebark pine. Descend fairly gradually from the pass and wade across the outlet of Smedberg Lake at the edge of a meadow. Beyond, the lake lies at the foot of blocky Volunteer Peak. There is good camping at the lake, but the best is on the shore opposite the trail.

After leaving Smedberg Lake, reach a junction at the steep west base of Volunteer Peak, at 26.5 miles. Here you leave the PCT, which cuts off westerly toward Seavey Pass. Continue south, climb an open grassy hump, and descend to Rodgers Lake at the base of flat-topped, red Regulation Peak, with pointed West Peak to the south. Continue descending a short spur to Neall Lake in a little hollow fringed by forest. Camping is best near the lake's outlet by forest.

Soon after leaving Neall Lake, meet a junction in Rodgers Canyon, at 30.1 miles, turn left (south) and follow along the meandering creek through a broad meadow. The grade steepens as you head down Rodgers Canyon toward the Tuolumne River Canyon. Eventually the trail swings west and leaves Rodgers Creek, your last source of water if the season is late. Cross a low saddle, then meet the Piute Creek junction, at 34.9 miles. Turn left (west) and tighten your boots for the long, long, knee-bashing, toe-squashing descent to the river. As you lose elevation, the vegetation changes to ponderosa pine, incense-cedar, and black oak in the places where there is still some tree cover, and it can become uncomfortably hot. At last you reach the cool green pools and refreshing cascades along the Tuolumne, at 39.5 miles, at the upper end of Pate Valley. Your route goes upstream to the left, but there is camping downstream in the lower part of the valley. Watch out for rattlesnakes in this low country. Pate Valley is a notorious bear hangout, too.

From Pate Valley, follow Hike 41 in reverse back to Glen Aulin High Sierra Camp and on to the trailhead at Tuolumne Meadows.

62 McCabe Lakes

General description:	Out-and-back overnight hike to Lower McCabe Lake and the base of Sheep Peak.
Total distance:	30.4 miles.
Difficulty:	Moderate–strenuous.
Elevation gain:	2,100 feet.
Trail traffic:	Moderate.
Best months:	July–September.
Maps:	USGS Dunderberg Peak, Tioga Pass, Matterhorn Peak, and Falls Ridge quads.
Permits:	Required, available from the USDA Forest Service ranger station in Bridgeport.

McCabe Lakes

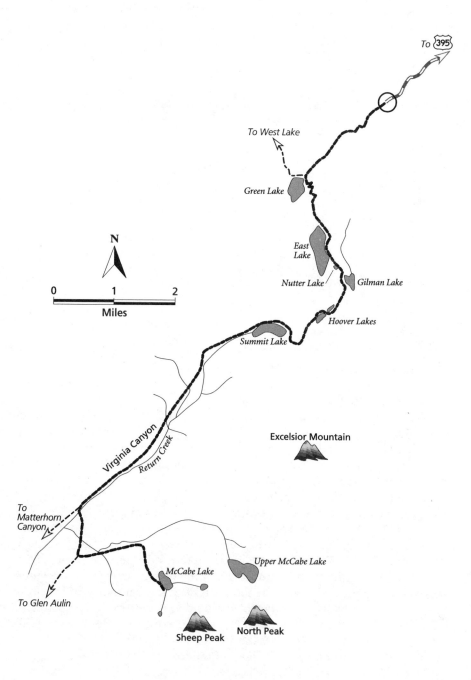

To 395

To West Lake

Green Lake

East Lake

Nutter Lake

Gilman Lake

Hoover Lakes

Summit Lake

N

0   1   2
Miles

Virginia Canyon

Return Creek

Excelsior Mountain

To Matterhorn Canyon

To Glen Aulin

McCabe Lake

Upper McCabe Lake

Sheep Peak

North Peak

Finding the trailhead: From U.S. Highway 395, turn west on Green Creek Road 21 miles north of Lee Vining, 4.7 miles south of Bridgeport. Follow the dirt road for about 10 miles just past the Green Creek Campground to the parking area.

Trailhead facilities: Drinking water and toilets at the Green Creek Campground.

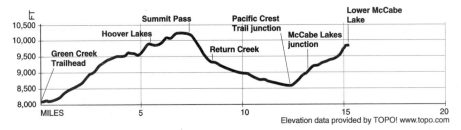

Elevation data provided by TOPO! www.topo.com

Key points:
- 0.0   Green Creek Trailhead.
- 5.8   Upper Hoover Lake.
- 6.2   Green Creek/Virginia Lakes trail junction.
- 7.2   Summit Pass (Yosemite Park boundary).
- 8.2   Return Creek.
- 12.2 Pacific Crest Trail junction.
- 13.2 McCabe Lakes junction.
- 15.2 Lower McCabe Lake.

The hike: Follow Hike 53 to Hoover Lakes, 5.8 miles. The trail follows the eastern boundary of upper Hoover Lake, crosses the inlet, and toils up a sunny slope dotted with sparse whitebark pine to a junction with the Virginia Lakes Trail, at 6.2 miles. This trail heads off to the southeast (left) to meet "Burro" Pass, from which Hike 54 may be followed in reverse to make a nice weekend shuttle trip. Your trail, however, continues to the right up a flower-filled gully along a gurgling creek to Summit Lake. The views here are stupendous, and this seems a natural place to camp, but it is usually very windy, and the few sheltered spots among the whitebark pines are carpeted with very fragile and slow-growing vegetation, easily trampled and destroyed. Much of the area near the lake is closed to camping. Continue on along the north shore of the lake to a sign that marks the Yosemite boundary at Summit Pass, at 7.2 miles, the highest point on this hike. From here, switchback steeply downhill into Virginia Canyon and arrive at the Virginia Pass Trail junction at Return Creek, 8.2 miles. You can make a detour to Virginia Pass by turning right (north) and following Return Creek upstream, then scrambling up a steep slope to the pass, an extra 1.6 miles each way. To continue to McCabe Lakes, cross the creek and follow the trail to the left. A mediocre campsite can be found just off the trail to the right. You can usually rock-hop the creek, but there is a big log to cross on downstream, if the water is high.

Soon the forest opens as you very gradually descend along Return Creek, passing massive Excelsior Peak on your left. The slopes above the canyon for the next couple miles have been scarred with repeated avalanches. Notice how, in some cases, the force was so great that trees were flattened, not only down the side of the slope but also across the canyon floor and even a short distance up the other side. The height of the new little trees in the avalanche path gives a hint of how recently the last one occurred.

The trail eventually nears the creek, where it flows over sculpted granite in picturesque cascades and falls. There are some campsites nearby. It's a great place for lunch, a snack, a nap, or a swim. Just beyond is the junction with the Pacific Crest Trail, at 12.2 miles. Turn left (south) here and follow the PCT for a short distance, climbing steeply. At a junction at 13.2 miles, turn left (east), leaving the PCT. Continue climbing, more gently now, up a wooded slope through an occasional meadow to Lower McCabe Lake, with Sheep Peak as its backdrop, at 15.2 miles. There is good camping on both sides of the outlet. Be sure to stay away from the lakeside to avoid trampling. You can scramble to Upper McCabe for better views by following the green slope to the west uphill along an inlet stream to an intermediate small lake, then cross the low ridge to the northwest to reach the largest of the lakes. Return the way you came.

You can continue on down the PCT to Glen Aulin High Sierra Camp and then to Tuolumne Meadows. You can also approach McCabe Lakes from Tuolumne Meadows via Glen Aulin and Cold Canyon. The distance is roughly the same, about 15 miles.

63 Peeler Lake

General description:	A challenging overnight loop hike that goes by many lakes.
Total distance:	48.7 miles.
Difficulty:	Moderately strenuous.
Elevation gain:	3,410 feet.
Trail traffic:	Light.
Best months:	Mid-July–September.
Maps:	USGS Buckeye Ridge, Dunderberg Peak, Falls Ridge, Matterhorn Peak, Piute Mountain, and Twin Lakes quads.
Permits:	Available from the USDA Forest Service ranger station in Bridgeport.

Finding the trailhead: From Bridgeport turn west off U.S. Highway 395 onto Twin Lakes Road and follow it about 23 miles to its end at Mono Village. Supervised overnight parking is available for a flat rate of $5. Drive to the kiosk in front of the campground for a parking permit and directions to the backpackers' lot.

Peeler Lake

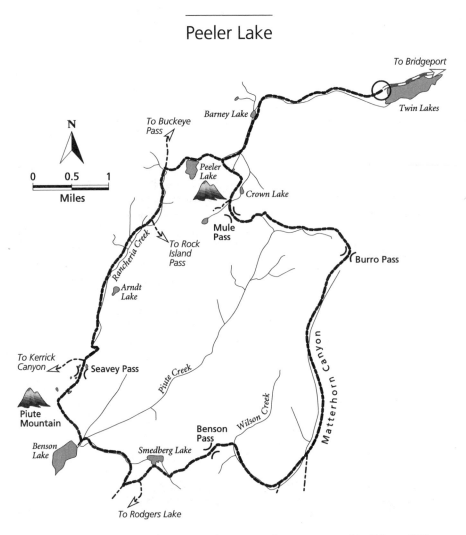

Trailhead facilities: Café, store, phones, and campground in Mono Village at Twin Lakes.

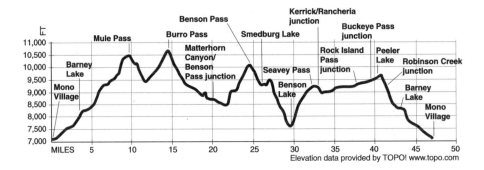

Elevation data provided by TOPO! www.topo.com

Key points:

19.0 Matterhorn Canyon/Benson Pass junction.
26.5 Rodgers Lake junction.
27.1 Benson Lake junction.
30.1 Benson Lake spur.
33.5 Kerrick/Rancheria junction.
38.7 Rock Island Pass junction.
39.7 Buckeye Pass junction.
40.2 Peeler Lake.
40.7 Robinson Creek junction.

The hike: Follow Hike 60 to the Benson Pass Trail junction, at 19 miles. The Pacific Crest Trail makes a sharp dogleg here cutting back southwest, crossing Matterhorn Creek, and following alongside its broad meandering course downstream for more than a mile. The trail swings northwest, climbing along Wilson Creek, which it must cross several times before it turns west and climbs switchbacks to wide, grassy Benson Pass, decorated with whitebark pine. Descend fairly gradually from the pass and wade across the inlet of Smedberg Lake at the edge of a meadow. Beyond, the lake lies at the foot of blocky Volunteer Peak. There is good camping at the lake, but the best is on the shore opposite the trail.

After leaving Smedberg Lake, reach at a junction at the base of Volunteer Peak, at 26.5 miles. Now make a short climb through forest to another junction, at 27.1 miles, and turn right (north) toward Benson Lake, dropping down to cross, then follow the stream connecting Smedberg and Benson lakes. Leave the stream to cross a rocky shoulder and descend to a boggy

Barney Lake.

flat blooming with corn lilies, onions, wild geraniums, and other water-loving flowers, to meet the spur trail to the lake, at 30.1 miles. This is a big lake in a beautifully ice-polished rocky bowl. It is surprisingly popular for such a remote spot, probably because of its good camping and beautiful beach at the end nearest the trail.

Leaving the lake, the trail climbs up open manzanita-covered slopes heading toward the pointed beacon of Piute Mountain, directly ahead. Near the peak, it swings northeast, climbs more steeply along the cascading stream, then levels out beside the first of several little lakes to Seavey Pass, a rather long, open ridge, studded with shining domes and tarns. A short distance down the north side of Seavey Pass, the Pacific Crest Trail leaves your route and heads off down Kerrick Canyon, at 33.5 miles. Turn right and begin climbing easily along Rancheria Creek, which you soon cross in a meadow, tinged pale lavender in July with shooting stars and little elephant heads. Continue upward out of the meadow through a beautiful rocky gorge that opens once again into another wide, sandy grassy area. Arndt Lake, just off the trail to the east, feeds this meadow and its several little ponds.

Meet the Buckeye Pass junction at 38.7 miles. Walk northward along the edge of Kerrick Meadow, then turn right at a junction, at 39.7 miles, toward Peeler Lake, at whose northwest shore you leave Yosemite, at 40.2 miles. There is good camping and lots of human activity at this lake, beneath the scenic backdrop of Crown Point. Cross the inlet stream and climb around a rock ridge, then drop, winding through rocks, to a junction with Robinson Lakes, at 40.7 miles. Here you turn left (northeast) and descend switchbacks to Barney Lake, at 44.7 miles. Then retrace your steps to Twin Lakes and the trailhead.

Two Famous Trails

Two Famous Trails

The John Muir and Pacific Crest trails traverse some of the most spectacular high country anywhere. Both pass through Yosemite, and for a time become one and the same.

The John Muir Trail follows the crest of the Sierra Nevada for roughly 211 miles between Yosemite Valley, at a mere 4,000 feet, and Mount Whitney, at around 14,500 feet, in Sequoia National Park. It begins in Yosemite at Happy Isles, swings northeast to pass through Tuolumne Meadows, then turns south to leave the park at Donohue Pass. The trail was scouted by Theodore Solomons and named in honor of John Muir, who did so much to preserve the wild country of the Sierra Nevada for the public to enjoy. Congress appropriated the funds to begin the trail in 1915, and it was completed in 1938.

The entire trail takes anywhere from three to six weeks to finish, although the Yosemite section takes only a few days. It is enjoyable in either direction, but I describe it here beginning at Happy Isles. In this direction you do have more uphill, but starting low gives you a chance to adjust to higher elevations gradually. There is no trailhead at Donohue Pass, so if you plan to hike only the Yosemite section, you will have to divide it into two parts: Tuolumne to Donohue Pass, and Tuolumne to Yosemite Valley (or vice versa).

The Pacific Crest Trail, dedicated in 1993, is part of the National Trails System authorized by Congress in 1968. It begins at the Mexican border and runs through the most scenic parts of the Western states for 2,650 miles to the Canadian border. Hiking the entire trail takes a long summer season, but you can sample one of its finest sections as it goes through Yosemite from Donohue Pass in the south to Dorothy Lake Pass on the northern park border in about two weeks.

Most PCT through-hikers begin in Mexico and hike north, following the summer snowmelt to reach Canada in fall. They usually reach the northern part of Yosemite by June, and frequently find the deep snow and swift, high river crossings challenging, or at worst, impossible. The Yosemite section is described here in the usual south-to-north direction, but wait until mid-July for the most rewarding, least frustrating experience. The Pacific Crest Trail Association has lots of good information about current trail conditions and trip planning. You can contact them at 5325 Elkhorn Boulevard 256, Sacramento, CA 95842. Phone (916) 349-2103, or on-line at www.pcta.org.

64 The John Muir Trail

General description:	Popular overnight shuttle hike with knock-your-socks-off views.
Total distance:	35.3 miles.
Difficulty:	Moderate.
Elevation gain:	7,059 feet.
Trail traffic:	Heavy.
Best months:	July–September.
Maps:	USGS Half Dome, Koip Peak, Merced Peak, Tenaya Lake, Vogelsang Peak quads.
Permits:	Required. Apply in advance. See section on wilderness permits.

Finding the trailhead: Leave your car in the backpackers' lot east of Curry Village and ride the shuttle bus to Stop 16, Happy Isles, or follow the signs along the footpath to Happy Isles.

Trailhead facilities: Full range of goods and services in Yosemite Valley.

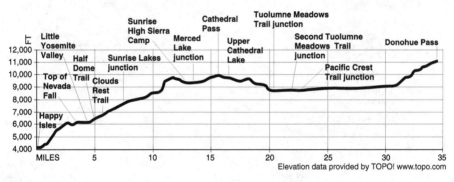

Elevation data provided by TOPO! www.topo.com

Key points:

0.0	Happy Isles Trailhead.
4.8	Little Yosemite Valley.
5.3	Half Dome Trail.
5.8	Clouds Rest Trail.
7.7	Sunrise Lakes junction.
7.8	Second Sunrise junction.
12.3	Sunrise High Sierra Camp.
13.2	Merced Lake junction.
16.3	Upper Cathedral Lake.
20.7	Tuolumne Meadows Trail junction.
22.4	Second junction to Tuolumne Meadows campground.
23.1	PCT junction.
35.3	Donohue Pass.

The hike: Follow Hike 18 to 4.8 miles, Little Yosemite Valley. Turn left (north) through the campground, passing the junction with another trail heading back down to Nevada Fall. Climb the well-beaten path toward Half

The John Muir Trail and The Pacific Crest Trail

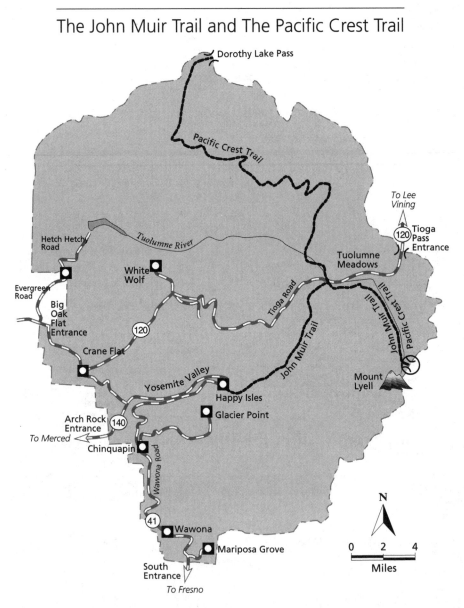

Dome along with the crowd of hikers heading for the summit to the Half Dome Trail junction, at 5.3 miles. Turn right (east), and at 5.8 miles, keep right again at the Sunrise Lakes junction and climb along Sunrise Creek. At 7.7 miles, meet a junction with a lateral trail to Echo Valley. Keep left (north) here, and very soon arrive at a second junction, at 7.8 miles, where the John Muir Trail turns right (east.) Climb gently, then steeply to a ridgetop where there are views of the Cathedral Range, then descend to the big meadow and the Sunrise High Sierra Camp, at 12.3 miles. Now follow the trail, eastward at first, then northward, skirting the meadow's edge to meet the trail to Merced Lake at 13.2 miles. Continue straight ahead into the forest, cross

Echo Peak from the John Muir Trail.

Echo Creek, then skirt the creek on its east side through aptly named Long Meadow. Veer northwest and climb toward Columbia Finger, rounding its base and reaching an open rocky saddle.

Here, one of those awe-inspiring Yosemite vistas bursts upon you. The grand, sweeping, sculptured white granite of Cathedral Peak, Echo Peak, and Matthes Crest looks like the spine of the world. Descend the hillside to the meadow below Cathedral Peak. At the end of the meadow, the trail drops over Cathedral Pass, revealing another knock-your-socks-off view. The spire of Cathedral Peak rises above a green meadow filled with flowers and the impossibly blue Upper Cathedral Lake, embellished with windblown pines and back-dropped by the park's northern ranges. Descend the pass and cross the marshy meadow to Upper Cathedral Lake, at 16.3 miles.

Now follow Hike 36 in reverse to the junction with the trail to Tuolumne Meadows, just after crossing Budd Creek, south of Tioga Road, at 20.7 miles. The trail passes behind the visitor center, Tuolumne Village, and the Tuolumne Meadows Campground, in case you need supplies or information. Pass several junctions leading to Tioga Road and the other facilities to the north, then pass the campground, the Elizabeth Lake Trailhead, and a second campground turnoff, at 22.4 miles. Follow along the north shore of the Lyell Fork of the Tuolumne River until you meet the junction where the Pacific Crest Trail joins the John Muir Trail, at 23.1 miles.

Now follow Hike 39 to Donohue Pass, at 35.3 miles, where the John Muir and Pacific Crest trails leave the park.

65 The Pacific Crest Trail

See map on page 212

General description: Overnight shuttle hike providing an excellent opportunity to experience Yosemite's diverse beauty.
Total distance: 79.4 miles.
Difficulty: Strenuous.
Elevation gain: 3,020 feet.
Trail traffic: Moderately heavy near Tuolumne Meadows, light toward the park boundary.
Best months: Late July–August, though PCT through-hikers must begin sooner.
Maps: USGS Koip Peak, Vogelsang Peak, Tioga Pass, Tenaya Lake, Falls Ridge, Matterhorn Peak, Piute Mountain, Tiltill Mountain, and Tower Peak quads.
Permits: Required in advance (see wilderness permits).

Finding the trailhead: This hike is described from border to border of Yosemite. There are no trailheads at either end. The only road the trail crosses is at Tuolumne Meadows.

Facilities: Tuolumne Meadows is the only source of supplies on the trail.

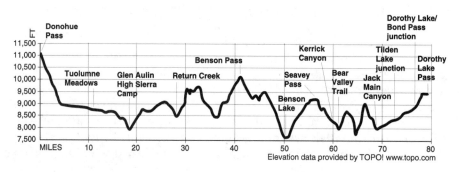

Elevation data provided by TOPO! www.topo.com

Key points:
0.0 Park boundary at Donohue Pass.
12.4 Dog Lake parking lot.
13.0 Glen Aulin Trailhead.
52.5 Seavey Pass/Rodgers Lake junction.
53.1 Second Seavey Pass junction.
55.5 Benson Lake spur trail.
58.9 Kerrick Canyon.
62.5 Bear Valley Trail.
68.2 Tilden Canyon/Wilma Lake junction.
68.3 Second Wilma Lake junction.
70.3 Jack Main Canyon.
72.2 Tilden Lake junction.
78.7 Dorothy Lake/Bond Pass junction.

The hike: Follow Hike 39 in reverse to the Dog Lake parking area in Tuolumne Meadows, at 12.4 miles. Walk along this secondary road heading west until it meets Tioga Road. Continue west along Tioga Road for less than a half mile until you can see the Lembert Dome parking lot on the north side. Cross Tioga Road to the parking lot, turn left (west), and continue along the road that parallels Tioga Road to the Glen Aulin Trailhead. It begins at the closed gate, at 13 miles. Follow Hike 61 to the Seavey Pass junction, at 52.5 miles. Continue toward Seavey Pass for about a half mile, where you meet a second Seavey Pass junction at 53.1 miles. Head north toward Seavey Pass and Benson Lake, dropping down to cross, then follow, the stream connecting Smedberg and Benson lakes. Leave the stream to cross a rocky shoulder and descend to a boggy flat blooming with corn lilies, onions, wild geraniums, and more, to meet the spur trail to Benson Lake, at 55.5 miles. This is a big lake in a beautifully ice-polished rocky bowl. It is surprisingly popular for such a remote spot, probably because of its good camping and beautiful beach at the end nearest the trail.

Leaving the lake, the trail climbs up open manzanita-covered slopes heading toward the pointed beacon of Piute Mountain directly ahead. Near the peak, it swings northeast, climbs more steeply along the cascading stream, then levels out beside the first of several little lakes to Seavey Pass, a rather long, open ridge studded with shining domes and tarns. A short distance down the north side of Seavey Pass, reach the junction with Kerrick Canyon, at 58.9 miles.

Turn left (west) down the shady floor of Kerrick Canyon, pass an avalanche chute, and proceed to the junction with the Bear Valley Trail, at 62.5 miles. Switchback up out of the gully and follow a roller-coaster route, then drop down steeply into the next valley, wading Thompson and Stubblefield creeks in Stubblefield Canyon, then labor your way up and down over

Dorothy Lake from the Pacific Crest Trail.

Macomb Ridge. Finally, cross Tilden Creek and meet the Tilden Canyon/ Wilma Lake junction, at 68.2 miles. Turn right (north) here and proceed a very short distance to a second junction, at 68.3 miles, toward Wilma Lake. The trail follows very close to the southwest shore of Wilma Lake and crosses a short stream that connects the lake to Falls Creek. Through much of July this is a soggy morass, and earlier in the year it may be so deeply flooded that it is impassable.

Once on the west side of Falls Creek, turn right (north) at the junction, at 70.3 miles. Soon you pass through a gate and wander along the flat valley floor to 72.2 miles, where a trail cuts off to the right (east) to the shore of Tilden Lake. A visit to this lake is worth a detour, and there is good camping at the southeast shore of this long, narrow finger of water, with Tower Peak above its far end.

Back on the Pacific Crest Trail, continue north, passing Chittenden Peak, then a pretty waterfall, and level out to follow miles of grassy meadow. Pass briefly through forest, then into the even wider expanse of Grace Meadow. Ascend out of the meadow at its north end to reach the Dorothy Lake/Bond Pass junction, at 78.7 miles. Turn right (east) here and skirt Dorothy Lake in its broad meadow to reach the park boundary at Dorothy Lake Pass, at 79.4 miles.

Appendix A: Further Reading

Further Reading

Barrett, S.A. and Gifford, E.W. *Miwok Material Culture.* Yosemite: Yosemite Natural History Association, 1933.

Browning, Peter. *Place Names of the Sierra Nevada.* Berkeley: Wilderness Press, 1991.

Gaines, David. *Birds of the Yosemite Sierra.* Oakland, 1977.

Grater, Russell K. *Discovering Sierra Mammals.* Yosemite: Yosemite Natural History Association and Sequoia Natural History Association, 1978.

Harmon, Will. *Leave No Trace.* Helena: Falcon Publishing, 1997.

Huber, N. King. *The Geologic Story of Yosemite National Park.* U.S. Geological Survey Bulletin 1595. U.S. Department of the Interior, 1987.

Johnson, Verna R. *Sierra Nevada.* Boston: Houghton Mifflin Company, 1970.

Moynier, John. *Avalanche Aware.* Helena: Falcon Publishing, 1998.

Paruk, Jim. *Sierra Nevada Tree Finder.* Yosemite Association, 1997.

Preston, Gilbert. *Wilderness First Aid.* Helena: Falcon Publishing, 1997.

Sax, Joseph L. *Mountains without Handrails.* Ann Arbor: University of Michigan Press, 1980.

Schneider, Bill. *Bear Aware.* Helena: Falcon Publishing, 1996.

Schneider, Bill and Russ. *Backpacking Tips.* Helena: Falcon Publishing, 1998.

Storer, Tracy I. and Usinger, Robert L. *Sierra Nevada Natural History.* Berkeley: University of California Press, 1966.

Swedo, Suzanne. *Wilderness Survival.* Helena: Falcon Publishing, 1998.

Weeden, Norman. *A Sierra Nevada Flora.* Berkeley: Wilderness Press, 1996.

Whitney, Stephen. *The Sierra Nevada: A Sierra Club Naturalist's Guide.* San Francisco: Sierra Club Books, 1979.

Wiese, Karen. *Sierra Nevada Wildflowers.* Helena: Falcon Publishing, 2000.

Woodmencey, Jim. *Reading Weather.* Helena: Falcon Publishing, 1998.

Zwinger, Ann H. and Willard, Beatrice E. *Land Above the Trees.* New York, Harper & Row, 1972.

Appendix B: Hiker's Checklist

Always make and check your own checklist!

If you've ever hiked into the backcountry and discovered that you've forgotten an essential, you know that it's a good idea to make a checklist and check the items off as you pack so that you won't forget the things you want and need. Here are some ideas:

Clothing
- ☐ Dependable rain parka
- ☐ Rain pants
- ☐ Windbreaker
- ☐ Thermal underwear
- ☐ Shorts
- ☐ Long pants or sweatpants
- ☐ Wood cap or balaclava
- ☐ Hat
- ☐ Wool shirt or sweater
- ☐ Jacket or parka
- ☐ Extra socks
- ☐ Underwear
- ☐ Lightweight shirts
- ☐ T-shirts
- ☐ Bandana(s)
- ☐ Mittens or gloves
- ☐ Belt

Footwear
- ☐ Sturdy, comfortable boots
- ☐ Lightweight camp shoes

Bedding
- ☐ Sleeping bag
- ☐ Foam pad or air mattress
- ☐ Ground sheet (plastic or nylon)
- ☐ Dependable tent

Hauling
- ☐ Backpack and/or day pack

Cooking
- ☐ 1-quart container (plastic)
- ☐ 1-gallon water container for camp use (collapsible)
- ☐ Backpacking stove and extra fuel
- ☐ Funnel
- ☐ Aluminum foil
- ☐ Cooking pots
- ☐ Bowls/plates
- ☐ Utensils (spoons, forks, small spatula, knife)
- ☐ Pot scrubber
- ☐ Matches in waterproof container

Food and Drink
- ☐ Cereal
- ☐ Bread
- ☐ Crackers
- ☐ Cheese
- ☐ Trail mix
- ☐ Margarine
- ☐ Powdered soups
- ☐ Salt/pepper
- ☐ Main course meals
- ☐ Snacks
- ☐ Hot chocolate
- ☐ Tea
- ☐ Powdered milk
- ☐ Drink mixes

Photography
- ☐ Camera and film
- ☐ Filters
- ☐ Lens brush/paper

Miscellaneous
- ☐ Sunglasses
- ☐ Map and a compass
- ☐ Toilet paper
- ☐ Pocketknife
- ☐ Sunscreen
- ☐ Good insect repellent
- ☐ Lip balm
- ☐ Flashlight with good batteries and a spare bulb
- ☐ Candle(s)
- ☐ First-aid kit
- ☐ Your FalconGuide
- ☐ Survival kit
- ☐ Small garden trowel or shovel
- ☐ Water filter or purification tablets
- ☐ Plastic bags (for trash)
- ☐ Soap
- ☐ Towel
- ☐ Toothbrush
- ☐ Fishing license
- ☐ Fishing rod, reel, lures, flies, etc.
- ☐ Binoculars
- ☐ Waterproof covering for pack
- ☐ Watch
- ☐ Sewing kit

About the Author

Suzanne Swedo has taught natural science seminars for the Yosemite Association in Yosemite National Park for 20 years. During the same period, she has conducted wilderness survival, outdoor skills, and natural history outings as founder and director of W.I.L.D., an international and domestic adventure travel company. She has also led nature and wilderness trips for various educational organizations including the University of California Extension, the National Outings Program of the Sierra Club, Wilderness Institute, Pacific Wilderness Institute, and Outdoor Adventures. She has demonstrated wilderness skills in a ten-week television series Alive and Well and served as a survival consultant for Warner Brothers Television. Her writings on travel and the outdoors have appeared in publications such as the *Los Angeles Examiner* and *California Magazine*. Other books for Falcon are *Wilderness Survival* and *Best Easy Day Hikes in Yosemite*.

Elevation profile data compiled from TOPO!, a registered trademark of Wildflower Productions. For more information on available products or to order TOPO! interactive maps on CD-ROM, contact

Wildflower Productions
375 Alabama Street, Suite 400
San Francisco, CA 94110

tel: 415-558-8700
fax: 415-558-9700
info@topo.com

or visit www.topo.com.

FALCON GUIDES ® Leading the Way™

HIKING GUIDES

Best Hikes Along the Continental Divide
Hiking Alaska
Hiking Arizona
Hiking Arizona's Cactus Country
Hiking the Beartooths
Hiking Big Bend National Park
Hiking the Bob Marshall Country
Hiking California
Hiking California's Desert Parks
Hiking Carlsbad Caverns
  and Guadalupe Mtns. National Parks
Hiking Colorado
Hiking Colorado, Vol. II
Hiking Colorado's Summits
Hiking Colorado's Weminuche Wilderness
Hiking the Columbia River Gorge
Hiking Florida
Hiking Georgia
Hiking Glacier & Waterton Lakes National Parks
Hiking Grand Canyon National Park
Hiking Grand Staircase-Escalante/Glen Canyon
Hiking Grand Teton National Park
Hiking Great Basin National Park
Hiking Hot Springs in the Pacific Northwest
Hiking Idaho
Hiking Indiana
Hiking Maine
Hiking Maryland and Delaware
Hiking Michigan
Hiking Minnesota
Hiking Montana
Hiking Mount Rainier National Park
Hiking Mount St. Helens
Hiking Nevada
Hiking New Hampshire
Hiking New Mexico
Hiking New Mexico's Gila Wilderness

Hiking New York
Hiking North Carolina
Hiking the North Cascades
Hiking Northern Arizona
Hiking Northern California
Hiking Olympic National Park
Hiking Oregon
Hiking Oregon's Eagle Cap Wilderness
Hiking Oregon's Mount Hood/Badger Creek
Hiking Oregon's Central Cascades
Hiking Pennsylvania
Hiking Ruins Seldom Seen
Hiking Shenandoah
Hiking the Sierra Nevada
Hiking South Carolina
Hiking South Dakota's Black Hills Country
Hiking Southern New England
Hiking Tennessee
Hiking Texas
Hiking Utah
Hiking Utah's Summits
Hiking Vermont
Hiking Virginia
Hiking Washington
Hiking Wisconsin
Hiking Wyoming
Hiking Wyoming's Cloud Peak Wilderness
Hiking Wyoming's Teton
  and Washakie Wilderness
Hiking Wyoming's Wind River Range
Hiking Yellowstone National Park
Hiking Yosemite National Park
Hiking Zion & Bryce Canyon National Parks
Wild Country Companion
Wild Montana
Wild Utah
Wild Virginia

■ *To order any of these books, check with your local bookseller*
or call FALCON ® at 1-800-582-2665.
Visit us on the world wide web at:
www.Falcon.com

FALCON®

FALCONGUIDES ®Leading the Way™

BEST EASY DAY HIKES SERIES
Beartooths
Boulder
Canyonlands & Arches
Cape Cod
Colorado Springs
Denver
Glacier & Wateron Lakes
Grand Staircase-Escalante and
 the Glen Canyon Region
Grand Canyon
Grand Teton
Lake Tahoe
Mount Rainier
Mount St. Helens
North Cascades
Northern Sierra
Olympics
Orange County
Phoenix
Salt Lake City
San Diego
Santa Fe
Shenandoah
Yellowstone
Yosemite

12 SHORT HIKES SERIES
Colorado
Aspen
Boulder
Denver Foothills Central
Denver Foothills North
Denver Foothills South
Rocky Mountain National Park-Estes Park
Rocky Mountain National Park-Grand Lake
Steamboat Springs
Summit County
Vail
California
San Diego Coast
San Diego Mountains
San Francisco Bay Area-Coastal
San Francisco Bay Area-East Bay
San Francisco Bay Area-North Bay
San Francisco Bay Area-South Bay
Washington
Mount Rainier National Park-Paradise
Mount Rainier National Park-Sunrise

■ *To order any of these books, check with your local bookseller*
*or call FALCON ® at **1-800-582-2665**.*
Visit us on the world wide web at:
www.Falcon.com

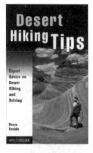